International Perspectives on Knowledge and Curriculum

Also available from Bloomsbury

Developing Culturally and Historically Sensitive Teacher Education: Global Lessons from a Literacy Education Program, edited by Yolanda Gayol Ramírez, Patricia Rosas Chávez and Peter Smagorinsky

International Perspectives on Knowledge and Quality: Implications for Innovation in Teacher Education Policy and Practice, edited by Brian Hudson, Niklas Gericke, Christina Olin-Scheller and Martin Stolare

Knowledge, Policy and Practice in Teacher Education: A Cross-National Study, edited by Maria Teresa Tatto and Ian Menter

Picture Pedagogy: Visual Culture Concepts to Enhance the Curriculum, by Paul Duncum

Reflective Teaching in Further, Adult and Vocational Education, by Margaret Gregson, Sam Duncan, Kevin Brosnan, Jay Derrick, Gary Husband, Lawrence Nixon, Trish Spedding, Rachel Stubley and Robin Webber Jones

Reinventing the Curriculum: New Trends in Curriculum Policy and Practice, edited by Mark Priestley and Gert Biesta

Teacher Agency: An Ecological Approach, by Mark Priestley, Gert Biesta and Sarah Robinson

Teaching Personal, Social, Health and Economic and Relationships, (Sex) and Health Education in Primary Schools: Enhancing the Whole Curriculum, edited by Victoria Pugh and Daniel Hughes

The Bloomsbury Handbook of Reading Perspectives and Practices, edited by Bethan Marshall, Jackie Manuel, Donna L. Pasternak and Jennifer Rowsell

The Promise and Practice of University Teacher Education: Insights from Aotearoa New Zealand, by Alexandra C. Gunn, Mary F. Hill, David A.G. Berg and Mavis Haigh

Transforming Education: Reimagining Learning, Pedagogy and Curriculum, by Miranda Jefferson and Michael Anderson

International Perspectives on Knowledge and Curriculum

Epistemic Quality across School Subjects

Edited by
Brian Hudson, Niklas Gericke,
Christina Olin-Scheller and Martin Stolare

BLOOMSBURY ACADEMIC
LONDON • NEW YORK • OXFORD • NEW DELHI • SYDNEY

BLOOMSBURY ACADEMIC
Bloomsbury Publishing Plc
50 Bedford Square, London, WC1B 3DP, UK
1385 Broadway, New York, NY 10018, USA
29 Earlsfort Terrace, Dublin 2, Ireland

BLOOMSBURY, BLOOMSBURY ACADEMIC and the Diana logo are
trademarks of Bloomsbury Publishing Plc

First published in Great Britain, 2022
Paperback editon published 2023

Copyright © Brian Hudson, Niklas Gericke, Christina Olin-Scheller,
Martin Stolare and Bloomsbury, 2022

Brian Hudson, Niklas Gericke, Christina Olin-Scheller, Martin Stolare and
Bloomsbury have asserted their right under the Copyright, Designs and
Patents Act, 1988, to be identified as Author of this work.

For legal purposes the Acknowledgements on pp. xix–xx constitute an
extension of this copyright page.

All rights reserved. No part of this publication may be reproduced or transmitted
in any form or by any means, electronic or mechanical, including photocopying,
recording, or any information storage or retrieval system, without
prior permission in writing from the publishers.

Bloomsbury Publishing Plc does not have any control over, or responsibility for,
any third-party websites referred to or in this book. All internet addresses given
in this book were correct at the time of going to press. The author and publisher
regret any inconvenience caused if addresses have changed or sites have
ceased to exist, but can accept no responsibility for any such changes.

A catalogue record for this book is available from the British Library.

Library of Congress Cataloging-in-Publication Data
Names: Hudson, Brian, 1951-editor.
Title: International perspectives on knowledge and curriculum: epistemic
quality across school subjects / edited by Brian Hudson, Niklas Gericke,
Christina Olin-Scheller, Martin Stolare.
Description: London; New York: Bloomsbury Academic, 2022. |
Includes bibliographical references and index.
Identifiers: LCCN 2021035385 (print) | LCCN 2021035386 (ebook) |
ISBN 9781350167094 (hardback) | ISBN 9781350167100 (pdf) | ISBN 9781350167117 (ebook)
Subjects: LCSH: Education–Curricula. | Curriculum planning. | Knowledge, Theory of.
Classification: LCC LB1570.I569 2022 (print) | LCC LB1570 (ebook) | DDC 375–dc23
LC record available at https://lccn.loc.gov/2021035385
LC ebook record available at https://lccn.loc.gov/2021035386

ISBN: HB: 978-1-3501-6709-4
PB: 978-1-3502-2508-4
ePDF: 978-1-3501-6710-0
eBook: 978-1-3501-6711-7

Typeset by Integra Software Services Pvt. Ltd.

To find out more about our authors and books visit www.bloomsbury.com
and sign up for our newsletters.

We dedicate this book with our appreciation to all the teachers, students and those working to support them who participated in the studies included in this book.

Contents

List of Figures		ix
Contributors		xi
Preface		xiv
Foreword		xvii
Acknowledgements		xix

1 Researching Powerful Knowledge and Epistemic Quality across School Subjects *Niklas Gericke, Brian Hudson, Christina Olin-Scheller and Martin Stolare* 1

2 Evaluating Epistemic Quality in Primary School Mathematics in Scotland *Brian Hudson* 17

3 Epistemic Quality of Physical Education in a High School in France *Monique Loquet, Brian Hudson and Anke Wegner* 37

4 Epistemic Quality of Language Learning in a Primary Classroom in Germany *Anke Wegner, Brian Hudson and Monique Loquet* 55

5 Powerful Knowledge of Language and Migration in Norwegian and Swedish Textbooks *Birgitta Ljung Egeland and Lise Iversen Kulbrandstad* 79

6 Powerful Reading and Epistemic Quality in first Language and Literature Education *Satu Grünthal, Pirjo Hiidenmaa and Liisa Tainio* 99

7 Teaching Practices in Transformation in Connected Social Science Swedish Classrooms *Marie Nilsberth, Christina Olin-Scheller and Martin Kristiansson* 117

8 Epistemic Quality in the Intended Mathematics Curriculum and Implications for Policy *Jennie Golding* 137

9 A Material-dialogic Perspective on Powerful Knowledge and Matter within a Science Classroom *Mark Hardman, John-Paul Riordan and Lindsay Hetherington* 157

10 Investigating the Nature of Powerful Knowledge and Epistemic Quality in Education for Sustainable Development *Per Sund and Niklas Gericke* 177

11 Trajectories of Epistemic Quality and Powerful Knowledge across School Subjects *Niklas Gericke, Brian Hudson, Christina Olin-Scheller and Martin Stolare* 197

Index 222

Figures

2.1	Trajectory in the development of subject-specific powerful knowledge in mathematics	23
2.2	John's drawings of the River Tay and the River Amazon	27
2.3	First example of a child's working	28
2.4	Second example of a child's working	29
3.1	Trajectory of development in the epistemic capacities of choreographic activities	40
3.2	Example of one picture of a sculpture by Ndary Lo taken by Yves Guigon	43
3.3	Picture of the sculpture in iron by Ndary Lo taken by Charles Jousselin	44
3.4	Edmond, with his group, mimics the gestures of a boxer (in the middle of the picture at the start of lesson 5)	45
3.5	Students imitate the teacher's monstration of a symbolic representation of the scene	47
3.6	Reciprocal game of imitation between teacher (T) and students (St) in a problematic situation: 'symbolic gesture' is difficult to explain	50
4.1	Levels of teacher–student interaction and co-operation in the instructional process	58
4.2	Trajectory of development in relation to language and language use	60
4.3	Placement of the tables, chairs and shelves for teaching material in the classroom	63
4.4	The schedule for the day – student participation in lesson planning	64
4.5	The daily routine, maths and German language exercises	66
4.6	The teacher directly instructing the whole class	67
4.7	The students holding up their cards to answer the quiz questions	69
7.1	The teacher's introduction	122
7.2	Stina is copying the blue text from Prezi	123
7.3	Watching the YouTube clip about the counsel for the defence	124
7.4	Watching the YouTube clip about the counsel for the claimant	126
7.5	Stina writes the blue text down in OneNote	127

7.6	'Tiny cards', a game about concepts and terms related to Law and Order	129
7.7	Searching for concepts with Google	131
9.1	Research design	163
9.2	The chromatograms engaged with over the lessons	167
9.3	The classroom whiteboard: a dialogic space	167
9.4	Pupil explanations of chromatography on mini whiteboards	168
10.1	Venn diagram representation of SD and its dimensions	182
10.2	Different ways of organizing cross-curricular work	184
10.3	The representation shows the different subject areas' contributions of educational content to ESD	191
11.1	Trajectory in the development of subject-specific powerful knowledge in mathematics (Hudson, 2022)	217
11.2	Trajectory of development in relation to language and language use (Wegner et al., 2022)	218

Tables

5.1	Categories of the content analysis	84
5.2	Transformation processes through student roles	87

Contributors

Birgitta Ljung Egeland is Senior Lecturer in Swedish language at Karlstad University, Sweden, where she is a member of the Research on Subject-Specific Education (ROSE) research group and a senior researcher at the Centre for Language and Literature Education (CSL), particularly interested in multilingualism and second language learning.

Niklas Gericke is Professor in Science Education and director of the SMEER (Science, Mathematics and Engineering Education Research) Research Centre at Karlstad University, Sweden, and Guest Professor at NTNU in Trondheim, Norway.

Jennie Golding is Associate Professor of Mathematics Education at the UCL Institute of Education, University College London, UK. She is Department Graduate Tutor and researches the interface between education policy, knowledge and practice through the lenses of teachers and learners.

Satu Grünthal is Docent at the University of Helsinki, Finland and at the University of Turku, Finland. She is Senior Lecturer in Finnish Language and Literature Education at the University of Helsinki, Finland.

Mark Hardman is Associate Professor at the Centre for Teachers and Teaching Research at the UCL Institute of Education, University College London, UK. Originally a secondary science teacher in London, he has been a teacher educator and researcher since 2007.

Lindsay Hetherington is Associate Professor of Science Education at Exeter University, UK, where she is the Head of Initial Teacher Education and a member of the Centre for Research in STEM Education and the Creativity and Emergent Education Futures Network.

Pirjo Hiidenmaa is Professor of Non-Fiction Literature and Dean of the Faculty of Arts at the University of Helsinki, Finland.

Brian Hudson is Guest Professor in the Department of Educational Studies at Karlstad University, Sweden, and Emeritus Professor of Education at the

University of Sussex, UK. He is a Fellow of the Institute of Mathematics and its Applications, an honorary member of EERA Network 27 Didactics – Learning and Teaching and was awarded a National Teaching Fellowship in 2004.

Martin Kristiansson is Senior Lecturer in Civics at Karlstad University, Sweden. He is a member of the Research on Subject-Specific Education (ROSE) group and a senior researcher at the Centre for Social Science Education (CSD).

Lise Iversen Kulbrandstad is Professor in Norwegian and Head of the PhD in Teaching and Teacher Education at the Inland Norway University of Applied Sciences, Norway. She was also a member of the ROSE group at Karlstad University, Sweden.

Monique Loquet is Professor in Didactics in the Department of Educational Sciences at Rennes University, France. She is also Researcher in the Centre for Education, Learning and Didactics (CREAD), at Rennes University, France, and is particularly interested in cross-cultural comparisons of the teaching-learning in bodily activities, sport and artistic activities.

Marie Nilsberth is Associate Professor in Educational Work and Senior Researcher in the Centre for Literature and Language Studies (CSL) at Karlstad University, Sweden. She is interested in classroom practices of teaching and learning in relation to the digitalization of education.

Christina Olin-Scheller is Professor of Educational Work and Director of the Centre of Language and Literature in Education (CSL) Research Centre and co-Director of the Research on Subject-Specific Education Research Group (ROSE) at Karlstad University, Sweden. She coordinates the Swedish National Literacy Network and participates in the Quality in Nordic Teaching Research Centre (Nordic QUINT).

John-Paul Riordan is Senior Lecturer in Education at Canterbury Christ Church University, UK. He is interested in initial teacher education, science education, video-based pedagogy analysis, science 'misconceptions', conceptual change strategy, educational technology and inclusion.

Martin Stolare is Professor of History at Karlstad University, Sweden. He is also co-Director of the Research on Subject-Specific Education Research Group

(ROSE) and Senior Researcher in the Centre for Social Science Education (CSD) at Karlstad University, Sweden.

Per Sund is Docent of Science Education in the Department of Mathematics and Science Education at Stockholm University, Sweden. He is the former link-convenor (2013–17) of the Environmental and Sustainability Education Research Network, collaborating within the European Educational Research Association.

Liisa Tainio is Professor of Finnish Language and Literature Education at the University of Helsinki, Finland, where she works as a member of the Research Community for Humanities and Social Sciences Education (HuSoEd).

Anke Wegner is Professor of Language Didactics in the Department of German Studies at Trier University, Germany. She is especially interested in plurilingualism, German as a second language, transnational education, citizenship education, comparative studies in classroom research, and professional development of teachers.

Preface

This book arises from the work of the KOSS Network *Knowledge and Quality across School Subjects and Teacher Education* funded by the Swedish Research Council (2019–22). The network brings together cross-disciplinary educational research groups from Sweden, England and Finland specializing in different school subjects. The research groups involved are *ROSE* (Research on Subject-specific Education) at Karlstad University in Sweden, *SSRG* (Subject Specialism Research Group) at the University College London in the UK, and *HuSoEd* (Research Community for Humanities and Social Sciences) at the University of Helsinki in Finland. Central aims of the KOSS research programme are to study how content knowledge in different school subjects is defined and transformed and to consider the implications for innovation in teacher education policy and practice. The book focuses on the former aspect and has been developed parallel to a second book published simultaneously by Bloomsbury Academic entitled *International Perspectives on Knowledge and Quality: Implications for Innovation in Teacher Education Policy and Practice* (Hudson et al. 2022).

The application made to the Swedish Research Council built on prior collaboration between the research groups and was developed in some detail at a seminar held in Apertin, Sweden in February 2018. The grant was awarded in November 2018 and the first meeting of the network took place in Stockholm in May 2019. The majority of chapters in this book are based on papers first presented at symposia at the European Conference on Educational Research (ECER) and the Nordic Conference on Teaching and Learning in Curriculum Subjects (NOFA). In particular, most of these papers formed contributions to symposia on *Powerful Knowledge across School Subjects* as part of ECER 2018 at the University of Bolzano in September 2018, on *Powerful Knowledge, Epistemic Quality and Transformations* as part of NOFA7 at Stockholm University in May 2019, and on *Powerful Knowledge and Epistemic Quality across School Subjects and Teacher Education* as part of ECER 2019 at the University of Hamburg in September 2019. Several other chapters arose from the development of the KOSS network's wider activities during this period of time.

The network is hosted by the ROSE group at Karlstad University, which designated it a strong research group in 2016. The group has developed from three subject-specific research centres at Karlstad University which focus on subject-specific research in close cooperation with teachers, students, teacher educators and a range of other stakeholders. The SSRG group at the UCL Institute of Education has specific interest and expertise in all areas of curriculum, pedagogy and assessment, especially the role of knowledge in school teaching. The HuSoEd group at Helsinki University has specific interest in subject didactics of different school subjects and in the humanities and social sciences particularly. The groups within the network share their expertise and interests in exploring and developing aspects of powerful knowledge, epistemic quality and transformation processes and how these hold implications for innovation in teacher education policy and practice.

The primary forms of collaboration in the network are workshops and research mobility, supplemented by webinars, joint conference presentations and publications. The first workshop of the network took place in Stockholm following the Nordic Conference on Teaching and Learning in Curriculum Subjects (NOFA7) at Stockholm University in May 2019. The second workshop was hosted by the HuSoEd group at Helsinki University in October 2019 while the third one was hosted by the SSRG group in London in March 2020. This pattern has continued and been adapted to a post-COVID-19 world with webinars hosted by the ROSE group at Karlstad in October 2020 and the HuSoEd group at Helsinki in March 2021.

The book is arranged as eleven chapters featuring contributions from England, Finland, France, Germany, Norway, Scotland and Sweden that address a range of classroom subject-specific and cross-curricular contexts that include mathematics, physical education, language learning, migration studies, literature, social science, natural science and sustainable development. The first chapter by Niklas Gericke, Brian Hudson, Christina Olin-Scheller and Martin Stolare is entitled *Researching Powerful Knowledge and Epistemic Quality across School Subjects* and overviews the theoretical and methodological approaches adopted in the KOSS network. A central aim of the research programme is to study how content knowledge in different school subjects is defined and transformed, taking a comparative perspective across education systems in different national contexts. By using the theoretical concepts of *powerful knowledge, transformation* and *epistemic quality,* we study how these concepts form knowledge of importance for subject didactics. A central issue is to explore how transformation processes can enable knowledge of high epistemic quality to be taught in school classrooms. The concept of *powerful knowledge* (Young 2014) was developed as a curriculum principle in order to restore the importance of knowledge and teaching in curriculum development and research and as a way of overcoming the crisis in curriculum theory. In turn, the concept of *transformation* (Gericke et al. 2018) is seen as an integrative process through which specialized knowledge, developed in subject disciplines, is reshaped and re-presented in educational environments – via various processes outside and within the education system on societal, institutional and individual levels – as bodies and forms of knowledge to be taught and learned. Third, the concept of *epistemic quality* (Hudson 2018) relates to the quality of education in terms of what the students are expected to know, make sense of and be able to do through the school curriculum at the classroom level in particular.

Brian Hudson, Niklas Gericke, Christina Olin-Scheller and Martin Stolare

References

Gericke, N., Hudson, B., Olin-Scheller, C. and Stolare, M. (2018), 'Powerful Knowledge, Transformations and the Need for Empirical Studies across School Subjects', *London Review of Education*, 16 (3): 428–44. doi.org/10.18546/LRE.16.3.06.

Hudson, B. (2018), 'Powerful Knowledge and Epistemic Quality in School Mathematics', *London Review of Education: Special Issue on Knowledge and Subject Specialist Teaching*, 16 (3): 384–97. UCL IOE Press. https://doi.org/10.18546/LRE.16.3.03

Hudson, B., Gericke, N., Olin-Scheller, C. and Stolare, M. (2022), *International Perspectives on Knowledge and Quality: Implications for Innovation in Teacher Education Policy and Practice*, London: Bloomsbury Publishing plc.

Young, M. (2014), 'Powerful Knowledge as Curriculum Principle', in M. Young, D. Lambert, C. R. Roberts and M. D. Roberts, *Knowledge and the Future School: Curriculum and Social Justice*, 65–88, 2nd edition, London: Bloomsbury Academic.

Foreword

This book is a remarkable achievement. When Michael Young and Johan Muller opened up a rich seam of scholarship around the notion of powerful knowledge, it was not immediately apparent how challenging it would be to mount empirical studies – not only to develop further the idea of powerful knowledge itself but also to explore the related 'three futures' curriculum scenarios which appeared to distinguish more desirable curriculum arrangements from less robust (but far more commonplace) alternatives.

In theory at least, the three futures heuristic provided a means to distinguish high-quality, knowledge-rich curricula from other scenarios. However, in the absence of detailed empirical work with teachers from different subjects and focussed on classroom processes, this has not always been convincing. For instance, Tim Oates (2018: 159) has written that,

> ... the analysis of Future 1 (knowledge for its own sake); Future 2 (rejection of the epistemological basis of subjects and an assertion of 'skills'); and Future 3 (stipulation of concepts associated with different subjects) gives a misleading impression of the relative distance between the three perspectives (Young 2011). If Future 1 and Future 3 appear to have a "space" between them, then this could appear like the distance between the Earth and Moon. But if this is the analogy, then the distance between 1 and 3 is nothing compared to the difference between these and Future 2 – which in epistemological terms is in a galaxy far, far away. While Future 1 and Future 3 may require a short and intensive debate to resolve the practicalities of translation into legitimate curriculum policy, Future 2 was embedded in an entirely different and outdated conception of 'knowledge'.

Thus, Oates agrees with Young et al. that the main crisis in the curriculum lay in its apparent turn away from knowledge questions. But this passage apparently fails to grasp the significance of powerful knowledge, and in this Oates may not be alone. The problem is that powerful knowledge is not, in itself, fundamentally an analytical concept. It is not fruitful to set out identifying the powerful concepts in this or that subject. In my own subject (geography), for example, Alaric Maude found that the power of powerful knowledge in geography lay not so much in exactly which concepts were taught, nor in the precise selection from the infinite content possibilities of the subject: it lies in what the subject enables the learner to do. From this realization, he then proposed a 'typology' of geographical knowledge – in effect, an analytical device that has proved useful to practitioner researchers in this subject domain.

The brilliance of this book then lies in its willingness to tackle how to investigate empirically the 'power' or at least the potential and significance of subject teaching. It does this by putting powerful knowledge into the mix with two related, but far more *analytical*, concepts. The first of these, epistemic quality, invites us to make qualitative distinctions between epistemic practices: fundamentally, between those that focus heavily on *knowing that* as opposed to those that also impart forms of *know how* – including notions of how we know what we claim to know. The second is didactical (some readers may prefer, pedagogical) transformation, the work that must take place not only to 'recontextualise' disciplinary knowledge into forms appropriate to educational encounters with young people but also to relate such theoretical or 'academic' ideas to existing, local or everyday knowledges.

These studies grasp and describe the *emergent* nature of powerful knowledge and the crucial role played by agentive teachers driven by their sense of educational purpose – for instance, their joy in helping young people find 'new ways of thinking' about themselves and the external world. The book confirms my suspicions that it is unlikely that Future 3 curriculum scenarios, featuring high levels of epistemic quality, and enacted by highly knowledgeable and skilful specialist teachers, will result from '… a short and intensive debate to resolve the practicalities …'. And yet, if we want to lift the ambition of schools to engage young people with a curriculum fit for the twenty-first century, we need to build on the perspectives being explored here.

David Lambert
Honorary Professor of Geography Education
UCL Institute of Education

Acknowledgements

The editors are particularly grateful for the support from the Swedish Research Council received between 2019 and 2022 by the KOSS Network: 'Knowledge and Quality across School Subjects and Teacher Education' through the award of the Educational Sciences network grant (2018-03603).

We are also grateful to the ROSE research group (Research On Subject Specific Education) at Karlstad University, Sweden for its support in general and also for supporting many of the studies included in this book.

We thank Murray Bales for his careful work in the language editing process.

In addition, we thank the following for permission to publish or adapt figures for which they hold the copyright:

Figure 2.1 *Trajectory in the development of subject-specific powerful knowledge in mathematics*
Brian Hudson is the copyright holder.
Figure 3.1 *Trajectory of development in the epistemic capacities of choreographic activities*
Monique Loquet, Brian Hudson and Anke Wegner are the copyright holders.
Figure 3.2 *Example of one pictures of a sculpture by Ndary Lo taken by Yves Guigon*
Our thanks to Yves Guigon of Galerie Guigon in Paris for the granting permission to use the photograph of the '3 homme' sculpture by Ndary.
Figure 3.2 *Example of one picture of a sculpture by Ndary Lo taken by Yves Guigon*
Our thanks to Yves Guigon, of Gallerie Guigon, Paris for granting permission to use this image.
Figure 3.3 *Picture of the sculpture in iron by Ndary Lo taken by Charles Jousselin*
Our thanks to Charles Jousselin for granting permission to use this image: https://detoursdesmondes.typepad.com/dtours_des_mondes/2009/02/ndary-lo-un-art-des-passages.html
Figure 4.1 *Levels of teacher–student interaction and co-operation in the instructional process*
Our thanks to Verlag Barbara Budrich for granting permission to use this figure.
Figure 4.2 *Trajectory of development in relation to language and language use*
Anke Wegner, Brian Hudson and Monique Loquet are the copyright holders.

Figure 11.1 *Trajectory in the development of subject-specific powerful knowledge in mathematics (Hudson 2022)*
Brian Hudson is the copyright holder.

Figure 4.2 *Trajectory of development in relation to language and language use (Wegner et al. 2022)*
   Anke Wegner, Brian Hudson and Monique Loquet are the copyright holders.

1

Researching Powerful Knowledge and Epistemic Quality across School Subjects

Niklas Gericke, Brian Hudson, Christina Olin-Scheller and Martin Stolare

Introduction

Knowledge building in schools can be a transformative and empowering process, transforming pupils' capacities, sense of self-efficacy and agency, while also acting as a powerful engine of social justice and social transformation (Muller 2016). Still, knowledge building is notorious for sometimes being a dry and inert process that makes little difference to pupils' lives and entrenches social inequality (Young and Muller 2010). This book aims to develop understanding of how educators and education systems can ensure that school-based knowledge building reaches its transformative potential. In so doing, it draws on the concepts 'powerful knowledge' and 'epistemic quality' to help understand knowledge building's qualities when it is effective and empowering, and how educational processes can build and develop these characteristics. The underlying research studies focus on the ways in which knowledge itself is transformed as it is re-contextualised at the individual, institutional and societal levels. These three themes – *powerful knowledge, transformation processes* and *epistemic quality* – form the conceptual framework of the collaboration in the studies described and hold implications for curriculum innovation in policy and for practice, all of which this book seeks to explore. The concept of *powerful knowledge* (Young 2013) was developed as a curriculum principle in order to restore the importance of knowledge and teaching in curriculum development and research and as a way of overcoming the crisis in curriculum theory. In turn, the concept of *transformation* (Gericke et al. 2018) is seen as an integrative process through which specialized knowledge, developed in subject disciplines, is reshaped and re-presented in educational environments – through various processes outside and within the education system on societal, institutional and individual levels – as bodies and forms of knowledge to be taught and learned. Third, the concept of *epistemic quality* (Hudson 2018) relates to the quality of education in terms of what the students are expected to know, make sense of and be able to do through the school curriculum at the classroom level in particular.

When reviewing the literature from recent years we can see that these ideas, especially powerful knowledge, have gained great interest in the research community of subject-specific education, for example, in the fields of geography (e.g. Maude 2018), history (e.g. Nordgren 2017) and physics education (e.g. Yates and Millar 2016). Our ambition with this book is to create a common conceptual framework and language for subject-specific research and scholarship in relation to different disciplines and school subjects. To accomplish this goal, we need to operationalize and use these concepts in empirical studies, a quest called for by Gericke et al. (2018). In that way, we can compare the similarities and differences in terms of how this conceptual framework is expressed in different disciplinary traditions and school subjects when transformed. This book is a response to this call to empirically investigate how these concepts might be understood in different disciplinary and educational contexts so as to enrich our understanding of the role of disciplines and subjects across the school curriculum. A more comprehensive and ambitious goal of the book is to contribute to the development of new knowledge that ensures powerful disciplinary knowledge holds a prominent place in the curriculum, and to thereby help prepare schools to meet the possible educational needs of future citizens.

Research focus

This explorative book has emerged following invited responses to three key questions that reflect our aim to investigate and operationalize our conceptual framework of powerful knowledge, transformation processes and epistemic quality. These questions have in recent years guided the work of the KOSS network *Knowledge and Quality across School Subjects and Teacher Education*. The chapters in this book address the first two questions in particular:

1. How can the nature of powerful knowledge and epistemic quality in different school subjects be characterized?
2. How can the transformation processes related to powerful knowledge and epistemic quality be described?

The third question addresses the nature of teachers' *powerful professional knowledge* (Furlong and Whitty 2017) and the implications for teacher education policy and practice. These issues are the main foci of a second book developed parallel to this one and also published by Bloomsbury Academic and forming part of the *Reinventing Teacher Education* series (Hudson et al. 2022). Returning to this book, the focus of the studies illustrated in the following chapters is on how content knowledge in different school subjects is defined and transformed by taking a comparative perspective. The research studies look at how these concepts form knowledge of importance for subject-specific education and, in turn, how this has a role in curriculum innovation by using the theoretical concepts of *powerful knowledge, transformation* and *epistemic quality* elaborated below. A central issue is to explore how transformation processes can enable knowledge of high epistemic quality to be taught in school classrooms. This chapter introduces and overviews the book by providing the theoretical background that underpins our conceptual framework.

Powerful knowledge

Young's (2013) development of the *powerful knowledge* concept may partly be seen as a response to critics like Goodson and Marsh (1996), who had argued that curriculum theory had failed to address the historical and political dimensions of change in the latter decades of the twentieth century. They argued that the concern of most curriculum specialists was simply on how to implement policy changes, how to train teachers or how to develop 'pedagogic content knowledge'. This position is seen as too often simply playing 'the part of the facilitator of political will: ours not to reason why, ours but to do or die' (ibid.: 1). They further argued that the 'historical amnesia' of so much curriculum theory is both a symptom and a cause of this political posture. The failure to study school subjects historically and sociologically is seen to have resulted in school subjects becoming a normative aspect of schooling and treated as 'taken for granted givens'. In contrast, however, attention is drawn to the way in which the study of school subjects can rapidly lead to appreciating them as 'the most quintessential of social and political constructions'. From this perspective, school subjects are viewed as social constructions that intersect with patterns of social relations and social structure and are 'intimately implicated' in their reproduction and also in cultural transmission processes.

As indicated earlier, the concept of *powerful knowledge* was developed as a curriculum principle with a view to overcoming the crisis in curriculum theory in the way alluded to by Goodson and Marsh (ibid.). In discussing the question of what knowledge school students are entitled to have access to, Young (2013) developed the concept of powerful knowledge and argued that 'in all fields of enquiry, there is better knowledge, more reliable knowledge, knowledge nearer the truth about the world we live in and to what it is to be human' (Young 2013: 107). And yet this knowledge is always fallible and open to challenge, and Young highlights the difficulty of holding these two ideas at once. The concept is based on two key characteristics, both expressed in the form of boundaries. First, this knowledge is *specialized* in both how it is produced and transmitted, and this specialization is expressed in terms of the boundaries between disciplines and school subjects that serve to define their focus and objects of study. It is stressed that this is not general knowledge and that the boundaries are not fixed and unchangeable (Young 2013). It is also emphasized that cross-disciplinary research and learning depend on discipline-based knowledge. Second, this knowledge is *differentiated* from the experiences pupils bring to school or which older learners bring to college or university. Powerful knowledge is thus world-expanding and transformative. This differentiation is expressed in the conceptual boundaries between school and everyday knowledge (Young 2013).

Young identifies two main traditions or approaches in recent debates about knowledge in the educational sciences and philosophy. These traditions are extrapolated as trajectories into possible futures. In the first tradition, denoted Future 1, knowledge is underpinned by an 'under-socialized' epistemology (Young and Muller 2010) and defined as fixed sets of verifiable propositions or concepts that are evaluated in education, typically through standardized testing. The second tradition, denoted Future 2, arose in response to the first. Young and Muller (2010) claim the epistemology of knowledge in Future 2 is 'over-socialized' in that the character of knowledge is reduced to 'who knows' and the identification of knowers and their practices. This perspective is echoed in the work of Biesta (2012; 2017), who argues that the international turn towards generic skills-based curricula has resulted in the 'learnification' of education, which has undermined teaching and the teacher's role. He also argues that the point of education is never simply that children learn but that they learn *something* for *particular purposes* and that they learn this *from someone*.

Both of these approaches (Futures 1 and 2) can be viewed as deficient, according to Young (2014a, b). Future 1 has been shown to be unable to motivate and engage students with the body of knowledge to be learnt, and does not provide students with knowledge to tackle the complex problems of contemporary society (Young 2014a, b). The alternative approach, Future 2, suggests the integration of school subjects, the promotion of generic skills and facilitative teaching that, according to Young and Muller, has unintended negative consequences, rendering 'the contours of knowledge and learning invisible to the very learners that the pedagogy was designed to favour' (Young and Muller 2010: 19).

In response to these deficient ways of organizing and investigating curriculum, Young and Muller suggest a social realist theory that 'sees knowledge as involving sets of systematically related concepts and methods for their empirical exploration and the increasingly specialized and historically located 'communities of enquirers' (Young and Muller 2010: 14). Young and Muller denotes this alternative approach as a Future-3 solution to the problem of curriculum making. On this account, the most important part of curriculum making, and thus educational research, is to identify what constitutes 'powerful knowledge' in different school subjects and to identify how this type of knowledge can be built. Much of what has been published in curriculum studies on powerful knowledge has been part of a quest to investigate the nature of powerful knowledge in different disciplines and school subjects. In that quest, a normative perspective on knowledge is often taken, and the norm is to try to outline the Future-3 trajectory of different subjects.

In the disciplinary domain of geography education, Maude (2018; 2020) has explored the idea of powerful knowledge. Maude takes a more generic, and learner-centred, viewpoint on the issue, arguing that we should look at what the knowledge can establish for power within the learner. He claims that knowledge characterized by the following criteria may be classified as powerful within geography education: it provides students with new ways of thinking about the world; provides students with powerful ways of analysing, explaining and understanding; provides power over the students' own geographical knowledge; enables young people to follow and participate in debates on significant local, national and global issues of the world (Maude 2018; 2020). Hence, he sees powerful knowledge as knowledge that facilitates students' skills in those domains within a Future-3 trajectory.

With regard to physics, Yates and Millar (2016) asked physics teachers at both school and university levels about their beliefs regarding what lies at heart of their discipline, that is, what constitutes powerful knowledge. As argued by the authors, science and physics are school subjects that are in line with, and could be even considered 'role models', for Young's argument about disciplines creating powerful conceptual advances by using boundaries, rules and non-everydayness. Yet, the teachers in their study also argued that powerful knowledge is not conveyed by teaching specific bits of useful knowledge only but by having a sense of what physics is all about. Some teachers also emphasized physics as a field of inquiry, that is, more the practice than content, while questions of values, interest and identity were also raised (Yates and Millar 2016).

In music education, McPhail (2017) has explored what powerful knowledge might be in the school subject of music. This is a really interesting case because it is a subject in which experience, skills and aesthetics are important aspects. McPhail sees great merit in powerful knowledge as 'this knowledge occurs by placing abstract concepts at the centre of curriculum conception as means to mediate space between everyday knowledge and the more vertical discourse of school knowledge' (McPhail 2017: 524). McPhail claims the school subject of music chiefly has three dimensions: experiential (sensory and corporal), aesthetic and epistemic. Powerful knowledge would thus be the epistemic dimension, in which objective concepts like *tonality, intervals, scales* and *chords* create a disciplinary objective conceptual understanding through which the students can communicate and discuss the experiential and aesthetic dimensions. Yet, McPhail recognizes that this must be adapted to the different levels of the education system.

With regard to history, based on studies of history curriculum documents from South Africa and Rwanda Bertram (2019) highlighted that what counts as powerful knowledge in the school subject of history might vary greatly across countries. The post-apartheid South African curriculum focuses on sources and evidence, and history as a skill and enquiry to analyse historical documents. In contrast, the Rwandan history curriculum takes a collective, memory-history approach with a focus on nation-building and citizenship in the light of the country's experience of genocide.

These examples of empirical research on powerful knowledge in curriculum studies show the authors interpret powerful knowledge very differently, and must adapt it to the disciplinary contexts. This makes it of particular interest to add more studies to see whether powerful knowledge can be understood and defined in a unitary way, or if it always needs contextual adaptation. Of the reviewed studies, only Yates and Miller in physics and McPhail in music come close to the definition of Young. Most studies seem to struggle with the evaluation to name and define the normative quality of powerful knowledge. Furthermore, all the studies we reviewed addressed school curriculum documents and school teachers' views while investigating powerful knowledge, rather than taking the standpoint from the discipline, as argued by Young (2014a, b). We claim that this is necessary when empirically investigating powerful knowledge, and while addressing powerful knowledge in school settings we need to consider the issue of *transformation*, that is, the way knowledge is transformed when re-contextualized in school subjects. This concept is therefore elaborated in the next section.

Transformation processes

We recognize the need to develop the concept of powerful knowledge in two important ways (Gericke et al. 2018). First, rather than just discussing powerful knowledge as an idea related to educational practices, we take a research position which suggests that powerful knowledge can be used as a tool in educational research related to subject-specific education. In doing so, in line with Deng (2015) we propose to align the curricular concept of powerful knowledge with the European research tradition of didactics in general, and with subject didactics in particular. Second, we develop the concept of powerful knowledge by refuting the dichotomization suggested by Young (2014b) that curriculum ('what to teach') can be separated from pedagogy ('how to teach'). Instead, we view these two questions as interrelated in didactical research. We suggest an expansion of the concept of powerful knowledge by using transformation as a key analytical concept in describing powerful knowledge in different disciplines, institutions and school subjects.

The concept of transformation is central to the different didactical research traditions. Transformation, as we understand it, is an integrative process through which specialized knowledge, developed in subject disciplines, is reshaped and re-presented in educational environments – via various processes outside and within the education system at individual, institutional and societal levels – as bodies and forms of knowledge to be taught and learned. Such transformation processes are apparent in concepts related to several different frameworks, including 'transposition' (Chevallard 2007), 'omstilling' (Ongstad 2006) and 'reconstruction' (Duit et al. 2012), and are also reflected in the work of Bernstein (1971) in relation to 're-contextualisation' within the curriculum tradition. The school subject is never a simple reduction of the discipline, and the disciplinary knowledge is always transformed to fit the educational purpose of teaching. Hence, to study the concept of powerful knowledge within school subjects we must study its transformation processes and address the 'why' question in addition to the 'what' and 'how' questions.

As indicated above, the didactic approach is relational – the didactic questions are interconnected – they are not to be addressed separately. The relational perception holds consequences for selecting knowledge addressed in class. This is because the didactic questions of 'why', 'what' and 'how' are to be supplemented with questions addressing the specific educational situation and the role of the pupils. In planning and executing, the teacher also needs to handle the questions of 'for whom?' and 'when'. Hence, in connection to the German and Nordic Bildung-tradition, it may be said that there always is an objective as well as a subjective dimension to the process of selecting and transforming knowledge (Hopmann 2007; Jank and Meyer 2018). This means the question of 'what knowledge?' needs to be managed in relation to the intended students. The core of the teaching process thus becomes the interaction between the students and the selected knowledge, where the teacher has a watchful eye on the possible significance appropriation of the knowledge might have for the students today and in the future (Klafki 1995). Power (in terms of what knowledge enables you to pursue) is a dimension in the argument here but is also something Muller and Young (2019) highlight in their later texts on powerful knowledge. Still, in our conceptual framework, we need a concept that can encompass different aspects of 'why', 'what' and 'how' of the enacted curriculum in school subjects after being transformed, and it is here that the notion of epistemic quality becomes important.

Epistemic quality

The notion of epistemic quality (EQ), as discussed in Hudson et al. (2015) and Hudson (2016), arose from a perspective informed by concepts drawn from the framework of Joint Action Theory in Didactics (JATD), which has developed within the field of French didactics (Sensevy 2011). It arose in particular from a study on the development of mathematical thinking (Hudson 2015), which highlighted the ways in which the children actively engaged in the joint action between the teacher and students within the didactic system and the ways in which the teacher extended the *epistemic games* through the use of the open-ended topic-based approach combined with effective teacher questioning. It also highlighted the ways in which the discursive elements of *learning games* as part of these lessons proved to be very effective means in supporting the development of the students' mathematical thinking. These aspects are discussed further in Chapter 2 of this book (Hudson this volume). EQ is seen as a way of thinking that helps articulate aspects of what we mean by 'powerful knowledge' in different subjects. It has also developed as a response to the normative aspect of school referred to earlier, which treats school subjects simply as 'taken for granted givens' (Goodson and Marsh 1996: 1). The idea was developed as a theoretical outcome of a research study in the field of mathematics education, although it is seen to be very relevant for other subject domains. EQ links Powerful Knowledge to the classroom and the concrete teaching of a subject matter. The concept of epistemic quality captures the outcome of the selection and transformation process. EQ denotes the nature or quality of the teaching and learning embodied in the didactical interaction between teacher–pupil–subject matter, with a particular interest in the pupil's relation to the subject matter. Thus, EQ not only captures the content and its connection to Powerful Knowledge, but also the methods, what the student is expected to do and, by extension, the wider goal of the subject teaching. In this way, EQ connects to the didactic questions of why, what, how, for whom and when. The joint answers to these questions can be used to characterize orchestrated teaching and learning as permeated by low or high EQ.

In their study, Hudson et al. (2015) distinguish between *mathematical fallibilism* based on a heuristic view of mathematics as a human activity (Lakatos 1976) and *mathematical fundamentalism*. The former involves an approach that presents mathematics as fallible, refutable and uncertain, and which promotes critical thinking, creative reasoning, the generation of multiple solutions and of learning from errors and mistakes. In contrast, *mathematical fundamentalism* is characterized by an approach that presents the subject as infallible, authoritarian, dogmatic, absolutist, irrefutable and certain, and also involves an overemphasis on memorization, rule-following of strict procedures, and right or wrong answers. Moreover, this is seen as a question of 'epistemic quality' in terms of what the students are expected to know, understand and be able to do. Accordingly, the characteristics of mathematical fallibilism are used to describe school mathematics of *high epistemic quality* while those characterizing mathematical fundamentalism describe school mathematics of *low epistemic quality*. Mathematics is the example here, but the classification may be applied to the teaching of other subjects. For example, in history, one can contrast low epistemic quality approaches to learning about the past that do not – and high epistemic quality approaches that do – engage pupils in the key component processes of historical reasoning (Seixas and Morton 2013). In the first approach, school history largely consists of mastering large bodies of information or 'subject matter', to be assessed through multiple choice factual assessments or other strategies that prioritize recall. In the second approach, by contrast, school history consists of trying to engage pupils in authentic historical enquiries into the past that aim simultaneously to develop parallel aspects of pupils' historical knowing. In Chapter 2 of this book (Hudson this volume), the concept of epistemic quality is developed further by relating it to a trajectory of the *epistemic ascent* (Winch 2013) in the development of subject expertise. This is linked to a continuum that reflects a trajectory of the *epistemic ascent* in the development of subject expertise from the restricted 'knowledge by acquaintance' of the novice, the primary mode of knowledge being through the senses, towards the sophisticated higher-order 'knowledge that' and 'knowledge how' of an expert in the subject. This process reflects the increasing level of *know-that* and *know-how* on this trajectory of development.

The school's subjects are linked to academic disciplines, which in turn are rooted in different theoretical traditions. In the long run, this link means that perceptions of what can be considered EQ may differ between the subjects in school. A comparative cross-disciplinary approach presents an opportunity to determine what EQ can be in different subjects but also to point out the diversity among the subjects. In addition, when subjects and the different expressions of EQ are placed in relation to each other, this creates opportunities to define the concept at an analytical level. To do this, discussing the analytical power of the EQ concept, relating the concept to more established approaches like powerful knowledge and transformation, is an ambition of this book and something that will be done explicitly in the concluding chapter.

Overview of the chapters

This book is arranged into 11 chapters bringing empirical contributions from England, Finland, France, Germany, Norway, Scotland and Sweden. The texts address a range of classroom subject-specific and cross-curricular contexts, including arts, language, literature, mathematics, migration studies, natural science, physical education, social science, and sustainable development. An overview of the chapters is given below.

In Chapter 2, *Evaluating Epistemic Quality in Primary School Mathematics in Scotland*, Brian Hudson addresses the prior discussion of *epistemic quality* and develops a theoretical framework for evaluating the epistemic quality in primary school mathematics. Here epistemic quality is seen as a continuum of *epistemic ascent* in the development of expertise from the restricted 'knowledge by acquaintance' of the novice, towards the higher-order 'knowledge that' and 'knowledge how' of an expert. Ensuring high epistemic quality is important if we are to maximize the chances that every pupil has *epistemic access* to high-quality education in school mathematics. The third chapter, *Epistemic Quality of*

Physical Education in a High School in France by Monique Loquet, Brian Hudson and Anke Wegner, also considers epistemic quality, this time with regard to a series of dance lessons at a secondary school in France. The approach taken to the study is based on the Joint Action Theory in Didactics while the chapter considers the quality of teacher–student interaction in providing an epistemic quality of knowledge relative to the students' imagination and inventiveness. Epistemic quality is further developed in Chapter 4, *Epistemic Quality of Language Learning in a Primary Classroom in Germany*, where Anke Wegner, Brian Hudson and Monique Loquet draw on case study findings concerning a German language lesson at a primary school. The chapter is based on the perspectives of *Bildungsgangforschung and -didaktik* developed within the German didactics tradition in combination with the concept of epistemic quality. Epistemic quality in language and language use is highlighted, first by focusing on the epistemic quality of the content and, second, on the epistemic quality of the teacher–student(s) joint action.

Issues of language education are also considered by Birgitta Ljung Egeland and Lise Iversen Kulbrandstad in Chapter 5, *Powerful Knowledge of Language and Migration in Norwegian and Swedish Textbooks*. Their particular focus is on the academic disciplines of Norwegian/Swedish as second languages. Using the concept of powerful knowledge, they examine how knowledge is transformed in printed textbooks for middle school in these two countries. A main result is that the textbooks themselves offer students few possibilities to learn about second-language learning, multilingualism and comparisons between languages. First-language learning is in focus in Chapter 6, *Powerful Reading and Epistemic Quality in First Language and Literature Education*, by Satu Grünthal, Liisa Tainio and Pirjo Hiidenmaa. In Finland, first-language learning (L1) consists of both language and literature, with their study being based on a large reading motivation project and survey research carried out in primary schools. Seen through the powerful knowledge concept, the chapter discusses the diversity and profoundness of teaching methods, the books read and literature education in Finnish primary schools.

In Chapter 7, *Teaching Practices in Transformation in Connected Social Science Swedish Classrooms*, Marie Nilsberth, Christina Olin-Scheller and Martin Kristiansson address issues relating to digitalization and education. The chapter explores how transformation processes can enable knowledge of high epistemic quality to be taught in social science in a Swedish Grade 7 classroom. Through the lens of the literacy engagement model, instructional content is studied in terms of epistemic quality and powerful knowledge while using digital devices.

In Chapter 8, *Epistemic Quality in the Intended Mathematics Curriculum and Implications for Policy*, by Jennie Golding, the focus returns to the concept of *epistemic quality*. The chapter discusses how epistemic quality can, and should, be more explicitly addressed in the context of curriculum change and teacher education in mathematics.

Mark Hardman, John-Paul Riordan and Lindsay Hetherington study the situated, embodied and material nature of classroom contexts in Chapter 9, *A Material-dialogic Perspective on Powerful Knowledge and Matter within a Science Classroom*. This chapter extends the consideration of transformations from the intended curriculum to that enacted and learned by students. From video data involving a group of 13- to 14-year-olds in England, the text draws on a material-dialogic framework and explores how powerful knowledge is situated within the unique circumstances of a classroom. Their principal argument is that powerful knowledge emerges in the classroom not simply upon the interaction of teacher, student and content, but also via interaction with material resources. In Chapter 10, *Investigating the Nature of Powerful Knowledge and Epistemic Quality in Education for Sustainable Development*, Per Sund and Niklas Gericke address issues with collaboration on cross-curricular themes such as sustainable development. From a Swedish perspective, the chapter investigates the responses of teachers in the three different subject areas of language, science and social science, and describes how *powerful knowledge* of sustainable development can be characterized as the specific contribution of the various subject specialist teachers. However, the combined teaching from three subject areas together forms an educational content of greater *epistemic quality* in cross-curricular teaching that would not be offered to the students had sustainable development been taught separately within the subjects.

In the final chapter, *Trajectories of Epistemic Quality and Powerful Knowledge across School Subjects*, we reflect on the studies outlined in this book based on the KOSS research questions, regarding how the nature of powerful knowledge and epistemic quality in different school subjects can be characterized in the light of transformation. We begin that chapter by returning to Young's (2013) original description of powerful knowledge, and in particular to his focus on specialized knowledge in terms of the boundaries between disciplines and subjects, and outline how this way of understanding plays out in empirical studies of powerful knowledge in different school subjects. We also give particular consideration to the transformation process and the relationship between powerful knowledge and epistemic quality between and across school subjects. In doing so, we further develop the concepts of powerful knowledge, epistemic quality and transformation outlined in this chapter into a coherent system of interrelated analytical concepts that can be used in empirical studies in subject-specific research of different school subjects and disciplines. In that way, we aim to bridge the research communities across various school subjects into a combined area of comparative subject-specific research education.

References

Bernstein, B. (1971), *Class, Codes and Control. Vol. 1, Theoretical Studies towards a Sociology of Language*, London: Routledge.

Bertram, C. (2019), 'What is Powerful Knowledge in School History? Learning from the South African and Rwandan School Curriculum Documents', *The Curriculum Journal*, 30 (2): 125–43.

Biesta, G. J. J. (2012), 'Giving Teaching Back to Education: Responding to the Disappearance of the Teacher', *Phenomenology and Practice*, 6 (2): 35–49.

Biesta, G. J. J. (2017), *The Rediscovery of Teaching*, London and New York: Routledge.

Chevallard, Y. (2007), 'Readjusting Didactics to a Changing Epistemology', *European Educational Research Journal*, 6 (2): 131–4.

Deng, Z. (2015), 'Content, Joseph Schwab and German Didaktik', *Journal of Curriculum Studies*, 47: 773–86.

Duit, R., Gropengießer, H., Kattmann, U., Komorek, M., Parchmann, I. (2012), 'The Model of Educational Reconstruction – A Framework for Improving Teaching and Learning Science', in D. Jorde and J. Dillon (eds), *Science Education Research and Practice in Europe: Retrospective and Prospective*, 13–37, Rotterdam: Sense Publishers.

Furlong, J. and Whitty, G. (2017), 'Knowledge Traditions in the Study of Education', in J. Furlong and G. Whitty (eds), *Knowledge and the Study of Education*, 13–57, Oxford: Symposium Books.

Gericke, N., Hudson, B., Olin-Scheller, C. and Stolare, M. (2018), 'Powerful Knowledge, Transformations and the Need for Empirical Studies across School Subjects', *London Review of Education: Special Issue on Knowledge and Subject Specialist Teaching*, 16 (3): 428–44. UCL IOE Press. https://doi.org/10.18546/LRE.16.3.06

Goodson, I. F. and Marsh, C. J. (1996), *Studying School Subjects: A Guide*, London: Falmer Press.

Hopmann, S. (2007), 'Restrained Teaching: The Common Core of Didaktik', *European Educational Research Journal*, 6 (2): 109–24.

Hudson, B. (2015), 'Butterflies and Moths in the Amazon: Developing Mathematical Thinking through the Rainforest', *Education and Didactique*, 9 (2): 119–33. http://educationdidactique.revues.org/2322

Hudson, B. (2016), 'The Epistemology and Methodology of Curriculum: Didactics', in D. Wyse, L. Hayward and J. Pandya (eds), *SAGE Handbook of Curriculum, Pedagogy and Assessment*, 107–24, London: Sage Publications.

Hudson, B. (2018), 'Powerful Knowledge and Epistemic Quality in School Mathematics', *London Review of Education: Special Issue on Knowledge and Subject Specialist Teaching*, 16 (3): 384–97. UCL IOE Press. https://doi.org/10.18546/LRE.16.3.03

Hudson, B. (2019), 'Epistemic Quality for Equitable Access to Quality Education in School Mathematics', *Journal of Curriculum Studies*, 51 (4): 437–56. https://doi.org/10.1080/00220272.2019.1618917

Hudson, B., Gericke, N., Olin-Scheller, C. and Stolare, M. (2022), *International Perspectives on Knowledge and Quality: Implications for Innovation in Teacher Education Policy and Practice*, London: Bloomsbury Publishing plc.

Hudson, B., Henderson, S. and Hudson, A. (2015), 'Developing Mathematical Thinking in the Primary Classroom: Liberating Teachers and Students as Learners of Mathematics', *Journal of Curriculum Studies*, 47 (3): 374–98. http://dx.doi.org/10.1080/00220272.2014.979233

Jank, W. and Meyer, H. (2018), *Didaktische Modelle. [Didactic models. Handbook of Didaktik]*. (12. Aufl.), Frankfurt am Main: Cornelsen Scriptor.

Klafki, W. (1995), 'Didactic Analysis as the Core of Preparation for Instruction' (Didaktische Analyse als Kern der Unterrichtsvorbereitung), *Journal of Curriculum Studies*, 27 (1): 13–30.

Lakatos, I. (1976), *Proofs and Refutations*, Cambridge: Cambridge University Press.

Maude, A. (2018), 'Geography and Powerful Knowledge: A Contribution to the Debate', *International Research in Geographical and Environmental Education*, 27 (2): 179–90.

Maude, A. (2020), 'The Role of Geography's Concepts and Powerful Knowledge in a Future 3 Curriculum', *International Research in Geographical and Environmental Education*, 29 (3): 232–43.

McPhail, G. J. (2017), 'Powerful Knowledge: Insights from Music's Case', *The Curriculum Journal*, 28 (4): 524–38.

Muller, J. (2016), 'Knowledge and the Curriculum in the Sociology of Knowledge', in D. Wyse, L. Hayward and J. Pandya (eds), *SAGE Handbook of Curriculum, Pedagogy and Assessment*, 92–106, London: Sage Publications.

Muller, J. and Young, M. (2019), 'Knowledge, Power and Powerful Knowledge Re-visited', *The Curriculum Journal*, 30 (2): 196–214.

Nordgren, K. (2017), 'Powerful Knowledge, Intercultural Learning and History Education', *Journal of Curriculum Studies*, 49 (5): 663–82.

Ongstad, S. (red.) (2006), *Fag og didaktikk i lærerutdanning: kunnskap i grenseland*, Oslo: Universitetsforlaget.

Seixas, P. and Morton, T. (2013), *The Big Six Historical Thinking Concepts*, Toronto: Nelson.

Sensevy, G. (2011), 'Overcoming Fragmentation: Towards a Joint Action Theory in Didactics', in Hudson, B. and Meyer, M. A. (eds), *Beyond Fragmentation: Didactics, Learning, and Teaching*, 60–76), Opladen and Farmington Hills: Verlag Barbara Budrich.

Winch, C. (2013), 'Curriculum Design and Epistemic Ascent', *Journal of Philosophy of Education*, 47 (1): 128–46.

Yates, L. and Millar, V. (2016), '"Powerful Knowledge" Curriculum Theories and the Case of Physics', *The Curriculum Journal*, 27 (3): 298–312.

Young, M. (2013), 'Overcoming the Crisis in Curriculum Theory: A Knowledge-based Approach', *Journal of Curriculum Studies*, 45 (2): 101–18. http://www.tandfonline.com/doi/full/10.1080/00220272.2013.764505

Young, M. (2014a), 'Powerful Knowledge as Curriculum Principle, in M. Young, D. Lambert, C. R. Roberts and M. D. Roberts, *Knowledge and the Future School: Curriculum and Social Justice*, 65–88, 2nd edition, London: Bloomsbury Academic.

Young, M. (2014b), 'The Progressive Case for a Subject-based Curriculum', in M. Young, D. Lambert, C. R. Roberts, and M. D. Roberts (eds), *Knowledge and the Future School: Curriculum and Social Justice*, 89–109, 2nd edition, London: Bloomsbury Academic.

Young, M. and Muller, J. (2010), 'Three Educational Scenarios for the Future: Lessons from the Sociology of Knowledge', *European Journal of Education* 45: 11–27.

2

Evaluating Epistemic Quality in Primary School Mathematics in Scotland

Brian Hudson

Introduction

This chapter builds on the idea of *epistemic quality*, as discussed in Hudson (2018, 2019), which arose from the outcomes of the *Developing Mathematical Thinking in the Primary Classroom* (DMTPC) project (Hudson et al. 2015). It does so by relating epistemic quality to a continuum that reflects a trajectory of *epistemic ascent* (Winch 2013) in the development of expertise from the novice towards that of an expert in the subject. The significance of epistemic quality stems from the need to maximize the chances that all pupils will have *epistemic access* (Morrow 2008; Young 2013: 115) to high-quality education in school mathematics. This is regarded as a way of making quality education visible and as a precondition for addressing the challenges of UN Sustainable Development Goal 4 to ensure inclusive and equitable quality education for all (UN 2015). The idea of epistemic quality is in turn used as a theoretical framework for evaluating the quality in primary school mathematics by revisiting the data analysis from an earlier study that considered the development of a topic-based approach to teaching and learning mathematics on the theme of 'The Rainforest' (Hudson 2015, 2019). The analysis addresses the question of how the nature of epistemic quality in school mathematics can be characterized by focussing first on the epistemic quality of the content and second on the epistemic quality of the teacher–student(s) joint action. As such, the chapter addresses KOSS research questions 1 and 2 that look at how the nature of powerful knowledge and epistemic quality in different school subjects can be characterized and how the transformation processes related to powerful knowledge and epistemic quality can be described, respectively. The final discussion focuses on considering the implications for curriculum innovation in schools.

Developing mathematical thinking in the primary classroom project

The DMTPC project was funded by the Scottish Government (2010–12) and involved working with a group of practising teachers ($n = 24$), who were all participants in a newly developed Masters course designed with the aim of promoting the development of mathematical thinking in the primary classroom. The project as a whole was established within a design research framework, which sought to promote curriculum development through the process of classroom-based action research on the part of participants and also research and evaluation of the project as a whole. A Curriculum for Excellence Development partnership group was established to plan the course that included a teacher from each of the Local Education Authorities (LEA) together with LEA advisory staff members and members of the university project team. An important aspect of the case made for support in the grant application was the fact that most mathematics lessons at that time in Scotland still tended to feature some form of teacher-led demonstration followed by children practising skills and procedures from a commercially produced scheme (Scottish Executive Education Department 2005). The more recent Scottish Survey of Literacy and Numeracy highlighted that the highest percentage of pupils reported that the ways in which they participated 'very often' were to 'listen to the teacher talk to the class about a topic' (62 per cent in P4 and 64 per cent in P7 and S2) and to 'work on your own' (between 55 and 61 per cent) (Scottish Government 2012: 13).

The course was designed around three main questions, two core texts and an action research project. The key questions were:

- What is mathematics?
- What is mathematical thinking?
- What is good mathematics teaching?

Participants completed an action research project, with their reports forming the course assignment. The research questions of the associated study focused on the teachers' confidence, competence, attitudes and beliefs relative to mathematics and their expectations and experiences of the impact on pupil learning arising from this course. Empirical data were drawn from pre- and post-course surveys, interviews, observations of the discussion forums in the online environment and from the teachers' action research project reports.

Epistemic quality

The term 'epistemic' is concerned with the knowledge involved in a didactical or teaching-studying-learning situation (Hudson et al. 2020). In turn, the term 'epistemic quality' refers to the quality of what students come to know, make sense of and are able to do in school. The concept of epistemic quality arose from a perspective informed by concepts drawn from the field of subject didactics (Hudson et al. 2015; Hudson 2016) and is seen as a way of thinking that helps articulate aspects of what we mean by 'powerful knowledge' (Young 2013, 2015). It is also seen as a way of making quality education visible and as of particular significance for addressing the challenges of UN Sustainable Development Goal 4 to ensure inclusive and equitable quality education for all (UN 2015). It is especially significant in relation to the need to maximize the chances that all pupils will have *epistemic access* (Morrow 2008; Young 2013: 115) to powerful knowledge through the curriculum which is seen as 'access to the best knowledge in any field of study they engage in' (Young 2013: 115). The idea stemmed from the process of applying the theoretical framework of Joint Action Theory in Didactics (JATD), developed within the tradition of French didactics, to the analysis of classroom interaction. JATD is based on the theoretical principle that, in order to understand a didactic activity, which denotes an activity when someone teaches and someone learns, you need to understand a *system*, the *didactic system* (Brousseau 1997; Sensevy et al. 2005; Sensevy 2011). This is a system of three subsystems, namely knowledge, the teacher and the student. The didactic system is seen as indivisible, and it is regarded as impossible to grasp the meaning of the teacher's action without understanding the relations between this action, the students' action and the structure of the piece of knowledge at stake. A key concept drawn from JATD is that of a 'game' based on the concept of 'language games' (Wittgenstein 1997) specific to didactic systems, as discussed by Sensevy (2011). 'Game' is used to describe what happens in a given didactic situation and allows us to describe the joint dimension of the didactic activity by modelling the interactions between the student and the teacher as participants in the same 'game'. Particular attention has been given to two games through the ways in which students participate in *learning games* in connection with *epistemic games*. With regard to the latter, an *epistemic game* refers to the game of the mathematician as a subject expert in his or her professional activity and two aspects of this game are distinguished. On the one hand, the *source epistemic game* refers to the human practices that exist outside the didactic situation while, on the other hand, the *actual epistemic game* is based on the analysis of class practices as they occur *in situ*. Second, the *learning game* is the reciprocal game of the student in relation to the joint game. In turn, these are seen as games of a particular kind, that is, as games in which some specific pieces of knowledge are involved and as collaborative or joint games within joint action (Gruson, Loquet and Pilet 2012: 65). A second key concept influencing the evolution of the idea of epistemic quality is that of 'didactic transposition', which draws from the wider field of French didactics as outlined by Chevallard (2007). The basic principle underpinning this perspective on learning and teaching is that knowledge is not something that is to be taken as simply given and to be explained. Rather, it is the case that 'knowledge is potentially encapsulated in situations, and it is in going through those situations that the pupil, or whoever, can learn' (Chevallard 2007). This view of learning as 'learning from the situation' is a central principle of French didactics, which sees knowledge as built up and transformed or *transposed* in didactic situations. Underpinning this theory is an ecological approach to the social dynamic of knowledge (ibid.). The main point in didactic transposition theory is that it considers knowledge as a changing reality, which adapts to its institutional habitat. Accordingly, in relation to the school context, the knowledge in question is not knowledge for acting and solving problems in the social contexts in which it was created and where it is used, but instead is transposed into knowledge to be taught and learned. This is an example of a transformation process, as discussed in Gericke et al. (2018).

A significant situation that highlighted the issue of epistemic quality occurred within the DMTPC course and was a result of the powerful responses arising from the teachers' readings of the book *The Elephant in the Classroom* by Boaler (2009). In this book, Boaler highlights the fact that in many mathematics classrooms a very narrow subject is taught to children, one that involves copying methods that teachers demonstrate and reproducing them accurately over and over again. Furthermore, she argues that this narrow subject is not mathematics but that it is a strange mutated version of the subject that is taught in schools. This process of mutation is seen as a transformation process and in particular as an example of didactic transposition. The mutated version of mathematics is characterized by an approach that presents the subject as infallible, authoritarian, dogmatic, absolutist, irrefutable and certain, and also involves an overemphasis on memorization, rule-following of strict procedures and right or wrong answers. In Hudson et al. (2015), we describe this as *mathematical fundamentalism* (Hudson et al. 2015) and contrast it with *mathematical fallibilism* based on a heuristic view of mathematics as a human activity (Lakatos 1976). The latter involves an approach that presents mathematics as fallible, refutable and uncertain, and which promotes critical thinking, creative reasoning, the generation of multiple solutions and of learning from errors and mistakes. The central role of creative reasoning is considered further in Hudson (2018, 2019) by drawing on the work of Lithner (2006) who offers a conceptual framework that compares and contrasts creative and imitative reasoning in mathematics which fits with the distinctions between mathematical fundamentalism and mathematical fallibilism. In relation to imitative reasoning in mathematics, Lithner (ibid.) highlights two aspects: memorized reasoning and algorithmic reasoning. Memorized reasoning is seen to fulfil two conditions. First, the strategy choice is founded on recalling a complete answer and, second, the strategy implementation consists only of writing it down. In relation to algorithmic reasoning and with reference to Brousseau (1997: 129), an algorithm is defined as 'a finite sequence of executable instructions that allows one to find a definite result for a given class of problems'. Similarly, algorithmic reasoning meets two conditions. First, the strategy choice is to recall a solution algorithm regarding which the predictive argumentation may be of different kinds but does not necessitate the creation of a new solution. Second, the remaining reasoning parts of the strategy implementation are trivial for the reasoner, and only a careless mistake can prevent an answer from being reached. Lithner (ibid.) also stresses how textbooks and teachers can serve to guide such superficial memorized and algorithmic reasoning. In contrast, creative mathematical reasoning involves novelty, plausibility and mathematical foundation, while creativity is seen as an orientation or disposition towards mathematical activity that can be fostered broadly in school. This perspective is reflected in US Standards of the National Council of Teachers of Mathematics (NCTM 2000) that recognize reasoning and proof as fundamental aspects of mathematics. 'People who reason and think analytically tend to note patterns, structure, or regularities in both real-world situations and symbolic objects; they ask if those patterns are accidental or if they occur for a reason; and they conjecture and prove' (ibid., 56). Such reasoning can have many functions in mathematics, including verification, explanation, systematization, discovery, communication, construction of theory and exploration.

In relation to epistemic quality, the characteristics of mathematical fundamentalism are used to describe school mathematics of *low epistemic quality*, while those characterizing mathematical fallibilism describe school mathematics of *high epistemic quality*. It is further argued (Hudson et al. 2015) that high epistemic quality is promoted through an approach based on assessment *for* learning involving low stakes formative and self-assessment. This is engaging and motivating for individual learners and can create the conditions leading to a sense of enjoyment and fulfilment of mathematics as a creative human activity. In contrast, the excessive pressure from high-stakes external testing and inspection and the associated heavy emphasis on memorization, drill and practice establish circumstances that can degrade epistemic quality into the mutated form of mathematical fundamentalism and lead to an experience for learners of mathematics that is fearful and anxiety-inducing, boring, demotivating and alienating from the subject itself.

In this chapter, the concept epistemic quality is developed further by considering it in relation to the idea of *epistemic ascent* (Winch 2013) in the development of subject expertise. This is based on a continuum that reflects a trajectory in developing expertise from that of a novice towards that of an expert in the subject. In his discussion of curriculum design and epistemic ascent, Winch (2013: 129) identifies three distinct yet related kinds of knowledge: *knowledge by acquaintance*, propositional knowledge or *knowledge that* and procedural knowledge or *knowledge how*. By doing so, he highlights the importance of each and also the relationships between them for the process of curriculum design. The primary mode of *knowledge by acquaintance* is through the senses so that one may be acquainted with objects, events, processes, states and persons. Examples of how such *knowledge by acquaintance* can arise include hearing a piece of music, smelling a flower and tasting a fruit. Furthermore, it is highlighted that not only is this an important part of any curriculum but also it is often a challenge for the curriculum designer to provide such knowledge. In relation to powerful knowledge, there is a correspondence between *knowledge by acquaintance* and Young's (2013) use of the term 'everyday knowledge'. While discussing *knowledge that*, Winch (ibid.) argues that this cannot consist solely in the identification of true but isolated propositions, but that this is embedded within a conceptual structure which is itself embedded within further related propositions. In developing subject expertise, it is stressed that it is not only the quantity of propositions that is important but also the ability to understand and, with reference to Brandom (2000), to make inferences employing the concepts embodied within the subject matter. It is also stressed (Winch 2013: 132) that it is necessary to be able to distinguish within the subject between claims that can be counted as knowledge and those which count as true beliefs. He also highlights that this distinction can be especially hard for a novice because the source of such beliefs is authoritative testimony. Third, as concerns *knowledge how*, it is argued that knowing how to do something is an epistemic capacity that is related to *knowledge by acquaintance* and *knowledge that* given that knowing how to do something usually requires elements of the other two kinds of knowledge. In thinking about the nature of expertise, it is argued that this applies to both *knowledge how* and *knowledge that* and also their inferential relationships with each other. Subject expertise in turn also involves knowledge of how to make and understand inferences to a very significant extent. Beginning to learn a subject involves beginning to use the language associated with the concepts of the subject, and this is primarily a practical ability that is learned. Accordingly, a central dimension of learning about a subject is learning to take part in conversations and discussions that employ those concepts. This process is part of a gradual transition from novice to expert as, with reference to Wittgenstein (1969), 'light dawns gradually over the whole'.

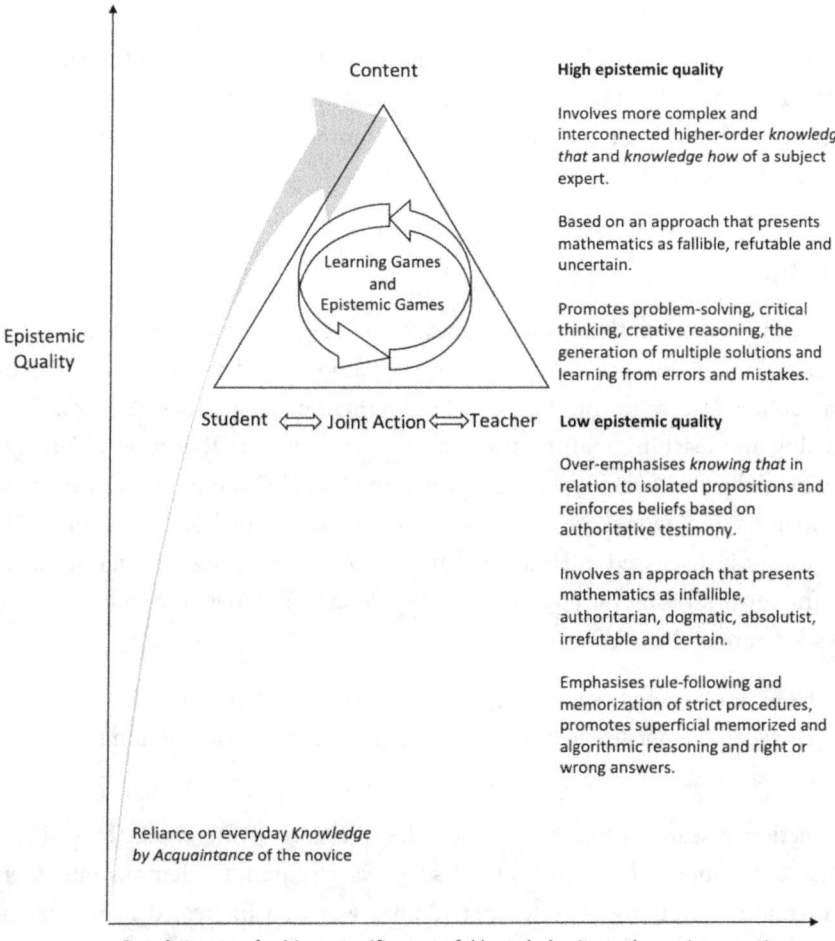

Figure 2.1 Trajectory in the development of subject-specific powerful knowledge in mathematics.

This stress on the crucial role of language in the process of developing subject expertise reflects the emphasis placed on this aspect in JATD through the central focus within this framework on language games. Hence, in the process of epistemic ascent the novice moves from a position in which *knowledge by acquaintance* and isolated beliefs based on authoritative testimony are predominant towards the more complex and interconnected higher-order *knowledge that* and *knowledge how* of an expert in the subject. This trajectory of development in relation to school mathematics is captured in Figure 2.1.

The framework based on *epistemic quality* outlined above is used in this chapter to evaluate the quality in primary school mathematics by revisiting the data analysis of an earlier study. This focuses on two aspects; first, the epistemic quality of the content knowledge and, second, the epistemic quality of the teacher–student(s) joint action. The idea of joint action is a fundamental starting point for JATD and is based on a view articulated by Loquet (2011) of teaching and learning as co-operative and asymmetric joint action between the teacher and the students.

The study

The study is based on the analysis of one sequence of classroom interaction from a series of mathematics lessons in a primary school. The data collection was part of an action research project on the development of a topic-based approach to teaching and learning mathematics on the theme of 'The Rainforest'. This was conducted by one teacher who took part in the DMTPC project already referred to. Analysis of data taken from the series of lessons as a whole using the JATD framework is discussed in Hudson (2015, 2019). In revisiting the analysis using the framework based on epistemic quality described above, the following two questions are addressed:

i. How can the epistemic quality of content be characterized?
ii. How can the epistemic quality of teacher–student(s) joint action be characterized?

The action research project addressed the question of the extent to which a topic-based approach to mathematics allows children to demonstrate their mathematical thinking. The teacher (Anna) was also interested in the extent to which topic-based mathematical questions allow children to verbalize their thinking and also the effect of such an approach on children's levels of engagement. This study took place in a five-class, rural primary school in Angus in North East Scotland, with a mixed-age class of Year 5 and Year 6 pupils, aged between 9 and 11 during the Spring and Summer terms of 2012. The overall topic for the action research project was 'The Rainforest' and, as a result, 23 pupils were given 4 questions to explore, analyse and record during a period of 3 weeks. The mathematical content was 'measurement', which chiefly related to measuring length and weight. The four questions the pupils worked on were:

1. How could we measure these life-sized insects accurately?
2. How could we mark out the different layers of the rainforest in our playground?
3. Can you compare the length of the River Tay and the Amazon River?
4. Is there a relationship between the weight of an animal and the layer it lives on in the rainforest?

Accounts of happenings in teaching and learning situations were recorded by collecting data in three ways. First, children's talk was recorded informally during conversations with peers. Second, notes were made of what children said during class feedback sessions and comments on the lessons in feedback sessions were recorded. Furthermore, observations were made of the levels of engagement within the class and various parts of the activities were filmed to watch and analyse on a later date. In this paper, one extract from Lesson 3 in response to question 3 is used for the analysis.

Data collection

Lesson 3 focused on addressing the question: 'Can you compare the length of the River Tay and the Amazon River?' Anna described her expectation for the children to be able to 'discuss length confidently in kilometres and to demonstrate an understanding of the enormity of the Amazon River in relation to the River Tay'. Prior to the lesson, the children had investigated the length of a kilometre, and most were able to convert between metres and kilometres. To begin the activity, children had 30 minutes to research the lengths of the two rivers by making use of the Internet.

A Year-5 boy (Andrew) explained his thinking as he was beginning to engage in the activity:

'The Amazon is like a snake, so some people might be measuring it from when it's just a wee stream and some might just be measuring it from the start of the big river'.

The children were then asked by Anna to present their findings in a sentence, paragraph or diagram. Anna saw this as a successful exercise for observing and recording the children's understanding of kilometres in a relaxed yet focused atmosphere. Some of the children's findings are listed below to illustrate the progress of the activity:

A Year-5 boy (Joseph) simply noted that:

The Tay is shorter than the Amazon.

Another Year-5 boy (Andrew) went further:

'The Amazon is the second biggest river in the world at around an amazing 6,400 kilometres long. So, the Amazon is longer'.

A Year-6 boy (Keith) described more extensive use of the Internet:

'We only found our results in miles but we found an online converter and put them both into kilometres'.

A Year-5 girl (Karen) stated that:

'We took away 193 from 6,360 to find the difference between the two rivers.'

This comment intrigued the rest of the class and prompted the activity of repeating the calculation to see if Karen had calculated correctly.

Anna describes how, following this activity, a Year-5 boy (John) wanted to explain the diagram that he and his partner had created.

He stated, 'I drew the Amazon and the River Tay on my piece of paper. I measured the paper and it was about 300 millimetres so we narrowed it down and got that every 5 centimetres was about 1,000 kilometres. The River Tay is only 186 kilometres, so it's only that size'.

She describes how he then pointed to the part of their diagram labelled 'River Tay' at the very bottom of the page shown in Figure 2.2.

Anna noted how this comment and diagram not only confirmed John's understanding of kilometres, but also how it demonstrated his understanding of centimetres and millimetres. Furthermore, she noted how from the teacher's perspective it had been an excellent opportunity to not only see the children's mathematical thinking unfold in their diagram but also listen to their explanation and observe their enthusiasm. The other children in the class were very interested in this and one Year-6 girl (Tracy) continued by commenting that:

The Tay is tiny compared to that, you could fit like, a hundred of the Tay into the Amazon!

Anna notes how this comment was explored and extended, leading her to question:

'How many times would the Tay fit into the Amazon River?' (Anna).

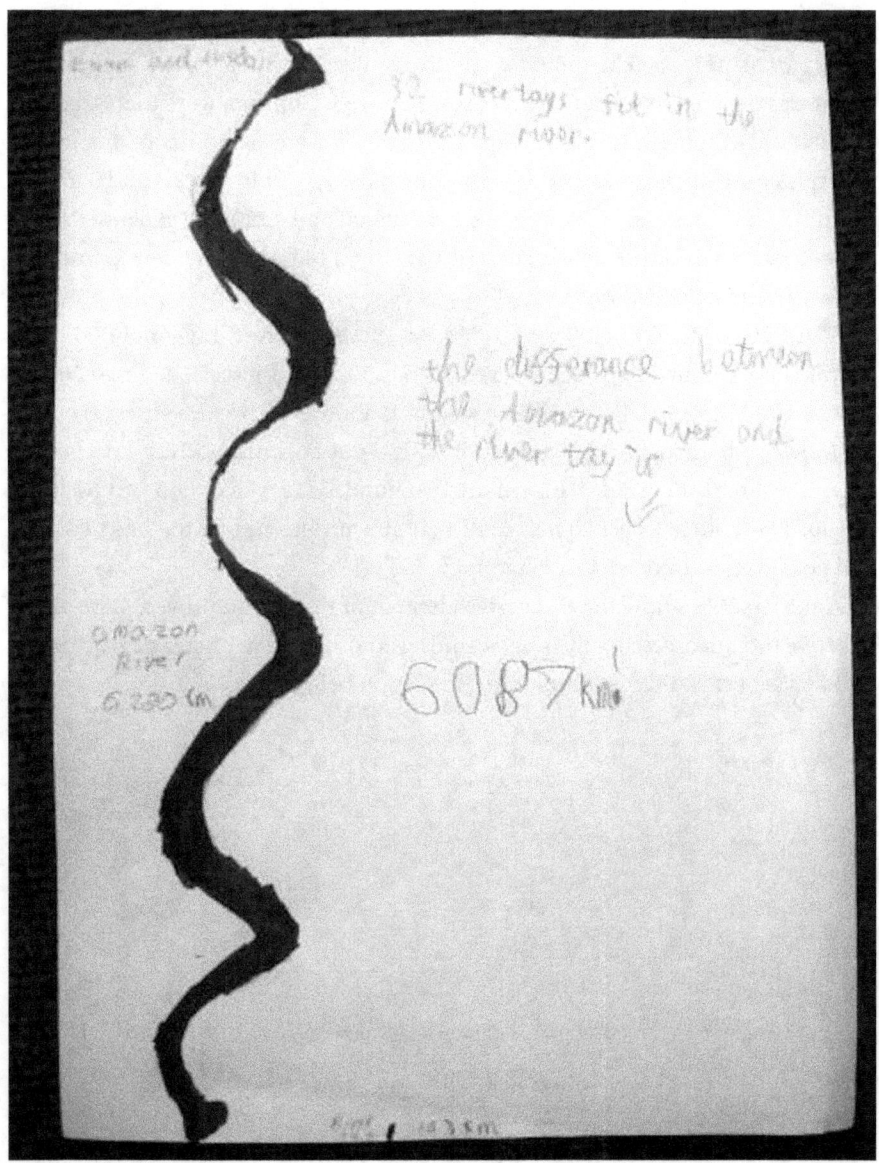

Figure 2.2 John's drawings of the River Tay and the River Amazon.

Subsequently, Anna described this as a 'light bulb moment' and this aspect is discussed further in the section below.

One Year-6 boy (Michael) suggested that both numbers should be rounded off to make it easier. In response, a Year-6 girl (Charlotte) said:

That would be …. 190 kilometres?

Michael then replied: 'It'd be good to do it to 200, to the hundred instead.'

As part of the whole class activity, Anna organized a vote on the two suggestions, and it was decided to work to the nearest hundred. Children were then set a task to solve this problem in pairs. Various methods were demonstrated, and two examples of the children's working are shown below in Figures 2.3 and 2.4.

To finish the lesson, the results were discussed and strategies explained. Here are two examples of the children's writing, which highlight the development of their mathematical thinking.

'I did 200, 400, 600, 800 and 1,000, so there's 5 River Tays in 1,000. That means there's 30 in 6,000 because 5 times 6 is 30, then I just needed two 200s to get the 400 kilometres left. So, the Amazon is about 32 River Tays.'

'I did 6,400 divided by 200 as a sum to find out how many River Tays I could get in the Amazon. I said, "How many two hundreds are in 6, none, in 64 none, in 640, 3 with 40 left over". Then I put that 40 with the zero in the units column and got two hundreds in 400. That made 32.'

Anna describes how the discursive element of this lesson proved to be a very effective tool for assessing the pupils' understanding and mathematical thinking, and this aspect is discussed more in the section below.

Figure 2.3 First example of a child's working.

Figure 2.4 Second example of a child's working.

Data analysis

The data is analysed by addressing the question of how the nature of epistemic quality in school mathematics can be characterized, and consideration is paid to the implications for curriculum innovation in the final discussion. With regard to epistemic quality, two aspects are addressed in particular; first, the epistemic quality of the content and, second, the epistemic quality of the teacher–student(s) joint action.

Epistemic quality of the content

In addressing the question 'Can you compare the length of the River Tay and the Amazon River?', Anna had designed a classroom activity that drew on the children's *knowledge by acquaintance*. One of her aims was that the children would build on their prior knowledge and be able to discuss length confidently in kilometres and demonstrate an understanding of the enormity of the Amazon River in comparison with the River Tay. The children's *knowledge by acquaintance* was based on two aspects. The first aspect was their general knowledge of the Amazon River, which may already have been gained through popular culture but was introduced and/or extended through the project on 'The Rainforest'. The second aspect was their knowledge of the River Tay as a very familiar feature of the local environment in which they lived. Prior to the lesson, the children had developed their *knowledge that* by investigating the length of a kilometre, and most had developed the *knowledge how* in terms of converting between metres and kilometres. The classroom activity was developed by the children having some time at the outset to research the lengths of the two rivers by making use of the Internet.

Andrew demonstrated his engagement in the activity by comparing the Amazon to a snake, while Joseph demonstrated a basic *knowledge how* in terms of comparison by making the inference that the Tay is shorter than the Amazon. Similarly, Andrew concluded that the Amazon is longer by also noting that it is the second-biggest river in the world at around 6,400 kilometres in length. Keith demonstrated how his *knowledge how* had been extended by the fact that his group could only find distances in miles, leading them to find an online converter to convert them both kilometres. Karen also demonstrated *knowledge how* of subtraction in finding the difference between the two rivers. This contribution intrigued the rest of the class and was used by Anna to extend the activity by engaging the class in repeating the calculation to see if Karen had calculated correctly. She describes how John wanted to explain the diagram he and his partner had created, as illustrated in Figure 2.2. In drawing pictures of both the Amazon and the River Tay, he used his prior *knowledge how* of measuring and also of ratio and scale such that every 5 centimetres represented 1,000 kilometres. This resulted in a very striking overall representation of the size of the two rivers and Tracy's comment that the River Tay was tiny in comparison. Anna highlighted the extent of both John's *knowledge that* and *knowledge how* in noting that this confirmed his understanding not only of kilometres but also of centimetres and millimetres and the associated inter-relatedness between them. Anna also stressed the importance of language in emphasizing how it had been an excellent opportunity for her to not only see the children's mathematical thinking unfold in their diagram but to also listen to their explanation and observe their enthusiasm. She goes on to illuminate how she built on Tracy's comment, leading to her key question of 'How many times would the Tay fit into the Amazon River?'

In summing up, Anna noted that it was evident the children were able to take their investigation further according to their level of understanding and previous knowledge. A particularly significant aspect of Lesson 3 was the incident Anna described as a 'light bulb moment'. This marked a situation in which she responded at the moment and built on the children's contributions to extend the classroom activity in a very spontaneous and creative way. As a result, the epistemic quality of the content was greatly enhanced into one concerned with both *knowledge that* and *knowledge how* in relation to estimation, scale and calculations involving addition, subtraction, division and multiplication with up to four-digit numbers.

Epistemic quality of teacher–student(s) joint action

In relation to the quality of the teacher–student(s) joint action, Anna describes how the discursive element of this lesson proved to be a very effective tool for assessing the pupils' understanding and mathematical thinking. Anna's original learning intention for this lesson was for the children to become confident in measuring with millimetres and be able to convert between centimetres and millimetres. However, the children's *knowledge how* and mathematical thinking was extended through a process of creative reasoning to consideration of *knowledge that* in terms of the concept of scale, which involved estimation and also calculations entailing addition, subtraction, division and multiplication with up to four-digit numbers as outlined above. Since all pupils recognized the vast difference between the two rivers, their natural inquisitiveness and natural orientation towards creative reasoning drove them to extend their own thinking and the thinking of others. The question in Lesson 3 'Can you compare the length of the River Tay and the Amazon River?' in particular developed tremendously throughout the lesson. It was evident in this study that the children had very different prior knowledge and experiences to bring to the problem-solving elements of the tasks. Moreover, the mathematics became more accessible to all due to their ability to visualize the problems and to engage in collective creative reasoning. This resulted from the high quality of the teacher–student(s) joint action and the high epistemic quality of the content, which in turn can be seen to have produced an evolution in mathematical thinking and epistemic access (Morrow 2008; Young 2013: 115) to powerful knowledge *for all*.

Discussion

As indicated earlier, an important aspect of the case made for support in the grant application for the DMTPC project was that most mathematics lessons in Scotland at that time still tended to feature some form of teacher-led demonstration followed by children practising skills and procedures from a commercially produced scheme. The more recent Scottish Survey of Literacy and Numeracy of that time also reported the most common aspects of the classroom experience for pupils were 'listening to the teacher talk to the class about a topic' and 'working on your own'. Such approaches serve to reinforce the presentation of mathematics as being predominantly about memorization, rule-following of strict procedures and right or wrong answers that are associated with mathematical fundamentalism and low epistemic quality, as illustrated in Figure 2.1, as an over-emphasis on merely *knowing that.* In contrast, the case study discussed in this chapter illustrates the central role of children verbalizing their thinking, which was one of Anna's specific interests at the outset. In particular, this reflects an important aspect in the development of subject expertise from the knowledge by acquaintance of the novice to the *knowledge that* and *knowledge how* of an expert in the subject. This development involves knowledge of how to make and understand inferences and the use of language associated with the concepts of the subject, which is largely a practical ability that is learned. As such, a central dimension of learning about a subject is learning to take part in conversations and discussions that employ those concepts. This process can also be seen as part of a gradual transition from novice to expert such that 'light dawns gradually over the whole' (Wittgenstein 1969). Such an emphasis serves to develop a fallibilistic view of mathematics as refutable and uncertain and one which promotes critical thinking, creative reasoning, the generation of multiple solutions and of learning from errors and mistakes that is associated with high epistemic quality.

With regard to the implications for curriculum innovation in schools, Anna's approach may be seen as exemplary. This involved addressing the central question of the extent to which a topic-based approach to mathematics allows children to demonstrate their mathematical thinking. In addition, she was interested in the extent to which topic-based mathematical questions allow children to verbalize their thinking and the effect of such an approach on children's levels of engagement. The way in which this was approached as a whole through the DMTPC project is discussed further in Hudson (2022), which focuses on the processes involved in supporting the professional development of teachers as 'curriculum makers' (Lambert and Biddulph 2015) for school mathematics of high epistemic quality.

The interplay between curriculum innovation and teacher professional development is captured most effectively by Stenhouse (1980) in his observation below, which is an appropriate point for reflection on which to end this chapter:

> What is curriculum as we now understand the word? ... It is not a syllabus – a mere list of content to be covered – nor even is it what German speakers would call a Lehrplan ... Nor is it in our understanding of a list of objectives. Let me claim that it is a symbolic or meaningful object, like Shakespeare's first folio, not like a lawnmower; like the pieces and board of chess, not like an apple tree. It has a physical existence but also a meaning incarnate in words or pictures or sound or games or whatever ... by virtue of their meaningfulness curricula are not simply means to improve teaching but are expressions of ideas to improve teachers. Of course, they have day-to-day instructional utility: cathedrals must keep the rain out ....
>
> (Stenhouse 1980: 40)

References

Boaler, J. (2009), *The Elephant in the Classroom*, London: Souvenir Press Ltd.
Brandom, R. (2000), *Articulating Reasons: An Introduction to Inferentialism*, Cambridge, MA: Harvard University Press.
Brousseau, G. (1997), *Theory of Didactical Situations in Mathematics*, Dordrecht: Kluwer.

Chevallard, Y. (2007), 'Readjusting Didactics to a Changing Epistemology', in Hudson, B. and Schneuwly, B. (eds), *Special Issue of the European Educational Research Journal (EERJ) on Didactics: Learning and Teaching in Europe*, 6 (2): 131–4.

Gericke, N., Hudson, B., Olin-Scheller, C. and Stolare, M. (2018), 'Powerful Knowledge, Transformations and the Need for Empirical Studies across School Subjects', *London Review of Education*, 16 (3): 428–44. doi.org/10.18546/LRE.16.3.06.

Gruson, B., Loquet, M. and Pilet, G. (2012) Analyzing Semiosis Process in Primary Classrooms: Case Studies in Second Language and Gymnastics, *International Colloquium on Forms of Education and Emancipation Processes*, Centre for Research in Education and Didactics (CREAD), Rennes, 22–24 May 2012.

Hudson, B. (2015), 'Butterflies and Moths in the Amazon: Developing Mathematical Thinking through the Rainforest', *Education and Didactique*, 9 (2): 119–33. http://educationdidactique.revues.org/2322

Hudson, B. (2016), 'Didactics', in D. Wyse, L. Hayward and J. Pandya (eds), *SAGE Handbook of Curriculum, Pedagogy and Assessment*, 107–24, London: Sage Publications.

Hudson, B. (2018), 'Powerful Knowledge and Epistemic Quality in School Mathematics', *London Review of Education: Special Issue on Knowledge and Subject Specialist Teaching*, 16 (3): 384–97. UCL IOE Press. https://doi.org/10.18546/LRE.16.3.03

Hudson, B. (2019) 'Epistemic Quality for Equitable Access to Quality Education in School Mathematics', *Journal of Curriculum Studies*, 51 (4): 437–56 https://doi.org/10.1080/00220272.2019.1618917

Hudson, B. (2022), 'Teachers as Curriculum Makers for School Mathematics of High Epistemic Quality' in B. Hudson, N. Gericke, C. Olin-Scheller and M. Stolare (eds), *International Perspectives on Knowledge and Quality: Implications for Innovation in Teacher Education Policy and Practice*, London: Bloomsbury Publishing plc.

Hudson, B., Gericke, N., Loquet, M., Olin-Scheller, C. and Wegner, A. (2020), *Epistemic Quality and Powerful Knowledge: Implications for Curriculum Innovation and Teacher Education Policy & Practice*, Panel Discussion at European Conference on Educational Research (ECER 2020), University of Glasgow, 23–28 August 2020.

Lakatos, I. (1976), *Proofs and Refutations*, Cambridge: Cambridge University Press.

Lambert, D. and Biddulph, M. (2015), 'The Dialogic Space Offered by Curriculum-Making in the Process of Learning to Teach, and the Creation of a Progressive Knowledge-Led Curriculum', *Asia-Pacific Journal of Teacher Education*, 43 (3): 210–24.

Lithner, J. (2008), 'A Research Framework for Creative and Imitative Reasoning', *Educational Studies in Mathematics*, 67: 255–76.

Loquet, M. (2011), 'Swimming Babies, on Joint Didactic Action in Physical and Sports Activities: A Case Study in a Non-Schooling Institution', in Hudson, B. and Meyer, M. A. (eds), *Beyond Fragmentation: Didactics, Learning, and Teaching*, 60–76. Opladen and Farmington Hills: Verlag Barbara Budrich.

Morrow, W. (2008), *Bounds of Democracy: Epistemological Access in Higher Education*, Pretoria: HSRC Press.

NCTM (2000), *Principles and Standards for School Mathematics*, Reston, VA: The Council.

Scottish Executive Education Department (2005), *Assessment of Achievement Programme: Seventh Survey of Mathematics 2004*, Edinburgh: Scottish Executive Education Department.

Sensevy, G. (2011), 'Overcoming Fragmentation: Towards a Joint Action Theory in Didactics', in Hudson, B. and Meyer, M. A. (eds), *Beyond Fragmentation: Didactics, Learning, and Teaching*, 60–76. Opladen and Farmington Hills: Verlag Barbara Budrich.

Sensevy, G., Schubauer-Leoni, M.-L., Mercier, A., Ligozat, F. and Perrot, G. (2005), 'An Attempt To Model the Teacher's Action in the Mathematics Class', *Educational Studies in Mathematics*, 59 (1–3): 153–81.

Stenhouse, L. (1980), 'Curriculum Research and the Art of the Teacher', *Curriculum*, 1 (1).

UN (2015), Transforming Our World: The 2030 Agenda for Sustainable Development, https://sustainabledevelopment.un.org/?menu=1300

Winch, C. (2013), 'Curriculum Design and Epistemic Ascent', *Journal of Philosophy of Education*, 47 (1): 128–46.

Wittgenstein, L. (1997), *Philosophical Investigations = Philosophische Untersuchungen* (G.E.M. Anscombe, Transl.), Oxford: Blackwell (original work published 1953).

Wittgenstein, L. (1969), *On Certainty*, Oxford: Blackwell.

Young, M. (2013), 'Overcoming the Crisis in Curriculum Theory: A Knowledge-based Approach', *Journal of Curriculum Studies*, 45 (2): 101–18. http://www.tandfonline.com/doi/full/10.1080/00220272.2013.764505

Young, M. (2015), 'Powerful Knowledge as a Curriculum Principle', in M. Young, D. Lambert, C. Roberts, and M. Roberts (eds), *Knowledge and the Future School: Curriculum and Social Justice*, 2nd ed., 65–88. London: Bloomsbury Academic.

3

Epistemic Quality of Physical Education in a High School in France

Monique Loquet, Brian Hudson and Anke Wegner

Introduction

The study reported in this chapter was conducted in 2015 when, as part of a whole research team, we observed a dance lesson with a class in a high school in France. This was part of a case study (Loquet et al. 2017) within the Joint Action in Didactics in Europe (JADE) project which has cross-curricular foci on mathematics, physical education and first-language teaching in school. The dance lesson was one of a series of lessons in Physical Education (PE) held in November 2015 at the Rosa Parks College, which is a secondary high school that is part of a Priority Education Zone located within a Sensitive Urban Zone characterized by social, cultural and ethnic diversity. Students at the college originate from forty-seven different countries, and the particular class of twenty-five students was very diverse. Some students were studying special vocational training courses for the economic and industrial spheres, while others were from bilingual international sections or in sports sections with a specialization in football. The lessons were conducted by a PE teacher, who is an expert in teaching within a Sensitive Urban Zone, and a keen amateur dancer, although not a specialist in choreographic activities.

Theoretical framework

The theoretical framework for the study is based on Joint Action Theory in Didactics (JATD) and also draws on the concept of epistemic quality as discussed in the previous chapter of this book (Hudson this volume).

Joint Action Theory in Didactics (JATD)

JATD has developed within the tradition of French didactics and is based on the theoretical principle that, in order to understand a didactic activity, which denotes an activity where someone teaches and someone learns, you need to understand a *system*, the *didactic system* (Brousseau 1997; Sensevy et al. 2005; Sensevy 2011, 2012; CDpE 2019). This is a system of three subsystems, namely knowledge, the teacher and the student. The didactic system is seen as indivisible, and it is regarded as impossible to grasp the meaning of the teacher's action without understanding the relations between this action, the students' action, and the structure of the piece of knowledge at stake. In turn, JATD is based on an understanding of joint action as a process of reciprocal semiosis (Sensevy 2011: 61) involving the deciphering of verbal and bodily actions (or signs) of others in a certain situation. The argument is well made by (ibid.) that didactic research needs a new paradigm, a paradigmatic shift from an analytic stance to a holistic approach, in which the necessary analytic study is only part of the researcher's work. In this respect, the main purpose of the joint action theory is to grasp the dynamics and the unity of the joint action. The key concepts drawn from JATD and used in this study are 'game', 'contract' and 'milieu'. Concerning the first of these, the fundamental starting point for the JATD, as described by Loquet (2011), is to consider teaching and learning as a joint action, co-operative, and asymmetric, occurring between the teacher and the students based on 'language games' (Wittgenstein 1997) specific to didactic systems. The use of 'game' in JATD should not be understood as meaning a playful activity. It is a model in the scientific sense of the term, that is, a form of description to understand what happens in a given social situation. In a didactic situation, the notion of 'game' allows us to describe the joint dimension of the didactic activity by modelling the interactions between the student and the teacher as participants in the same 'game'. In particular, three games are identified, which might be seen in relation to the three aspects of the didactic triad, that is, content, learner and teacher. These are the 'epistemic game', the 'learning game' and the 'didactic game', respectively. First, the epistemic game refers to the game of the dancer in his/her professional activity and also that of the mathematician, writer, historian, physicist, chef or in any other profession. Two aspects of this game are distinguished, both the *source epistemic game*, which refers to the human practices that exist outside the didactic situation, and also the *actual epistemic game*, which is based on the analysis of class practices as they occur *in situ*. Second, the 'learning game' relates to learning as the first stake of the didactic action, in which some specific pieces of knowledge are involved. It relates to the game played by the students, seen as a collaborative game (Gruson, Loquet and Pilet 2012: 65), which occurs when the teacher and the students interact in the classroom. Indeed, one may observe that what is asked of the student is changing, and that the learning stake is evolving. Thus, the development of didactic transactions between the teacher and the students can be modelled as a succession of 'learning games', as the lesson progresses. Third, the 'didactic game' is that which brings the other two games together, the 'epistemic game' and the 'learning game', and which reflects the complex relation that characterizes the didactic relation linked to the knowledge at stake. The second key concept from JATD is the didactic contract (Brousseau 1997) used to describe the system of habits, which is largely implicit, between the teacher and the students regarding the knowledge in question. Based on those habits established in the didactic situation, each participant (teacher or student) attributes certain expectations to the other(s). The didactic contract provides a common background between the teacher and the students against which the didactic transactions occur. Finally, the third key concept from JATD is 'milieu', which refers to the system of material and symbolic objects in question that corresponds to the new knowledge the students are to acquire. According to this description, the older pieces of knowledge enable the teacher and the students to act jointly, whereas the new knowledge involves a kind of resistance to the students' action (Gruson et al. 2012: 65).

Epistemic quality

We see the term 'epistemic' as being concerned with the knowledge involved in a didactical situation (Hudson et al. 2021). In turn, the term 'epistemic quality' refers to the quality of what students come to know, make sense of and are able to do in school. We see this aspect as particularly significant for addressing the challenges of UN Sustainable Development Goal 4 to ensure inclusive and equitable quality education for all (UN 2015), especially as concerns the need to maximize the chances that all pupils will have *epistemic access* (Morrow 2008; Young 2013: 115) to powerful knowledge through the curriculum. Drawing on Loquet (2009, 2016, 2017), this chapter considers the presence of a didactic form prevalent in French school practices, based on 'monstration-imitation-reproduction'. In these classical lesson forms, the teacher's monstrations lead to the performance of tasks, to be accomplished and repeated in certain specified conditions defined by the teacher. This approach reflects a tendency for mechanical learning. In the classic school form, students do not encounter the complexity of the cultural practices that have been chosen as a reference at school, such as dancing. In this case, it is seen that there is a great distance between the 'epistemic capacities' developed by the students in a dance class, which make the teacher satisfied, and those attested by connoisseurs in choreographic practices, or 'savants'. In this chapter, we use the term 'epistemic' synonymously with the idea of 'concerning the knowledge involved' in a learning situation, while the expression 'epistemic capacity' is used to emphasize the action potentialities students possess as a system of knowledge and knowing-how. The term 'savant' is used in a generic sense to

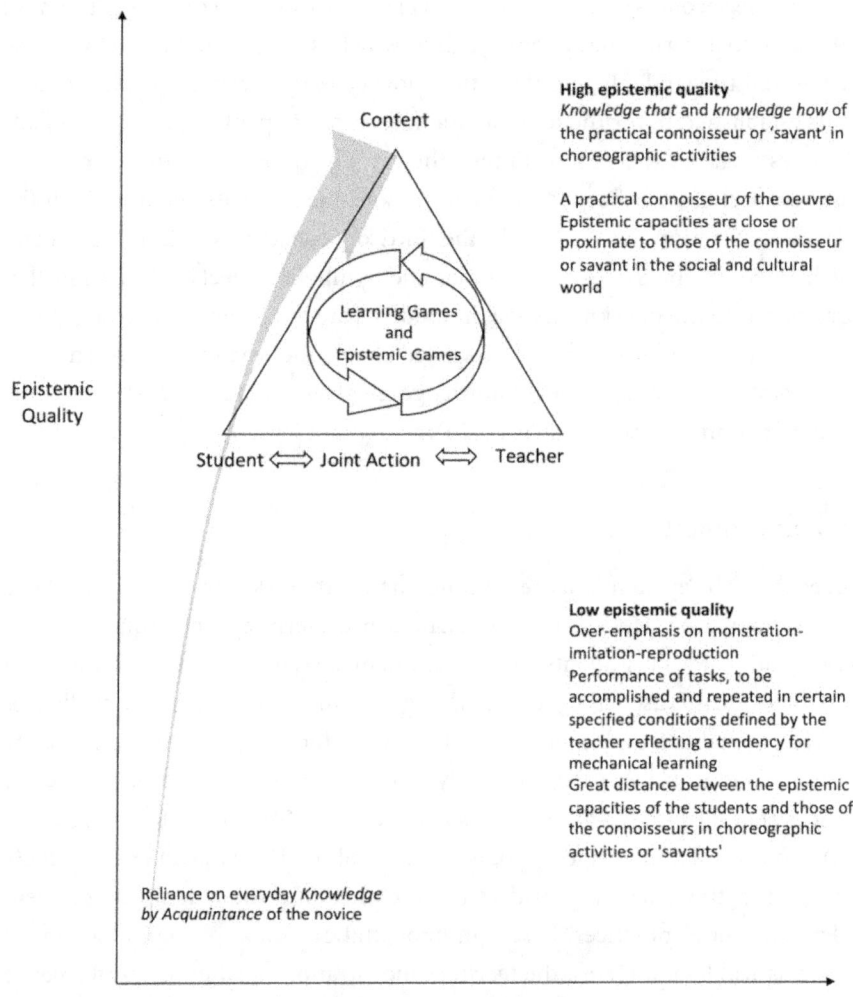

Figure 3.1 Trajectory of development in the epistemic capacities of choreographic activities.

qualify the oeuvre of those who invent and produce knowledge. Accordingly, one who is savant, in the social and cultural world, knows (or does) something (an oeuvre) as a 'practical connoisseur' of this oeuvre. For example, Fosbury is the savant (connoisseur or expert) of the Fosbury flop, the contemporary dancer is a savant of the contemporary choreographic oeuvre, etc. In traditional lesson forms, students can miss the challenges posed by essential problems in cultural practices. They can be far away from the situation that savants or connoisseurs would normally undertake in these cultural practices. This form is associated with low epistemic quality in classroom activities. Such a trajectory of developing epistemic capacities with respect to choreographic activities is related to that of development in subject knowledge in school mathematics presented in Hudson (this volume). The development from the everyday knowledge of the novice to the *knowledge that* and *knowledge how* of the practical connoisseur or 'savant' in choreographic activities is captured in Figure 3.1.

Research design

A major focus in the JADE project has been to question the conditions needed to ensure equitable school education and to ask which kinds of teaching activities can be equitable for all students. This emphasis brings a focus on the didactic system and, within this frame, we have focused on investigating two aspects:

- the epistemic quality of content; and
- the epistemic quality of teacher–student(s) interaction.

Our methodological approach is based upon studies conducted in three countries (UK, France and Germany) in relation to three specific subjects (mathematics, PE/dance and language learning). The aim has been to analyse different examples of epistemic quality in relation to content and teacher–student(s) joint action in classroom activities and to compare findings within a broadly shared theoretical framework. In doing so, we have adopted a primarily qualitative approach to this project using a case study approach (Stake 1995). The data collection, analysis and interpretation are based on a constructivist grounded theory approach (Charmaz 2000). This approach is described by Charmaz (2008) as an 'emergent method' (ibid.), meaning that it is inductive, indeterminate and open-ended. It begins with the empirical world and builds an inductive understanding of it as events unfold and knowledge accrues. From this same perspective, JATD involves a methodological approach towards the 'ascent from the abstract to the concrete' based on the dialectical vision of abstract–concrete relationship (initiated by Marx 1992 [1867]; Ilyenkov 1982; Engeström et al. 2012; and worked by Sensevy 2011; CDpE 2019). According to this approach, we give priority to the concreteness of practice over the abstract aspects of the research. Attention is thus given to selected examples of practice, seen as 'emblematic examples'. As a consequence, video analysis of practice plays an essential function in describing the 'epistemic quality' features.

The process started with each research team member making individual notes based on their observations of the lesson while another member was engaged in video recording the lesson's main elements. It continued with all team members sharing key aspects of the lesson observations in a review session immediately following the video observation, and further advanced through written accounts shared in the period soon afterwards. This approach allowed for checking the emerging categories that arose from successive levels of analysis and reasoning. This in turn led to significant episodes in the lesson being identified for greater levels of analysis through a process of progressive focussing. Selected episodes were then transcribed and translated into English by research team members. The process of dialogue and exchange within the research team was continued subsequently by way of digital communication and file sharing.

The study

The study was carried out in November 2015 when the research team as a whole observed a PE lesson with a class of students aged 14 to 16 years, whose content focused on the practice of dance and the aims of citizenship education. Access to the school had been agreed by the local co-ordinator of the Centre for Research in Education and Didactics (CREAD) at the University of Rennes 2 in liaison with the class teacher. Further, the College Principal certified that the parents of the pupils involved in the research had approved their participation in it.

According to the French Curriculum (MNE 2013),[1] 'artistic and cultural education' is a compulsory subject matter at school. The national purpose is to strengthen artistic culture and develop cultural democratization through 'the meeting of *oeuvres* and artists'. The dance teaching studied comprises part

---

[1] In France, art education consists of 'the meeting of oeuvres' organized throughout schooling depending on the 'cultural and artistic educational path' (Ministry of National Education, 2013).

of a course of study called 'Dance and Citizenship'. The teacher used different pictures of sculpture and artistic work to foster the students' imagination. The pictures came from the work of two authors: Ndary Lo, a Senegalese artist who pays special tribute to Rosa Parks, and Rania Omani, an artist whose family is from Algeria. Based on these pictures, students produced a personal danced *oeuvre (work)* about their idea of citizenship. An example from the work of Ndary Lo can be seen in Figure 3.2.

The teacher focused the lessons on the symbolization process of the dance gesture and aimed to develop relationships between the students' capabilities in building a symbolic gesture in dance while also developing citizenship practices in class.

The course of study consisted of ten lessons, divided into three main phases. The first phase, involving lessons 1 and 2, was classroom-based and concentrated on generally presenting the dance cycle, discussing various forms of dance, and debating the nature of citizenship. The second phase, entailing lessons 3 to 8, focused on teaching and learning dance and was devoted to choreographic activities held in the gymnasium. In this second phase, the successive teaching

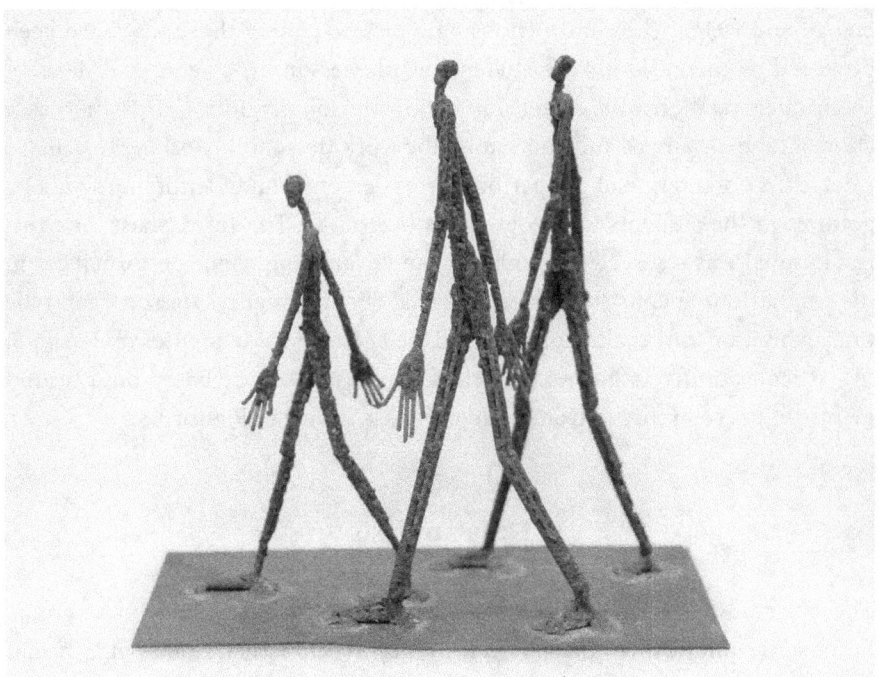

Figure 3.2 Example of one picture of a sculpture by Ndary Lo taken by Yves Guigon.

Figure 3.3 Picture of the sculpture in iron by Ndary Lo taken by Charles Jousselin.

topics were as follows: exploring the factors of movement: space, rhythm, energy and weight (lesson 3); choosing a picture among those that have been proposed as the basis for the students' work (lesson 4); staging and dancing as an interpretation of a citizenship action (lesson 5); 'lifting a partner' as a choreographic element and continuing the work (lesson 6); working to achieve a detached observation about performances (lesson 7) and identifying symbolic gestures in the students' choreographies (lesson 8). The third phase (the two last lessons) was reserved for exhibiting and evaluating dance performances in the gymnasium. It consisted of the rehearsal of performances (lesson 9) and the final exhibition and evaluation (lesson 10). The case study focuses on lesson 5, in particular on five students who chose to create a dance based on a second picture of the sculpture in iron by Ndary Lo, as shown in Figure 3.3.

Data analysis

The case study especially focuses on Edmond, one of the students in the group. Edmond is from Kosovo and arrived in France 2 years earlier. At that time, he did not speak French, and he joined a non-native speaker class. He is passionate about boxing and practised this sport in a club at a good level, as observed in Figure 3.4.

Figure 3.4 Edmond, with his group, mimics the gestures of a boxer (in the middle of the picture at the start of lesson 5).

For these students, the photograph represents a group of slaves. They collectively agreed to 'give them life back and restore their rights'. In the subsequent dance, Edmond played the character of the 'slaves' master' on the understanding that 'slaves must obey their master'. At the start of the lesson, we see Edmond (and others) acting as if he is straightforwardly directing a simple translation of a power relationship – the master dominating his slaves – into a bodily expression. He mimes familiar punching and kicking of 'his slave' partners repeatedly, using boxing gestures. Edmond seems to represent his body as a representation of an instrument of power and of violence. Thus, for him handling his slaves seems to be to 'beat them up' and dominate them as if he wants to recreate the reality of a street boxing match. Initially, he solves the task of translating a piece of art into dancing by telling a story of slaves and their master, in an immediate sense linked to his everyday knowledge, and by interpreting his role as an aggressive one and the situation as painful and fearful. The idea of citizenship is directly linked to this situation: the citizenship act then consists of freeing the slaves from the yoke of this master. Edmond and the other students create a hierarchical surrounding environment of power and violence, which probably corresponds to what they often experience and what fascinates them in their daily life on TV and in their social-media experience.

During the next episode, the teacher intervenes to help Edmond and his classmates to find a way into the 'symbolic' world. The teacher tries to explain the meaning of the term 'symbolic', which he admits is quite difficult. Finally, he takes on the role of the slaves' master, as if he were Edmond. He moves to the slaves and, when he is near them, turns his back to them and taps his feet rhythmically. The slaves fall to the ground one by one, in rhythm, behind the teacher's back. He thereby monstrates a symbolic interpretation of the scene by stamping his feet in rhythm. Coming back to Edmond, the teacher tries to explain his monstration: 'I have slapped them (the slaves' partners) … but I haven't slapped them really'. He draws Edmond's attention to how the gesture he has shown can be regarded as an example of symbolic expression. Edmond approves it 'Oh yeah, I like that!', and starts representing the movement by tapping and swinging the legs. The students start playing at the same dancing game – see Figure 3.5.

The dialogue within the research team immediately following the lesson observations led to a focus on Edmond's group and his performance, regarded as a particularly significant aspect of the lesson. This was partly due to the performance's dramatic impact and also to the interactions between the teacher and group members (especially Edmond) in the build up to it. The process

Figure 3.5 Students imitate the teacher's monstration of a symbolic representation of the scene.

Figure 3.5 Students imitate the teacher's monstration of a symbolic representation of the scene. (Continued)

of transcription and translation which then ensued led to increasing levels of dialogue and exchange around successive levels of analysis in the period following the lesson observation. During this process, two particular themes emerged with respect to the roles of imitation and creativity in the didactical situation. In part, these emerged from a comparison with the contrasts between creative and imitative reasoning in mathematics, referred to in Hudson (2022). This then led to questions about the role of imitation and creativity in the context of PE.

Discussion

As described earlier, we have focused on investigating both the epistemic quality of content and the epistemic quality of the teacher–student(s) interaction. We begin this discussion by first considering the epistemic quality of teacher–student(s) interaction, second the epistemic quality of the content and, finally, the differing roles of imitation across the two subject areas of mathematics and PE.

With regard to the epistemic quality of the teacher–student(s) interaction, the role of imitation emerged as a significant theme. Traditionally the role of imitation in relation to physical performance in PE has been strongly undervalued (Winnykamen 1990). At the same time, there is much criticism of the use of imitation in teaching because it is seen as a superficial process which assumes that students are unable to develop autonomous and creative behaviour. This is also often the case in dance teaching, in which context the dance teacher is regarded as the primary source of knowledge and students are perceived as learning through imitation and adherence to external instructions (Daniels 2009). The issue of imitation in dance is further complicated by the fact the relevant knowledge to be taught is not very stable, and defining knowledge content in dance is generally seen as problematic. In ordinary practices, dance contents are often characterized by an antinomy between imitation and creation. On the contrary, our case study shows that the teacher's monstration does not lead to a spontaneous imitation-replication. Rather, imitation is considered here as comprehension and creation that requires significant interaction between teacher and students. In addition, the teacher not only presents himself as a model, but the students also provide models to the teacher. He looks at the students' behaviour, adheres to what they spontaneously perform based on their everyday knowledge in terms of familiar mimic gestures. Then he re-enacts their movements by introducing a special point to be studied, some rhythmic element of a slapping symbolic gesture. In doing so, thanks to his monstration, he 'forces' the students to face the resistant properties of the *milieu* and to build new knowledge, that is, symbolic gestures, through an abstraction process. Further, certain actions, gestures and/or words more than others seem to 'make sense' to both the teacher and the students and influence them in return. Signs are exchanged, emitted and deciphered by each other. In the case study, teacher and students are used to sharing responsibilities of observer and dancer. This habit has developed at an early stage between them based on an empathic didactical relationship. For these reasons, we identify a 'reciprocal game of imitation' in the joint teacher–students action and consider it as an example of *high epistemic quality* of teacher–student(s) interaction, as summarized in Figure 3.6.

In relation to the epistemic quality of content, at the outset Edmond was acting out a drama based on his everyday knowledge by acquaintance as a novice. This one-way process of imitation resulted in knowledge of low epistemic quality. This 'low epistemic quality' of knowledge is characterized by a distant connection between the student's everyday knowledge (the only familiar mimic gesture) and the savant's or practical connoisseur's knowledge (symbolic gesture). However, by going through a reciprocal game of imitation with the teacher, he was able to both grasp and also enact the creative symbolism of dance as an art form and in so doing move along the trajectory of development towards becoming a practical connoisseur in the cultural practice. The content of the lesson developed to become of high epistemic quality thereby progressed as

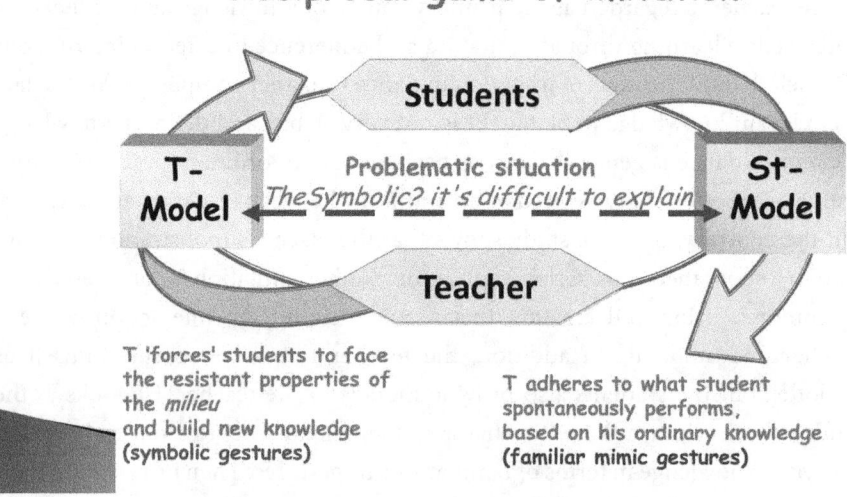

Figure 3.6 Reciprocal game of imitation between teacher (T) and students (St) in a problematic situation: 'symbolic gesture' is difficult to explain.

the proximity to cultural practice increased. This process of proximity between the students and savant's knowledge is referred to as 'epistemic kinship' (Loquet 2017), which is a guarantee of knowledge quality at school.

Finally, in comparing the roles of imitation and creativity across the two subject areas – mathematics and dance in PE – we may observe differences in the way these play out in practice. It is argued that these differences represent particular characteristics of each subject area. In relation to mathematics, the roles of both creativity and imitation, as discussed in this study, refer to abstract thinking and reasoning processes in general. With regard to imitative reasoning in mathematics, two aspects can be identified in particular: namely, memorized reasoning and algorithmic reasoning, which rely mainly on memory recall in response to which rote learning can all too often be seen as the pedagogical solution. This triggered questions about the role of imitation and creativity in the context of the dance lesson in which, however, the emphasis is more on the artistic expression of emotion and performance rather than on abstract reasoning.

Nevertheless, in both cases, the analysis shows that the dualism between imitation and creation is unfounded. Beyond the particularities of the subject-specific, if the teacher conceives imitation as the student's experience of creation, the implemented situation can have for him/her a meaning other than rote learning. Imitation not only consists in 'replicating' a gesture (artistic expression or performance) or abstract reasoning (memorized or algorithmic) but in creating a personal solution based on the understanding of these gestures or reasoning. The question then is: what does the student understand from what the teacher gives to imitate (algorithm completion, painting, dancing or crafting 'in the manner of', etc.). Imitating what others have already experienced is viewed as a necessity to understand things of the world, and makes it possible to invent a solution 'everywhere' when a problem arises, which is ultimately the guarantee of learning.

In particular, we can see how the *imitation-creation* relation links in with the social-constructivist perspective of imitation proposed by Winnykamen (1990), who notes that 'imitation activity consists in the intentional use of observed actions of others, as a source of information in order to achieve one's own goal' (1990: 105). We extend this approach in the theoretical framework of joint action in didactics by emphasizing the importance of the epistemic quality of the content involved in imitation. We consider that imitating is about being able to recognize in others an *essential unity of knowledge*. In other words, imitating requires one to identify the premises of an epistemic activity in others. The notion of imitation-creation is thus linked to the 'epistemic game', defined as the process through which the teacher, in the joint action, supports the students in developing *new capacities*, new possibilities in dance. In our study, we can observe the way in which the teacher helped Edmond understand the meaning of 'symbolic' in the context of dance and to appreciate that '*I slapped them but I haven't slapped them really*'.

References

Brousseau, G. (1997), *Theory of Didactical Situations in Mathematics*, Dordrecht: Kluwer.

CDpE (Collectif Didactique Pour Enseigner) (2019), *Didactique pour enseigner*, Rennes: PUR. http://pur-editions.fr/detail.php?idOuv=4850

Charmaz, K. (2000), 'Grounded Theory: Objectivist and Constructivist Methods' in N. K. Denzin and Y. S. Lincoln (eds), *Handbook of Qualitative Research*, 2nd ed., 509–35. Thousand Oaks, CA: Sage.

Charmaz, K. (2008), 'Grounded Theory as an Emergent Method', in S. N. Hesse-Biber and P. Leavy (eds), *Handbook of Emergent Methods*, 155–72. New York: The Guilford Press.

Daniels, K. (2009), 'Teaching to the Whole Dancer. Synthesizing Pedagogy, Anatomy, and Psychology', *The International Association for Dance Medicine and Science Bulletin for Teachers*, 1 (1): 8–10.

Engeström, Y., Nummijoki, J., and Sannino, A. (2012), 'Embodied Germ Cell at Work: Building an Expansive Concept of Physical Mobility in Home Care', *Mind Cult Act* 19 (3): 287–309.

Gruson, B., Forest, D. and Loquet, M. (2012) (dir.), *Jeux de savoir. Etudes de l'action conjointe en didactique*, Rennes: PUR.

Hudson, B., Gericke, N., Loquet, M., Olin-Scheller, C., Stolare, M. and Wegner, A. (2021), *Epistemic Quality and Powerful Knowledge: Implications for Curriculum Innovation and Teacher Education Policy & Practice*, Panel Discussion at European Conference on Educational Research (ECER 2021), University of Geneva, 6–10 September 2021.

Ilyenkov, E. (1982), *The Dialectics of the Abstract and the Concrete in Marx's Capital*, Moscow: Progress Publishers.

Loquet, M., Hudson, B., Meyer, M., Wegner, A. and Benberghout, F. (2017), '*I have slapped them but I haven't slapped them really': Epistemic Quality for Equitable Learning through Physical Education in France*, WERA 2017 Focal Meeting/Hong Kong Education Research Association International Conference, The Education University of Hong Kong, 30 November – 2 December 2017.

Loquet, M. (2017), 'La notion de parenté épistémique: une modélisation des savoirs entre la pratique des élèves et celle des savants', *Recherches en éducation*, 29: 38–54.

Loquet, M. (2016), 'The Epistemic Kinship: A Way to Bridge the Affirmed Gap between Student's and Expert's Knowledge, the Case of Dance Lessons', in Symposium Global Perspectives on Didactics, Learning and Teaching, at *Annual Focal Meeting of the World Education Research Association (WERA) Public Scholarship to Educate Diverse Democracies*, Washington, USA (8–12 April).

Loquet, M. (2009), *Jeu épistémique et jeu d'apprentissage dans les activités physiques sportives et artistiques: vers une approche comparatiste en didactique*. Note de synthèse pour l'habilitation à diriger des recherches. Université Rennes2.

Marx, K. (1992), *Capital: A Critique of Political Economy*, London and New York: Penguin Classics.

MNE (2013), Le parcours d'éducation artistique et culturelle. http://www.education.gouv.fr/pid25535/bulletin_officiel.html?cid_bo=71673

Morrow, W. (2008), *Bounds of Democracy: Epistemological Access in Higher Education*, Pretoria: HSRC Press.

Sensevy, G., Schubauer-Leoni, M.-L., Mercier, A., Ligozat, F. and Perrot, G. (2005), 'An Attempt To Model the Teacher's Action in the Mathematics Class', *Educational Studies in Mathematics*, 59 (1–3): 153–81.

Sensevy, G. (2011), 'Overcoming Fragmentation: Towards a Joint Action Theory in Didactics', in Hudson, B. and Meyer, M. A. (eds), *Beyond Fragmentation: Didactics, Learning, and Teaching*, 60–76. Opladen and Farmington Hills: Verlag Barbara Budrich.

Sensevy, G. (2012), 'About the Joint Action Theory in Didactics', *Zeitschrift für Erziehungswissenschaft*, 15 (3): 503–16. http://python.espe-bretagne.fr/sensevy/ZFE%20Sensevy%202012%20JATD.pdf

Stake, R. (1995), *The Art of Case Study Research*, London: Sage.

UN (2015), Transforming Our World: The 2030 Agenda for Sustainable Development, https://sustainabledevelopment.un.org/?menu=1300

Winnykamen, F. (1990), *Apprendre en imitant*, Paris: PUF.

Wittgenstein, L. (1997), *Philosophical Investigations = Philosophische Untersuchungen* (G.E.M. Anscombe, Transl.), Oxford: Blackwell (original work published 1953).

Young, M. (2013), 'Overcoming the Crisis in Curriculum Theory: A Knowledge-based Approach', *Journal of Curriculum Studies*, 45 (2): 101–18. http://www.tandfonline.com/doi/full/10.1080/00220272.2013.764505

4

Epistemic Quality of Language Learning in a Primary Classroom in Germany

Anke Wegner, Brian Hudson and Monique Loquet

Introduction

This chapter arises from the study of a German language lesson at a primary school in Frankfurt/Main, Germany carried out in March 2017. This was one of the case studies conducted as part of the Joint Action in Didactics in Europe (JADE) project (Wegner et al. 2019), which has cross-curricular foci on mathematics, physical education and first-language teaching in school. The theoretical framework for the study is based on the perspective of *Bildungsgangforschung and -didaktik* developed within the tradition of German didactics in combination with the concept of epistemic quality. The study focuses on the question of how the nature of epistemic quality in language and language use can be characterized and relates this to the three levels of interaction and co-operation in the instructional process that arises from consideration of *Bildungsgangforschung and -didaktik*. The analysis concentrates on the epistemic quality of the language and language use during the teacher–student interaction of a particular lesson sequence involving a quiz. It addresses the question of how the nature of epistemic quality in language and language use can be characterized by first focusing on the epistemic quality of the content and second on the epistemic quality of the teacher–student(s) joint action. The democratic quality of instruction through this analysis is also addressed. In conclusion, the final discussion looks at the implications for curriculum innovation in relation to language and language use in the primary classroom.

Theoretical framework

The theoretical framework for this study is based on the perspective of *Bildungsgangforschung and -didaktik* developed within the tradition of German didactics in combination with the concept of epistemic quality, as discussed in Chapter 2 of this book (Hudson this volume).

Bildungsgangforschung and -didaktik

The perspective of *Bildungsgangforschung and -didaktik* combines a scientific dimension on research and a normative dimension on didactics. It is best translated as research and didactics on learner development and educational experience and is centrally concerned with both the question of *Bildung* and the facilitation of learning and *Bildung* processes in the classroom. It focuses on the tension between social, institutional requirements and individual sense construction, interests and developmental goals of children and adolescents and aims to mediate between continuity and transformation. In its normative dimension, with regard to the target category of *Bildung* (Hericks 2008: 61), *Bildungsgangdidaktik* follows a concept of *Bildung* that not only includes the adoption of what has been handed down in society – the cultural heritage – but also the constant new development of self and world relation of students which potentially includes the joint construction and transformation of given institutional and societal structures (see Peukert 1998: 18; Peukert 2000: 519). An essential characteristic of the approach is its understanding of *Bildung* as a biographical or 'socializing process' (Meyer et al. 2001: 3). Students are understood as developing subjects, as 'designers of their subjective educational pathways' (Meyer 2005: 18) with their individual sense constructions, own interests and developmental goals. It is therefore necessary to ask how the institutional educational pathway and individual development pathway intertwine and what can be done so that teaching makes sense from the students' perspective. In the interest of communicating institutional requirements and individual concerns, the core of *Bildungsgangforschung and -didaktik* is the reconstruction of students' sense construction as an individual attribution of meaning to content (Müller-Roselius 2013: 113) and the reconstruction of learning and *Bildung* processes as individual perception, interpretation and processing of developmental tasks. *Bildungsgangforschung and -didaktik* thus connects the reconstruction of learning and *Bildung* processes and the didactic 'application' (Meyer 2005: 18) of findings; it combines normative, development-oriented or biographical and empirical dimensions (see Terhart 2009: 202; Wegner 2016).

From this perspective, the quality of teacher–student interaction is interpreted in relation to three levels of interaction and co-operation in the instructional process by Meyer (2011). In describing this model, Meyer (ibid.) draws on Wittgenstein's concept of 'seeing as' (Wittgenstein 1960: 503–42; Sensevy 2011). Seeing something means that you really 'see' it and, at the same time, you see it 'as' something, e.g. you might see the behaviour of a student as disobedience and mis-adaptation. 'Seeing as', in Wittgenstein's sense, depends on experience and action and implies that a change in how we see things is possible. Accordingly, at the *first level* of classroom interaction, teaching can be regarded simply as the transmission of knowledge, competence and values, in which circumstances the students adapt to what the teacher expects them to do. This one-directional action structure is sub-optimal in the long run merely because it does not take sufficient account of individual sense construction on the students' part. Therefore, the first level of classroom interaction must be transformed into a *second,* communicative *level* in order that students and teachers come to see instruction as a shared experience and joint action. The transfer of knowledge, skills and attitudes is understood as the product of negotiation in a *community of practice* of learners and teachers. Teachers and students 'see' teacher–student interaction and communication 'as' a communicative process. However, there is a *third level* of teacher–student interaction, which is needed in order to describe the processes of *Bildung*. The concept of Bildung is viewed as being more than the mastery of contents or the development of competencies and abilities and as far more than knowing something or being able to do it. In relation to the development of Bildung, whatever is done or learned is done or learned to develop one's own individuality and to unfold one's capabilities. The purpose of teaching and schooling from this perspective is not seen as being solely to transmit knowledge from society to a learner, nor to transpose knowledge from science or other domains to the classroom. Instead, the purpose is to use knowledge as a transformative tool for unfolding the individuality and sociability of the learner. In the long run, students thus will develop their own world views and self-concepts in a transformative process that can be fostered by teaching which, however, is the students' own task and their own success or failure. Seeing teacher–student interaction in this way allows *intergenerational communication* and the mutual *acceptance of 'otherness'* – i.e. fundamental differences of the self-concepts and world views of teachers and students. The levels are defined by their distance from or closeness to the central aim in education, namely

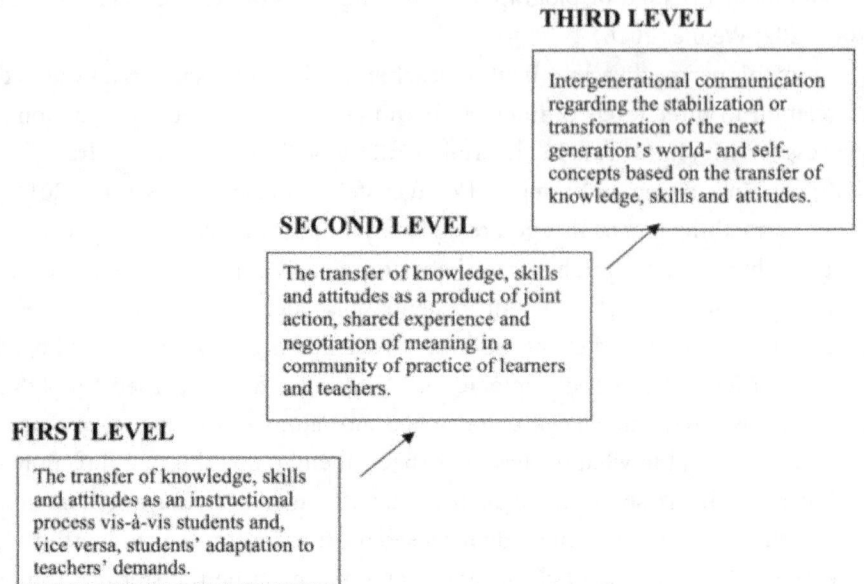

Figure 4.1 Levels of teacher–student interaction and co-operation in the instructional process.

knowledge and competence transfer *and* the transformation of world views and self-concepts by the students (Meyer 2008; Roselius and Meyer 2018). These levels are illustrated by Meyer (2011: 405), as shown in Figure 4.1.

Epistemic quality

As highlighted earlier, in this case study we draw on the concept of epistemic quality as discussed in Hudson (this volume). The term 'epistemic' is concerned with the knowledge involved in a didactical situation (Hudson et al. 2021), and the term 'epistemic quality' in turn refers to the quality of what students come to know, make sense of and are able to do in school. The idea arose from the process applying the theoretical framework of Joint Action Theory in Didactics (JATD), developed within the tradition of French didactics (Sensevy 2011), to the analysis of classroom interaction. Two games are highlighted in particular by the ways in which students are actively involved in *learning game*s in connection with *epistemic games*. An *epistemic game* is the game of subject expert in his or her professional activity of which two aspects are distinguished. First, the *source epistemic game* refers to the human practices that exist outside the didactic situation, and second, the *actual epistemic game* is based on the analysis of class practices. In turn, the *learning game* is seen as the reciprocal game of the student in relation to the joint game within the joint action. The aspect of epistemic quality is regarded as being particularly significant for addressing the challenges of UN Sustainable Development Goal 4 to ensure inclusive and equitable quality education for all (UN 2015) and especially in relation to the need to maximize the chances that all pupils will have *epistemic access* (Morrow 2008; Young 2013: 115) to powerful knowledge through the curriculum. Creative reasoning is stressed by Hudson (this volume) as a particular characteristic of high epistemic quality in school mathematics. Such creative reasoning is then contrasted with superficial memorized and algorithmic reasoning in mathematics that is seen as of low epistemic quality. Concerning this aspect, we see a correspondence with languages and language teaching and learning. As with the example of school mathematics, creativity is seen as an orientation or disposition that can be fostered in language teaching and learning in schools. In this context, teachers are confronted with the task of accepting their students' deliberate critical reasoning and creative language use, while they also have to teach correct mother tongue language, i.e. the German language for the students in this case study (Svalberg 2009; Dirim/Knappig 2018; Wegner 2018). High epistemic quality in languages and language teaching and learning would involve the recognition and promotion of the creative use of complex, individual linguistic repertoires in the classroom, and also the joint reflection and negotiation of language and language use in linguistically diverse contexts like everyday communication, institutions and societies as a whole. High epistemic quality furthermore would imply that students are given the right time and space to develop epistemic capacities, to stabilize or transform language and language use, to reason creatively and thereby overcome traditional standards of language teaching and language use in oral and written communication at school. An intergenerational, democratic discourse on language and language use would enable and promote language learning and *sprachliche Bildung*. The latter relates to subjective needs, interests and developmental goals and fosters expert, linguistic *fallibilism*, corresponding to the idea of mathematical fallibilism as discussed by Hudson (2018). Such linguistic fallibilism involves the *knowing how* of language and language use, of language change and linguistic diversity in the institution and beyond. Low epistemic quality in languages and language teaching and learning implies a mere repetition of given rules in the classroom, a verbalization of memorized knowledge on language norms and norms of language use in institutional contexts which are dominated by mono-linguistic, academic standards set by the older generation. Low epistemic quality involves an over-dependence on teacher-led fixed tasks that re-present academic and didactic traditions which are too narrow in their epistemic potential. Low epistemic quality thus implies an over-emphasis on knowing rules (*knowing that*), a reduction of linguistic complexity, a lack of creative reasoning and of democratic discourse in the classroom and reflects a linguistic *fundamentalism* (Hudson 2018). This ignores the fact that language use is individual and a constructive, dynamic process and that students do have epistemic capacities which should be used to enable

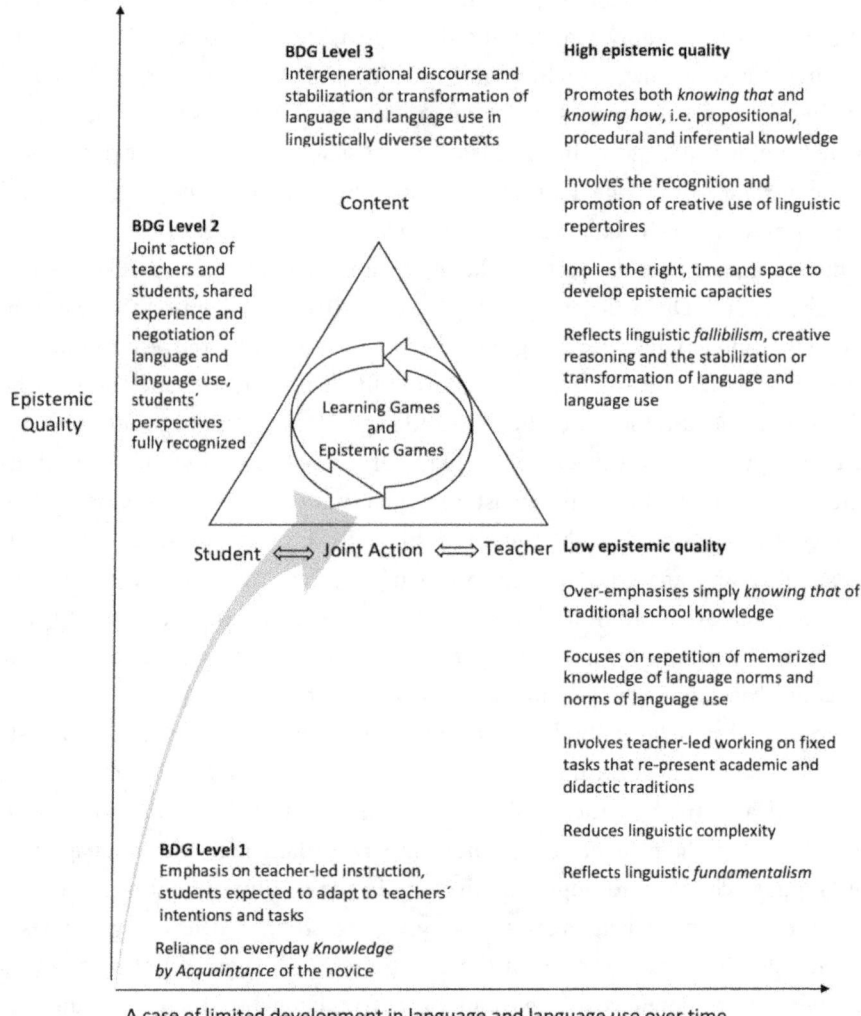

Figure 4.2 Trajectory of development in relation to language and language use.

learning and *Bildung*. The concept epistemic quality is developed further in Hudson (this volume) by considering it in relation to the idea of *epistemic ascent* (Winch 2013) in the development of subject expertise. This is based on a continuum that reflects a trajectory in the development of expertise from that of the novice towards that of an expert in the subject. We adopt this approach in this chapter by relating the trajectory of development to language and language use. In addition, we overlay the three levels of interaction and co-operation in the instructional process from the perspective of *Bildungsgangforschung and -didaktik (BDG)*. This trajectory of development of language and language use is related to that of development in subject knowledge in school mathematics presented in Hudson (this volume). The development from the everyday knowledge of the novice to the *knowledge that* and *knowledge how* of an expert in language and language use is summarized in Figure 4.2.

Research design

Like with the study reported in Chapter 3 of this book by Loquet et al. (this volume), a major focus of the JADE project has been to question the necessary conditions for ensuring equitable school education and to ask which kinds of teaching activities can be equitable for all students. This emphasis has brought a focus on both epistemic quality and the democratic quality of instruction in the didactic system. As a result, we have concentrated on investigating the following three aspects within this framework:

- the epistemic quality of content;
- the epistemic quality of teacher–student (s) interaction; and
- the democratic quality of instruction.

As outlined in Chapter 2 (ibid.), our methodological approach has involved case studies conducted in three countries (UK, France and Germany) in relation to three specific subjects (mathematics, PE/dance and language learning). We have adopted a primarily qualitative approach to this project using a case study approach (Stake 1995), while the data collection, analysis and interpretation have been based on a constructivist grounded theory approach (Charmaz 2000, 2008). The same process as followed in the earlier case study described in Chapter 2 was adopted for this study. This approach allowed for emergent categories to arise from the successive levels of analysis and for the identification of significant episodes in the lesson being subjected to greater levels of analysis through a process of progressive focussing.

The study

The empirical data for this study were gathered in March 2017 when the team observed a German language lesson (mother-tongue instruction) at a primary school in Frankfurt/Main with a large proportion of parents who were recent immigrants to the country. Parental permission to participate in monitored instruction was obtained. Children whose parents did not allow their children to participate were taught in a parallel class during the time of the programme. Two research team members were responsible for video recording the main elements of the lesson, and another took still images of the classroom environment. During the lesson, team members made individual notes based on their observations. Key aspects of the lesson observations were shared in the review session immediately following the observation, whereas written accounts were shared in the period soon afterwards. This process led to the identification of significant episodes in the lesson for deeper analysis through a process of progressive focussing. Selected episodes were then transcribed and translated into English by research team members. The language quiz discussed in this chapter was one such significant lesson episode. The process of exchange and dialogue within the research team continued in the process of preparing for, participating in and reflecting on the Round Table discussion of the ECER Conference held in Copenhagen in August 2017 (Hudson et al. 2017).

Didactic principles of teaching and learning

The class teacher is well known for fostering a specific way of individualized, self-organized learning, which follows the didactic principles of her supervisor, Meike Enders, with whom she had trained during the second (practical) phase of teacher education (*Referendariat*). Meike Enders published her pedagogical and didactic approach in a booklet (Enders 2015) entitled *Individuell lernen – gemeinsam arbeiten. Ein kompetenzorientiertes Unterrichtsmodell aus der Grundschulpraxis (Individual Learning and Cooperative Working. A Competence-oriented Didactical Model from Primary School Practice)*. Enders summarizes her didactic principles, which have a strong impact on the class teachers' teaching style, as follows:

Language Learning in a Primary Classroom in Germany 63

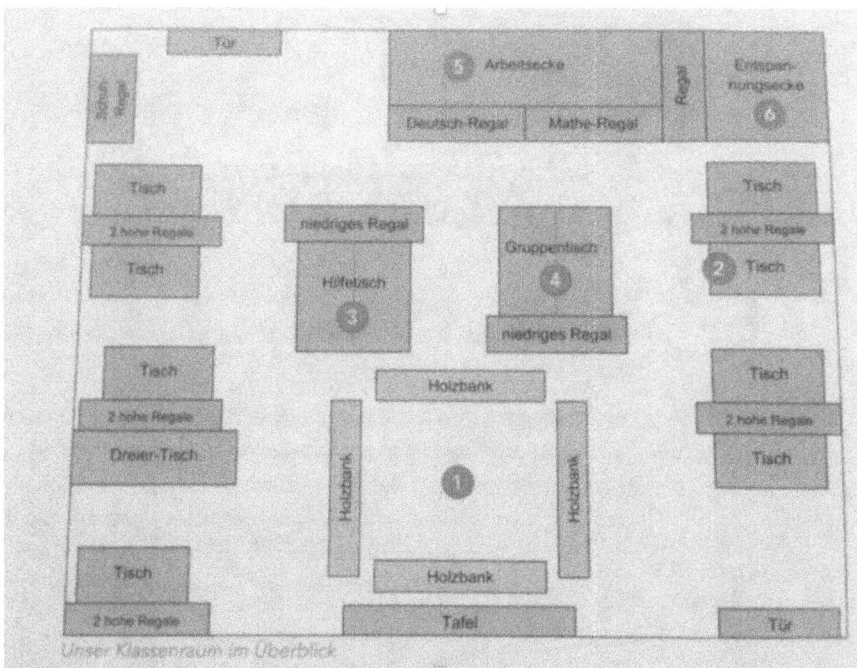

Figure 4.3 Placement of the tables, chairs and shelves for teaching material in the classroom.

- The *setting* of teaching and learning is very important: Students have the opportunity to work in their 'offices' (2) on their own, or at group desks (4) to communicate with their peers, or at a help desk (3) with the teacher; they also need to meet all together (1) or relax (6) or work with supplementary material (5) – see Figure 4.3.
- Teaching and learning follow a strict *day schedule* (*Tagesstruktur*): The school day begins with 'other subjects' (and other subject teachers). Every morning after this, there is a morning circle with the class teacher in which the students summarize and present their homework. This is followed by a maths and a German language lesson, a rest period, a second work period, an action period and another work period. The school day ends with a feedback circle (*Abschlusskreis*) and with feedback for other subjects (with other teachers) – see Figure 4.4.
- *Visualizing learning* and the definition of *learning fields* are two core principles of individualized work. The teacher lists topics/learning fields from grades 1 to 4, which are divided into learning areas, learning paths and learning signs. Learning areas and paths are done individually, whereas learning signs are worked on in joint phases.

Figure 4.4 The schedule for the day – student participation in lesson planning.

- *Individualized learning* is fostered by a variety of learning material, exercise boxes and subject shelves, time for mini-tests and self-evaluation. There are strict classroom rules such as silence phases and help systems.
- *Joint learning* is given in joint units or joint lessons, via joint topics, in plenary phases, revision lessons, so-called children's lessons (students as teachers), in the blackboard cinema (a plenary session in front of the blackboard) and in presentation phases.
- *Keeping an overview* includes defining and documenting the competence/performance of students, controlling the exercise books of the students, reports and weekly plans, helpdesk-work and documenting via exercise book lists, notes, weekly overviews and yearly lists.
- *Clear structures* are implemented by class rules, a rewards system, class services, class conferences, mediation of conflicts, seating arrangements, morning and close circles, round tables, e.g. on students' feelings, action and relaxation (Enders 2015).

Data collection

The teacher had worked to the principles outlined above as she aimed to enable student learning in a very clear and strict setting, as described below.

The day begins with a morning circle, a clear procedure which a chosen student has to moderate with the help of a laminated paper indicating step by step what he must do, ask, etc. The students initially note the date on the blackboard, describe how they feel, if they have done their homework, and which task they completed. Some students show their homework to everybody and read it out aloud, and the class applauds for everything presented. In the end, the 'homework service' hands out the exercise books and any material for the lesson and everybody looks for a place to sit down and work. The teacher asks some students to stay at her desk so she can help directly, more easily.

Before starting the working phase, the students have a look at the exercises they can choose, as marked on the blackboard (Figure 4.5). After reading aloud what is to be done, every child tells the teacher what they are planning to do during the work phase. Again, there are strong rules in place, every student tells the teacher what they intend to do, which is a question of patience and concentration, given that there are 18 students in the room and they are still sitting in the circle and nobody is allowed to move.

Figure 4.5 The daily routine, maths and German language exercises.

All students show the teacher their results after they have finished a task. They then all stand in a row with their exercises. The teacher whispers her comments to the students in a very simple, clear and direct way, and almost no smiling is apparent, the atmosphere is busy and concentrated and the students seem to really want the teacher's comments.

From time to time, the teacher gives an input to assist the students in learning things in a more systematic way: this sequence will be described and discussed in the section below.

Data analysis: The quiz sequence

Following the first part of the lesson, after the end of the morning circle and the handing out of the exercise books with the homework inside, the teacher tells the students to come into the 'blackboard cinema'. The students assemble before the blackboard, the teacher hands out cards in different colours and conducts a colour check during which the students have to hold up their colour – Figure 4.6.

The teacher then explains that they will have a German quiz; the students know how it works from maths lessons. She announces the quiz will be on parts of speech, on nouns, verbs and adjectives. She asks the students to explain what that means, and they answer that nouns are name words, verbs are doing-words, and adjectives are how-words. The quiz is thus on the question of whether the words the teacher shows are nouns, verbs or adjectives.

Figure 4.6 The teacher directly instructing the whole class.

T: Exactly, we are going to do a German quiz today (..) with our (…) what were they called?
S: Nouns, verbs and adjectives.
T: Exactly. And what are they then?
S: Words and these …
T: Nouns, verbs, adjectives. (..) What are they then?
S: Nouns are name words.
T: Correct.
S: Verbs are doing words.
T: Exactly, verbs are doing words.
S: Adjectives are how words.
T: Exactly. Brilliant. Okay, and we do the quiz like this today (..). I show you word after word (..) and you have to decide, is it a noun, a verb or an adjective. (..) Okay? (….) So, no more playing/flattering with the cards. Anybody got a question?
S: (Unv.) like the maths quiz? (unv.)
T: Exactly. (..) -

The sequence neither represents competence-oriented and individualized learning nor the use of settings in the classroom to be chosen by the students themselves (see Ender 2015). The teacher asks everybody to sit together in front of the blackboard in order to do some 'joint learning' in 'visualizing' grammar in a table (nouns, verbs, adjectives) on the blackboard (ibid.), repeating grammar with a quiz. As the students follow the teacher's intention, the students and the teacher see teaching and learning in class as (see Wittgenstein 1960) a game in which the teacher leads and the students follow, the teacher decides what to learn and how and the students answer questions the teacher asks. This is what we identify as level 1, teacher-led instruction at best. The repetition of three rules which are very narrow and reductive illustrates content in relation to language and language use of low epistemic quality. The teacher intends that the students simply know, memorize and repeat the chosen rules that represent traditional school knowledge and linguistic *fundamentalism*. Further, there is no sign of democratic teaching and learning since any question of the students or any other students' impulse to be clarified or discussed in class is not given space.

The colors are important as the students belong to groups A and B and points are given to each colour, not individual students. The communication is dominated by phrases identifying groups and colours.

(The teacher chooses a word card.)
T: Everybody looks here.
(Students hold up their cards.)

T: (10) Purple.
S: Verbs.
T: Aloud.
S: Verbs.
T: Verb. (…) B. (…) Why is to sing a verb? (6) Yes, this is also a quiz question. Why is to sing a verb? (5) Lina.
S: Because you (…) um can do it.
T: (whispers) Because you can do it. What kind of group are you?
S: A.
(The teacher points to the blackboard. She pins the word card on the blackboard and chooses another word card.)
T: So. (12) Orange.
S: Noun, um, noun.
S: Do word, do, um verb.
T: So, now what is it, Emma?
S: Drawing -
T: - Drawing is a …
S: Doing word. Doing word.
T: A doing word. Exact. You are … ?
S: A.

Figure 4.7 The students holding up their cards to answer the quiz questions.

The quiz which brings two groups A and B into competition and the use of many different card colours requires a constant process of identifying group members by their card colour and writing down points gained on the blackboard – Figure 4.7. This leads to the neglect of the students as learning subjects in the classroom. It may be observed that there are students who do not follow the speed of the quiz (holding up cards quickly and giving answers immediately) and who get lost in the repetition of the three rules. The teacher does not 'keep an overview' here (Ender 2015) and does not give space to joint reflection.

After the first part of the quiz in which the students identify nouns, verbs and adjectives according to the word cards shown, the teacher changes her strategy and shows words with an 'incorrect' orthography, e.g. adjectives with capital letters (in German, the first letter of nouns is capitalized, but this does not apply to adjectives and verbs).

> T: B. (writing the verb onto the blackboard, showing the next word card). (24) Yellow!
> Yellow: Noun! (snickering)
> T: (3) Why? Hmmmm (….)
> S: //Verbs//.
> T: Don't guess! (..) (pointing to a student) Aloud.
> The student being pointed at: Adjective.
> T: Aloud! Why is this an adjective? (…) Joris.
> Joris: A.
> T: (turning to the blackboard, pushing the figure and turning her back to the students) (.) Why is this an adjective, Lea?
> Lea: Because you she ah because it (.) it is like (.) ah how to describe it?
> T: How is something? //unv.)//
> Emma: A.
> T: And why did Kenan think that it is a noun? (….) Dark blue.
> Dark blue: Because it starts with a capital letter.
> T: Yes. (..) And is it correct?
> Dark blue: No.
> T: No. (points to a student)
> Dark blue: A.
> T: How then are adjectives identified? (5) Green.
> Green: Äh (.)
> Light green: Small. B.
> T: Green.
> T: I didn't say light green.
> Light green: Hmm but (unv.) but it is written with a capital letter.

> T: (unv.) Did you pay attention right now?
> S: He said it.
> Green: Small.
> T: (7) (writing a word onto the blackboard) So, (.) they are written with small letters. (6) (The teacher pushes the figure on the blackboard). So (..) well (..) don't get (..) from the <u>orthography</u> (..), maybe I have made mistakes deliberately, but check. (6) (The teacher shows the next word card.) Light green.

The quiz finishes with the challenge to give 'correct' answers, although the orthography is 'incorrect'. The teacher had decided to unsettle the students as she wants the students to define and explain the function of the given words. In our view, three aspects are crucial in this interaction: the three rules are still to be repeated constantly, and the students still follow the teacher. The change in the teacher's strategy results in much greater uncertainty for the students compared with the first part of the quiz. In essence, they are misled by the teacher's possible 'deliberate mistake' and still repeat the rule she taught that adjectives do not start with capital letters. Kenan is misled into thinking the word is a noun but is not even asked why he chose his answer.

At the end of the quiz, the teacher asks the students to collect the cards and meet in the circle to prepare for the working phase.

> T: Good, okay, (13) okay! So, the (...) (teacher looks behind the blackboard) distribution service, Ni- (.) Nicole and (incomplete), please collect the cards and come together in the circle please, (....) (whispering) and the circle kid fetches the red ball.

The teacher's whispering seems to have different functions in her interaction with the students. She uses it when she repeats and thus reinforces correct answers (echo strategy), when giving direct orders (the circle kid fetches the red ball), and when giving individual students feedback on their work in the middle of the class publicly. In all three cases, the teacher in a way glosses over and at the same time underlines her power, strength and leadership in the classroom.

Discussion

As already described, we have focused on investigating the epistemic quality of the content, the epistemic quality of the teacher–student(s) interaction and the democratic quality of the instruction. We begin this discussion by considering each aspect in turn and in the conclusion consider the implications of this study for curriculum innovation in schools.

The analysis of the quiz sequence from the perspective of *Bildungsgangforschung* offers a particular way of viewing the conditions needed to promote equitable access to high-quality learning and education, the barriers that hinder equitable access to high-quality learning and education, and how these barriers can be overcome. In contrast to the case studies concerning the maths lesson (Hudson this volume) and the dance lesson (Loquet et al. this volume), we have now witnessed a sequence of comparatively low epistemic quality. This is because the teacher reduced the complexity of the language used, and the students were asked to repeat three rules of categorizing language that were too narrowly conceived. It is also because the given task follows academic and didactic traditions on grammar teaching, aspects of which are misleading and do not necessarily promote the development of epistemic capacities. Individual questions and experiences, subjective sense construction and creative reasoning of the students are ignored. High epistemic quality in languages and language teaching and learning would at least imply a *knowing how* as well as a critical, joint reflection and negotiation of language and language use, and would also open doors to a critical view on academic and didactic traditions at school and the potential of linguistic diversity in the classroom and of language change as a whole. Finally, the students' developmental tasks do not play a role in the teaching and learning concept of our teacher. Although the development of fundamental skills in reading and writing is a fundamental developmental task for children, the quiz remains a formal act in a teacher-directed curriculum that does not take the developmental tasks of the students into consideration.

The quality of teacher–students' interaction, our second focus, differs in the chosen sequence from the concept of individualized learning. Whereas generally the teacher takes the role of a facilitator giving feedback on students' work, she leads her group with simple impulses that need short answers which do not allow any divergent thinking, any utterance of subjective interest or need. Nor is there any discussion of their concerns on language phenomena, etc. We witness teacher–students' interaction which represents a teacher-led stimulus–response interaction during which the students follow the teacher's intention and recall what she had taught. The quiz also hinders any joint negotiation and intergenerational discourse in class. In general, the idea of the quiz further implies the concept of concurrence so that there is a double constraint in subject-specific interaction. Further, the quality of instruction as a creative process cannot be identified in this sequence. Rules and definitions are put in place, and creativity does not play a role here. Both the lack of quality of the teacher–students' interaction and the lack of quality of instruction as a creative process increase the effect of the low epistemic quality of the teaching and thus of a low level for enabling language learning, *sprachliche Bildung*.

As far as the democratic quality of instruction is concerned, the complex system of rules and principles the teacher follows indeed generally does allow the students to decide individually what to work on and when. Yet, at the same time, the given rules and strictness and routine of the teacher's communication with the students make schooling and instruction a power game in which students use their right to decide on the tasks to be done, but no more. Students are asked to moderate the morning circles but must adhere to a laminated sheet of paper indicating every single question to be asked and answered. Democratic schooling and instruction would mean enabling and encouraging students to become actively involved in decisions on curriculum, content, methods and practice. In the quiz sequence, at least, there is no democratic quality at all.

The model of teacher–student interaction and co-operation in the instructional process represents and allows empirical research on *Bildung* processes. It also helps illuminate implications for curriculum innovation in language and language use in the classroom. In deciding to study the practice in this particular classroom, we were strongly influenced by our knowledge of the reputation of the class teacher who was then well known for fostering a specific way of individualized, self-organized learning, which followed the didactic principles of Enders (2015). The classroom organization was highly complex but very well ordered, the classroom environment was very attractive and the students were all fully engaged in the activities at the start of the day. It was clear from these initial impressions that the teacher was a highly skilled classroom practitioner who could be described in terms of Shulman (1987) as demonstrating a high level of pedagogical knowledge (PK). Her organization and management of the quiz was especially impressive and became the focus of further analysis as it was identified as a particularly significant lesson episode.

However, our closer analysis revealed classroom activity that focused on the repetition of memorized knowledge of language norms and norms of language use, involved teacher-led working on fixed tasks that re-presented academic and didactic traditions, reduced linguistic complexity and reflected linguistic *fundamentalism*. As concerns sense construction and processes of *Bildung*, the activity reflected an emphasis on teacher-led instruction based on an expectation that students would adapt to teachers' intentions and tasks. With regard to Shulman's (1987) other categories of content knowledge (CK) and pedagogical content knowledge (PCK), it could be seen that too little attention had been given to both the epistemic quality of the content and the epistemic quality of the classroom interaction. Little attention was paid during this episode of classroom interaction to the joint action of the teacher and the students, to the shared experience of language and language use or to the students' perspectives. More attention could have been given to the recognition and promotion of creative use of linguistic repertoires and to a joint reflection and negotiation of language and language use. Consideration could have been paid to principles underpinning the democratic quality of instruction which would have helped to address such aspects related to higher epistemic quality.

A well-established approach to the development of language and language use that might contribute to addressing some of the shortcomings identified in this study is that offered by Hawkins (1987), James and Garrett (1991) and others on language awareness. This depends on the development of various domains' basic principles that, among others, allow students to develop a creative understanding of language teaching and learning, invite the teacher and students to develop their cognitive capacities, and promote social encounter and joint negotiation of language, language use and linguistic diversity. In turn, the principles outlined above hold implications not only for curriculum innovation but also for the continuing professional development of teachers in relation to language and language use and in promoting high epistemic quality of content in the primary classroom.

Acknowledgement

We dedicate this chapter to our highly respected colleague and very dear friend professor Meinert Meyer who passed away in 2018 and who contributed so much to the JADE project until he was taken ill at the end of 2017.

References

Charmaz, K. (2000), 'Grounded Theory: Objectivist and Constructivist Methods' in N. K. Denzin and Y. S. Lincoln (eds), *Handbook of Qualitative Research*, 2nd ed., 509–35. Thousand Oaks, CA: Sage.

Charmaz, K. (2008), 'Grounded Theory as an Emergent Method', in S. N. Hesse-Biber and P. Leavy (eds), *Handbook of Emergent Methods*. 155–72, New York: The Guilford Press.

Dirim, İ., Knappig, N. (2018), 'Deutsch in allen Fächern', in İ. Dirim and P. Mecheril (eds), *Heterogenität, Sprache(n) und Bildung. Eine differenz- und diskriminierungstheoretische Einführung*, 227–45, Bad Heilbrunn: Julius Klinkhardt.

Enders, M. (2015): *Individuell lernen – gemeinsam arbeiten. Ein kompetenzorientiertes Unterrichtsmodell aus der Grundschulpraxis*, Mühlheim an der Ruhr: Verlag an der Ruhr.

Hawkins, E. (1987), *Awareness of Language. An Introduction*, Cambridge: Cambridge University Press.

Hericks, U. (2008), Bildungsgangforschung und die Professionalisierung des Lehrerberufs – Perspektiven für die Allgemeine Didaktik, *Zeitschrift für Erziehungswissenschaft*. Sonderheft 9, 61–75.

Hudson, B., Loquet, M., Meyer, M., Wegner, A. and Gerin, M. (2017), Comparative Perspectives on Joint Action in Didactics: High Epistemic Quality for Equitable Access to High Quality Learning and Education in School. Round Table, *European Conference on Educational Research* (ECER 2017), University College UCC, Copenhagen, 22–25 August 2017.

Hudson, B. (2018), 'Powerful Knowledge and Epistemic Quality in School Mathematics', *London Review of Education: Special Issue on Knowledge and Subject Specialist Teaching*, 16 (3): 384–97. UCL IOE Press. https://doi.org/10.18546/LRE.16.3.03.

Hudson, B., Gericke, N., Loquet, M., Olin-Scheller, C., Stolare, M. and Wegner, A. (2021), *Epistemic Quality and Powerful Knowledge: Implications for Curriculum Innovation and Teacher Education Policy & Practice*, Panel Discussion at European Conference on Educational Research (ECER 2020), University of Geneva, 6–10 September 2021.

Hudson, B. (2022), 'Evaluating Epistemic Quality in Primary School Mathematics', in B. Hudson, N. Gericke, C. Olin-Scheller and M. Stolare (eds), *International Perspectives on Knowledge and Curriculum: Epistemic Quality across School Subjects*, London: Bloomsbury Publishing plc.

James, C. and Garrett, P. (1991), 'The Scope of Language Awareness', in C. James and P. Garrett, Peter (eds), *Language Awareness in the Classroom*, 3–20, London: Longman (Applied linguistics and language study).

Meyer, M. A. (2011), 'Professional Teacher Development and Educational Experience', in Hudson, B. and Meyer, M. A. (eds), *Beyond Fragmentation: Didactics, Learning, and Teaching*, 60–76, Opladen and Farmington Hills: Verlag Barbara Budrich.

Meyer, M.A. (2008), 'Unterrichtsplanung aus der Perspektive der Bildungsgangforschung', *Zeitschrift für Erziehungswissenschaft*. Sonderheft 9, 117–37.

Meyer, M. A. (2005), Die Bildungsgangforschung als Rahmen für die Weiterentwicklung der Allgemeinen Didaktik, in B. Schenk (ed.), *Bausteine einer Bildungsgangtheorie*, 17–46, Wiesbaden: VS Verlag.

Meyer, M.A. et al. (2001), *Antrag auf Einrichtung und Förderung eines Graduiertenkollegs zur Bildungsgangforschung*, Manuskript Hamburg Universität, Hamburg.

Morrow, W. (2008), *Bounds of Democracy: Epistemological Access in Higher Education*, Pretoria: HSRC Press.

Müller-Roselius, K. (2013), 'Bildungsgangdidaktik', in K. Zierer (ed.), *Jahrbuch Allgemeine Didaktik. Thementeil: Neuere Ansätze in der Allgemeinen Didaktik*, 17–46, Baltmannsweiler: Schneider Verlag Hohengehren.

Peukert, H. (2000), 'Reflexionen über die Zukunft von Bildung', *Zeitschrift für Pädagogik, 46* (4): 507–24.

Peukert, H. (1998), 'Zur Neubestimmung des Bildungsbegriffs', in M.A. Meyer and A. Reinartz (eds), *Bildungsgangdidaktik. Denkanstöße für pädagogische Forschung und schulische Praxis*, 17–29, Opladen: Leske + Budrich.

Shulman, L. S. (1987), 'Knowledge and Teaching: Foundations of the New Reform', *Harvard Educational Review*, 5 (1): 1–22.

Sensevy, G. (2011), 'Overcoming Fragmentation: Towards a Joint Action Theory in Didactics', in Hudson, B. and Meyer, M. A. (eds), *Beyond Fragmentation: Didactics, Learning, and Teaching*, 60–76, Opladen and Farmington Hills: Verlag Barbara Budrich.

Stake, R. (1995), *The Art of Case Study Research*, London: Sage.

Svalberg, A. (2012), 'Language Awareness in Language Learning and Teaching. A Research Agenda', *Language Teaching*, 445 (3): 376–88.

Terhart, E. (2009), *Didaktik. Eine Einführung*, Stuttgart: Reclam.

UN (2015), Transforming Our World: The 2030 Agenda for Sustainable Development, https://sustainabledevelopment.un.org/?menu=1300

Wegner, A., Hudson, B. and Loquet, M. (2019), *What Epistemic Quality for Equitable Access to Powerful Knowledge? A Case Study of Language Learning in a Primary Classroom in Germany, through the Lenses of Bildungsgangforschung and JATD*, 1st International Congress on the Joint Action Theory in Didactics, 25–27 June 2019, ESPE de Bretagne-UBO, Site de formation de Rennes, 2, 190–201.

Wegner, A. (2018), 'Biographie und professionelle Entwicklung im Kontext der Mehrsprachigkeit von Schule und Unterricht', in İ. Dirim and A. Wegner (eds), *Normative Grundlagen und reflexive Verortungen im Feld Deutsch als Fremd- und Zweitsprache*, 249–75, Opladen: Budrich.

Wegner, A. (2016), 'Bildungsgangforschung und -didaktik: Zum Potenzial Allgemeiner Didaktik für die Gestaltung von Unterricht', in Wegner, Anke (ed.), *Allgemeine Didaktik: Praxis, Positionen, Perspektiven*, 87–112, Opladen: Budrich.

Wittgenstein, L. (1960), *Philosophische Unersuchungen* Frankfurt am Main: Suhrkamp Verlag.

Young, M. (2013), 'Overcoming the Crisis in Curriculum Theory: A Knowledge-based Approach', *Journal of Curriculum Studies*, 45 (2): 101–18. http://www.tandfonline.com/doi/full/10.1080/00220272.2013.764505

Powerful Knowledge of Language and Migration in Norwegian and Swedish Textbooks

Birgitta Ljung Egeland and Lise Iversen Kulbrandstad

Introduction

Waves of global migration and increased cultural and linguistic diversity are bringing about societal changes in the two neighbouring countries of Sweden and Norway. In 2020, 25.5 per cent of persons living in Sweden were either themselves born outside the country or both of their parents were (SCB 2020). The corresponding share for Norway is 18.2 per cent (SSB 2020). Classrooms in these two countries include a growing number of multilingual students – with several being second language learners of Swedish or Norwegian. This greater societal diversity is challenging the education system, especially the language subjects, Swedish and Norwegian, respectively, since they developed as school subjects within a monolingual tradition (Lindberg 2009; Kulbrandstad 2018). However, the most recent curricula for compulsory school in both Sweden and Norway stress the need to address diversity. A Swedish student should, for example, be able to 'understand [his or her] own reality in a global context' (Skolverket 2018: 8), while a Norwegian student should experience 'that being proficient in a number of languages is a resource, both in school and society at large' (Utdanningsdirektoratet 2017: 6). Meeting these new challenges requires new teacher competencies as well as new teaching aids. The topic of diversity is slowly finding its way into teacher education programmes but is still considered a matter which needs to be better covered (Følgjegruppa 2015; Lärarutbildningskonventet 2018).

In this article, we explore teaching aids in the light of the diversity caused by modern migration. We ask how and in which ways subject content related to language and migration is transformed into the school subjects Swedish and

Norwegian through printed textbooks for middle school (students aged 10 to 12). We look at both the content and the roles students are invited to enter through textbook assignments.

Teaching aids of various kinds are an important facet of how schools introduce and adapt content to students. Norwegian primary school teachers, for example, describe textbooks as central for structuring classroom activities and for ensuring work towards the learning goals established by the national curriculum (Gilje et al. 2016). Lately, the complex transformation of content through different teaching aids has been studied in terms of questions of equality as well as inherent norms and expectations of students' competencies (Vinde 2018).

Two theoretical perspectives are used as our point of departure: multilingualism as part of language awareness (Hélot 2012; A. Young 2018) and the transformation and selection of knowledge (M. Young 2009/2016; Gericke et al. 2019; Hudson 2019). Of special interest is M. Young's concept *powerful knowledge* since we argue that knowledge of linguistic diversity in societies characterized by super-diversity created by new patterns of migration (Vertovec 2007, 2019) is knowledge which can provide young people with 'new ways of thinking about the world' (M. Young 2009/2016: 110). Vertovec (2019: 126) makes the point that super-diversity is producing novel hierarchies of social positions and 'new patterns of inequality and prejudice'. In both Norway and Sweden, the educational legislation and regulations emphasize the importance of equality and equal rights and prescribe that school 'shall present knowledge and promote attitudes which safeguard these values' (Utdanningsdirektoratet 2017: 4), and 'actively resist discrimination and degrading treatment of individuals or groups' (Skolverket 2018: 10).

In the following, we first expand on the theoretical perspectives and then present and discuss the results of a textbook study in view of these perspectives. Finally, we address the consequences for teacher education.

Multilingualism as part of language awareness

In her review of research of language awareness in primary education, Andrea Young (2018) asks why language awareness matters in schools characterized by linguistic diversity caused by migration. Her answer is that raising language awareness might be a way to handle inequality, linguistic prejudices and negative attitudes to differences, and as such to 'make a positive contribution to anti-discrimination education' (Young 2018: 24). She argues that inclusive practices might be favoured by taking account of all languages and dialects spoken in the classrooms as a basis. Learning to understand language, multilingualism, multiple identities and how we acquire language(s) are among topics listed that might 'have the potential to unlock children's prior knowledge and skills brought from home to school', help children 'to better comprehend the complexities of our multilingual worlds' and help them 'feel more confident and better prepared to negotiate linguistic and cultural differences, viewing it as a resource and a right rather than a problem' (ibid.).

The teaching of languages has traditionally concentrated on linguistic competence. Language awareness adds new dimensions, raising the importance of both knowledge about languages and linguistic tolerance (James and Garrett 1991: 13; Hélot 2012: 220). An observation made by several researchers is that it still seems difficult to bring the multilingualism and linguistic diversity developed outside school into classrooms. The monolingual norm based on European nation state ideology appears to remain dominant in many places (Gogolin 2008; Hélot 2012; A. Young 2018; Pujata 2018).

Textbooks might be helpful for raising language awareness. However, previous textbook studies show that societal diversity is still presented as the exception, not the norm (Niehaus 2018: 337). Loftsdóttir (2009: 257), for example, studies textbooks in Iceland and concludes that children of diverse backgrounds should be allowed to 'better identify and position themselves as part of Icelandic society'. L.A. Kulbrandstad (2001) analysed content on language variation and multilingualism in Norwegian textbooks for the lower secondary level published in the 1990s. He found that questions of migration-related linguistic diversity held a peripheral position, while Sami languages were slightly better covered. Content knowledge about multilingualism was, however, not dealt with at all.

Transformations of knowledge

Michael Young's concept of *powerful knowledge* provides a starting point for this study. It gives inspiration while we analyse the relationship between specialized academic knowledge and the school subjects, and we employ it to explore the potential intellectual power that knowledge can give students, for example, through new ways of seeing the world. The ROSE-project at Karlstad University, to which this study belongs, sums up the use of Young's concept in the project as follows:

> Powerful knowledge is defined by Young as subject-specific, coherent, conceptual disciplinary knowledge, that, when learned, will empower students to make decisions and become action-competent in a way that will influence their lives in a positive way.
>
> (Gericke et al. 2018: 428)

Young (2013) understands powerful knowledge as both an analytic concept in educational sociology and a curriculum principle. Powerful knowledge is both specialized by being developed in academic disciplines and differentiated by being distinct from the everyday knowledge students bring to school. While everyday knowledge is tied to particular situations, knowledge that is part of the school subjects should enable students to 'generalize beyond their experience', according to Young (2013: 110). His focus is the content of schools, not the ways schools work to adapt content as part of their teaching. Hudson (2018: 395) therefore criticizes Young for overlooking the importance of research on subject didactics. Following up on such a critique, Gericke et al. argue for an extended understanding of powerful knowledge with use of the concept of *transformation*.

> Transformation [...] is defined as an integrative process in which content knowledge is transformed into knowledge that is taught and learned through various transformation processes that take place outside and within the educational system at the individual, institutional and societal levels.
>
> (Gericke et al. 2018: 432)

Gericke et al. (2018: 433) emphasize that since school subjects can never be seen as simple reductions of academic disciplines, the study of school content must include transformations of content in the light of the didactical questions of why, what, for whom, when and how. While all of these questions are interwoven in our textbook study, our focus is on the *what* and *how* questions. We first sum up the results of earlier analysis of the content of the textbooks, that is, the what question (Kulbrandstad and Ljung Egeland 2019) and then more closely look at a sample of textbook activities aiming to explore language and migration in different ways, that is, the *how* and *when* questions. The why question motivates the study since we assume there is a need for changes to the curriculum due to the increase in cultural and linguistic diversity. These changes are not only relevant for the teaching content, but the composition of students in school is also ever more linguistically heterogeneous, leading to calls for new awareness of who the students in class are, that is, the who question.

The project language and migration: Identifying areas of focus

The first step in the analysis was to identify topics from academic disciplines possibly able to provide students with powerful knowledge about language and migration. Traditionally, the school subjects Swedish and Norwegian are built on knowledge from Nordic linguistics and literature studies while multilingualism and linguistic diversity form parts of the quite new academic field of second language research, which developed following the new waves of migration during the 1970s. To identify areas of focus for the textbook study, we analysed the content of university courses in Swedish and Norwegian as a second language (Kulbrandstad and Ljung Egeland 2019). These courses are based on second-language research and studied by prospective teachers. We concentrated on the four universities that established research and teaching in this field early on, namely the universities in Oslo and Bergen in Norway, and Stockholm and Gothenburg in Sweden. We found that the course descriptions had three overall topics in common:

- Swedish/Norwegian in a comparative perspective
- Multilingualism
- Second language learning

Thus, these three topics represent core content emerging from second-language research. At the same time, they represent new areas of knowledge for the school subjects in question. In the project, we consider the extent to and in which ways knowledge from these topics is transformed through the textbooks into the school subjects.

Material and method of the textbook study

We examined 24 printed textbooks in Swedish from three different publishers issued between 2011 and 2017 and a total of 27 Norwegian textbooks from four publishers, released between 2006 and 2017. The books are written for middle school, which refers to grades 4–6 in Sweden and 5–7 in Norway. More details of this first part of the study are given in Kulbrandstad and Ljung Egeland (2019) and Kulbrandstad (2019).

Table 5.1 Categories of the content analysis

Multilingualism					Swedish/Norwegian language in a comparative perspective	Second language learning	
Representation of languages other than Swedish and Norwegian	Texts about multilingualism				Language comparisons	Texts which thematize learning a second language	Texts which thematize learning through a second language
Words or phrases	Texts	In general	About Sami languages	About minority languages			

The textbooks were examined through qualitative content analysis. We worked deductively, looking for examples of the three topics found in the analysis of the university courses (cf. upper row, Table 5.1). As part of the process of going through the books, more specific categories emerged (the two lower rows, Table 5.1). We first worked individually with the Norwegian or the Swedish textbooks and then together with all of the books, discussing typical and less typical examples of each category and adjusting the analysis. Table 5.1 sums up categories used to register occurrences.

Transformation of powerful knowledge of language and migration through textbooks

A main result of the comparative study is that the three topics derived from second-language research are only occasionally covered as content knowledge in the textbooks (Kulbrandstad and Ljung Egeland 2019). Second-language learning is almost absent, while language comparisons are the most frequently found topic of the three. Most often, the neighbouring languages Norwegian, Swedish and Danish, which are mutually understandable, are compared. In the Norwegian textbooks, even more frequent are comparisons of different dialect forms and of the two written standards of Norwegian, Bokmål and Nynorsk.

In the textbook sample, there is one example we consider to be quite a thorough treatment of multilingualism as content knowledge for the age group in question. We characterize this coverage as in-depth because it defines concepts and describes multilingualism as both a phenomenon in society and something pertaining to the individual.

> *Norwegian and other languages*
> We say that Norway is a *multilingual* society because it is a society where we use more than one language. There are two official languages in Norway: Norwegian and Sámi. The fact that a language is official means that it is used on road signs, in newspapers and on television, in schools and other public places. In some places in Norway, the road signs are in both Norwegian and Sami.
>
> *To be multilingual*
> In addition to the two official languages, many more languages are used in Norway. Most people speak Norwegian as their *mother tongue*, but many speak another language at home. If you know more than one language, you are a *multilingual* person. For example, if you speak Persian at home and Norwegian at school, you are multilingual.
>
> (Anly, Lissner and Nome 2015: 106, our translation)

Both the Swedish and the Norwegian textbooks include examples of words, phrases and texts from other languages, for instance, the word 'hello' in different languages, greeting phrases in Sami, and a text message exchange in Faroese. Still, only one text is directly connected to migration: a short postcard in Bosnian. We find the same tendency when it comes to the way the textbooks choose single words and phrases from other languages. All in all, there are examples of words from 34 different languages across all the Norwegian textbooks and 27 across the Swedish ones. However, the collection of single words does not cover all of the largest immigrant groups. For example, there are no occurrences of words from the following languages spoken by large immigrant groups of Norway in the Norwegian books: Polish, Lithuanian, Somali, Kurdish, Tigrinya, Pilipino, Thai, Persian or Dari.

To sum up: The textbook analysis shows that the three thematic topics of multilingualism, second language learning and Swedish/Norwegian compared with languages other than the Nordic are only occasionally relatively thoroughly covered in the textbooks. Thus, the content does not reflect the current multilingual situation of Sweden and Norway but includes examples of what we characterize as promising first steps away from a monolingual tradition. Still, the main conclusion is that the books offer few opportunities to explore linguistic diversity in ways that potentially will take students 'beyond the limits of their own experiences' (cf. M. Young) or help them better comprehend the complexities of our multilingual world (cf. A. Young).

Thus far, we have concentrated on the content presented in texts. Below, we present a study of textbook activities that constitute part of the textbook content. The purpose is to explore whether focusing on these activities will add new perspectives to the understanding of possible transformations of powerful knowledge through teaching materials. Studying activities is of special interest since classroom research shows that students in primary school spend an important part of their school day working on exercises individually, in groups or as part of whole-class teaching (Haug 2012; Skolinspektionen 2017). In the school subjects of Swedish and Norwegian, textbook activities are used in different ways to transform content knowledge into learning. For example, students are supposed to work on the knowledge content itself, on developing and using their oral and written language competencies, or on developing empathy and their own identity.

Framework for analysing textbook activities

The textbooks present several activities in each chapter. We decided to concentrate on activities linked to textbook content already found to be promising first steps away from a monolingual tradition. This allowed us to explore examples holding the possibility of helping to transform content into powerful knowledge.

As the main analytical framework, we further developed a typology originally presented in Otnes (2015) for describing the different roles students are invited to enter by writing assignments in middle-grade classrooms. We use four possible roles in the typology for analysing all kinds of assignments relating to the transformation of subject-specific content on language and migration. The roles were given the following labels: the subject-specific apprentice, the personal expert, the empathetic individual and the active citizen. Table 5.2 gives an overview of transformation processes that might be initiated through the different roles and how the roles connect to the development of powerful knowledge (cf. Young 2013; Maude 2016).

When students are invited to enter *the role of a subject-specific apprentice*, they perform activities in which they are supposed to work on learning the content presented in the textbook. These activities are often closely connected to the content, for example, answering questions about the text. As such, they might be considered an early phase in learning the content in question.

Table 5.2 Transformation processes through student roles

Roles students are invited to enter	Description of the roles within the subject Swedish/Norwegian	Possible contribution to powerful knowledge
Subject-specific apprentice	Doing activities to work on learning the textbook content	Basis for establishing knowledge and discovering new ways of thinking
Personal expert	Using the knowledge students have from before	Potential invitation to reflect on, generalize and develop identity, but in isolation there is a danger of only learning what students already know from earlier experience
Empathetic individual	Entering a role as another person in a different situation	Engaging with feelings, going beyond the limits of the students' own experience, generalizing from a particular situation
Active citizen	Participating by communicating opinions in different genres	Becoming action-oriented, being able to engage in current debates in society

When invited to take on *the role as a personal expert*, the students are supposed to use what they know from before, which very often means their everyday knowledge. Sometimes, such activities invite reflection and generalization by combining knowledge from the textbooks and from the students themselves. In these cases, one might say that the use of everyday knowledge aims at 'unlocking' the children's prior knowledge (A. Young 2018: 24) as part of the process of learning the school content. However, textbook activities sometimes only invite schoolchildren to rely on their personal knowledge, and they are thus not challenged to learn new content. While the term *personal expert* has a positive connotation, Michael Young's critical comment, 'students do not come to school to know what they already know from experience' (2013: 111), spurs our interest in observing how this role might be combined with other roles and integrated with a teaching sequence. By working together with classmates, students for example also have possibilities to share experiences.

The third role, the *empathetic individual*, is often linked to working with literature. The students are invited to enter roles as another person in a different life situation and to explore new worlds. Young (2013: 109) comments that literature might be powerful because literature engages with feelings that are 'experienced in particular contexts but common to all human beings'.

The fourth role is an *active citizen*. In the national curriculums of both Sweden and Norway, the importance of school's contribution to democracy and fostering active citizens is emphasized. One way of doing this is by developing the ability to communicate and participate (Skolverket 2018: 7; Utdanningsdirektoratet 2017: 8f). In the subjects of Swedish and Norwegian, fostering active citizens often means learning to present opinions in different genres, for instance, a letter to the editor. However, it also means finding the students' own voice and developing their ability to reflect and adopt a critical stance.

When we analyse the textbook activities below, we also characterize them as open or closed, which means they can either be solved in different ways or have a fixed answer. We also notice in which part of the teaching process the activities are used: Are they a way into the content, are they closely connected to working directly on the learning content (a text), or are they used to sum up or go beyond the content presented in the textbook?

All of the following textbook examples are translated to English from Swedish or Norwegian by the authors.

Analysis of textbook activities and student roles

The role of subject-specific apprentice: Learning about alphabets

The first example is from a Swedish textbook for grade 6 presenting language history by introducing the development of different writing systems (Eriksson and Sahlin 2017: 60–1). Relatively solid knowledge material on historical perspectives is presented. One double page contains the headings 'The Phoenician Alphabet' and 'The alphabet spreads out'. The Arabic writing system is explained, but no connections are made to contemporary use of Arabic writing in either Sweden or other countries. However, one speech bubble reads: 'Did you know that our numbers are Arabic?'

The exercises follow directly after the text. The students are invited to answer questions like: 'How many letters did the Phoenician alphabets consist of?', and 'Which similarities are there between the Phoenician and the Arabic alphabets?' In each case, the questions are used to check basic understanding since the answers might be found directly in the text. The questions are thus characterized as closed. We argue that here students are expected to practise the role of a subject-specific apprentice by processing the knowledge presented in the textbook by reading and probably copying the text. Such exercises might serve a purpose in an early phase of learning. Liberg et al. (2001) present a model for describing different ways of participating in learning activities within a community, from being a listener without a contribution of their own to an independent participant creating different kinds of texts. In between there are several steps, for example, participating through heavily controlled contributions like answering the above-cited closed questions on alphabets. The role of a subject-specific apprentice might be a necessary step, but in our material it is more often combined with other roles.

Combining the roles of a subject-specific apprentice and a personal expert: Multilingualism on the agenda

The second example is activities linked to the text about multilingualism that we already quoted (Anly, Lissner and Nome 2015: 105–8). In this textbook, students in grade 5 are invited to enter the role as a subject-specific apprentice combined with a role as a personal expert. The topic 'Talk about languages' is introduced with a picture showing a schoolyard with 'hello' written in different migrant languages. Four questions introduce the topic: Which languages do you recognize?, Which languages do you speak?, Which languages do you write?, How many languages do you know all together in class? All of these questions are open, and students are invited to use or mobilize their personal knowledge, that is, to enter the role as a personal expert in introducing the topic. The purpose here seems to be to start unlocking the students' everyday knowledge (cf. A. Young 2018). The next double-page contains the subject-specific substance. Following these texts, students are asked to talk about languages in Norway by answering eight questions together with a classmate. Four of these questions help grasp the content or control that the students already have knowledge about, like 'Which languages are official in Norway?' and 'What does it mean to be a multilingual person?' The answers to these questions are all found in the text. Thus, the questions are closed and reproducing but, as mentioned, represent a frequently used step to ensure that students work on the content knowledge by taking on a role of a subject-specific apprentice. The potential of these tasks depends on how the questions are formulated, what they focus on, how they are combined with other types of questions, and of course how they are used in the classroom. One mission might be to help the students attend to important parts of the text. In this example, such questions alternate with four open, often self-reflecting questions where students are again invited to assume roles as personal experts, like 'Are you multilingual?', and 'What are the benefits of speaking multiple languages?' In answering these questions, they are supposed to build on a combination of what they have learned from the text and their own experiences and to share them with their classmates.

Encounter with an illegal refugee by combining the roles of a subject-specific apprentice and an empathetic individual

This third example is connected to a fiction text from grade 7 in which a boy (Tony T) is confronted with a dilemma: A refugee girl is hiding from the immigration authorities in the attic of the boy's house. He discovers her by accident and must decide whether he should help her or tell his mother, who is a police officer (Bjerke and Pedersen 2017: 206–7). The activities presented after the text are partly meant to help the students understand the text by taking on the role of a subject-specific apprentice discussing both explicit and implicit information. In the end, the students are also challenged in an open activity to enter the role of an emphatic individual:

> Imagine that you are Tony T or the girl. Describe what you feel, think and do when you meet the other person in the attic.
> (Bjerke and Pedersen 2017: 207, our translation)

In our material, we often find activities in which students are supposed to assume the role of an empathetic person while working with fiction texts. Even though literary knowledge represents specific ways of knowing (Medway 2010; MacLean Davies and Sawyer 2018), the literature also offers knowledge about other areas, like in the example above – language and migration.

The role of an active citizen writing blogs after reading poetry

The final activity exemplifies the role of an active citizen. The exercise follows a text about a young author with a refugee background and two poems she wrote soon after she arrived in Norway (Bjørndal, Eide and Elvebakk 2016: 205–6). Several exercises are supposed to help students understand and reflect on the texts. One activity illustrates how they are asked to take on the role of an active citizen.

> Imagine that you are Marima or another refugee. Write a blog about your reflections after your arrival in a foreign country.
> (Bjørndal, Eide and Elvebakk 2016: 205, our translation)

The subjects Norwegian and Swedish aim to create active citizens by focusing on developing oral and written argumentation skills as well as learning to write in different genres on political or personal issues. The example just quoted is of one such genre, namely a personal blog, and one current issue of great concern: the refugee situation. However, there are few instances in our material where students are explicitly invited to take on the role of an active citizen when the topic is language and migration. It might be that the textbook authors consider topics related to migration to be too controversial for use in such activities for children aged 10 to 12.

Discussion

The four examples illustrate possible roles students might adopt while working with activities on the topic of language and migration. At the same time, they show how the language subjects can transform content in ways that might help students deal with knowledge in powerful ways. The core of the subjects Swedish and Norwegian is language and literature. By working on these areas of knowledge, students develop tools for reflection, communication and for building knowledge. Language as well as literature is also important for personal development and expressions of identity. Studies of language and literature thus help students to know the world, other people and themselves.

Taking the increased societal diversity as a point of departure, our aim was to study whether and how this new situation is influencing the school subjects we are concerned with. Overall, we find that linguistic diversity can hardly be said to be integrated into the subjects, at least not in the textbooks. Still, there are some promising examples of where multilingualism and migrant destinies are placed on the agenda. Such examples represent necessary first steps on the way towards more linguistic inclusive school subjects that acknowledge multilingualism as part of normality. This is in line with Andrea Young's emphasis that raising language awareness is one possible way to help children better comprehend 'the complexities of our multilingual world' and to handle inequality and linguistic prejudices (2018: 24). Integrating perspectives on diversity might accordingly amount to a contribution to an anti-discriminatory school from the language subjects.

The language subjects must always consider both historical and contemporary contexts, meaning the choice of teaching content can neither be static nor incidental. The concept of powerful knowledge draws attention to the important balance between the transmitting of past knowledge and building on this knowledge to create new knowledge. The question of what students are entitled to learn has no 'once and for all answer', as Michael Young stresses (2013: 101). The knowledge base of a school subject must, in other words, be dynamic enough to include new perspectives. At present, the growing societal diversity is a development that is challenging the subjects of Swedish and Norwegian to open up for new knowledge.

In classrooms, subject knowledge is transformed through the different ways in which teachers choose content and of how to work to ensure learning. Hence, the analysis of the textbook assignments and their potential contribution to the development of powerful knowledge is an exploration of transformation processes. The first example in our analysis, where the knowledge content is the alphabets of the world, uses the role of a subject-specific apprentice. Here the contribution to powerful knowledge will require an extension of the textbook content, for example, by adding a contemporary perspective to the historical one and by introducing new ways to work on the topic. Through knowledge about both the history of alphabets as well as their current use, students could have been invited to compare alphabets that are actually in use today. This might lead to the discovery of new ways of thinking about written languages, which go beyond the students' own experiences. At the same time, such extensions would invite those with knowledge of more than one alphabet to act as personal experts. In the second example, where the content knowledge is about multilingualism, we find that the textbook exercises already promote a combination of a subject-specific apprentice and a personal expert. In the first phase of the encounter with the content, students are invited to unlock their everyday knowledge and to then explore the content by focusing on developing concepts and making generalizations. In the final phase, they are again invited to rely on their personal experiences, but this time based on the subject knowledge and in a context in which they can share their experiences. Thus, this is a possible contribution to powerful knowledge since the combination of roles ensures that the students go beyond their prior knowledge.

The third example, where the schoolchildren read a fiction text about a young refugee on the run, invites the students to assume the role of an empathetic individual. This is a way of becoming familiar with another person's life situation and rising above one's own frames of reference, here possibly also with an emotional engagement. Experiences emerging from reading fiction also make it possible to generalize from one specific situation. The fourth example is an assignment presented in the last phase of the work on a topic. Through the textbook, the students first meet a young refugee girl and her story, then read two of her poems describing experiences in the new country, and are finally given the role of an active citizen and practise participating in society by stating opinions through blogs. This activity may contribute to powerful knowledge through the invitation to become action-oriented and engage in current debates.

The role perspective on learning activities has helped us better understand how transformations of powerful knowledge can be achieved through teaching materials. Although we have not counted different types of activities in the textbooks, the overall impression is that the role of a subject-specific apprentice is the most frequent. This role is considered a necessary step in the learning process, but it must be combined with one of the other roles, a personal expert, an empathetic person or an active citizen, for the students to connect knowledge about language and migration to their own lives or the lives of others, and to society. Yet, the students most often lack this opportunity even when the textbooks actually present relevant content, and we consider the texts to be promising first steps away from a monolingual tradition.

One weakness we observed is that assignments on language and migration sometimes stand more or less on their own. This means they are not connected to the content presented in the textbook. In such activities, students are often invited to enter roles as personal experts, but without a combination with the role of a subject-specific apprentice. They are thereby not offered help from the teaching material to conquer knowledge that provides them with new ways of thinking about the world and makes them go beyond the limits of their personal experiences, as powerful knowledge might do.

Implications for curriculum innovation and teacher education

Teachers' professional knowledge may be described as a combination of knowledge about the learners and their development, knowledge of the subject matter and curriculum goals, and knowledge of teaching (Bransford, Darling-Hammond and LePage 2005: 11). Super-diverse societies challenge all of these aspects of professional knowledge. The knowledge base of teacher education must open up to new perspectives and for adding new knowledge concerning diversity. Preparing teachers to teach diverse learners is characterized as a 'recurring theme for improving' across countries around the world (Darling-Hammond and Lieberman 2012: 159). In addition, the concept of super-diverse societies highlights the need to include knowledge of diversity in the teaching of *all* students. For the subjects Swedish and Norwegian, this means going from a monolingual norm to an inclusive linguistic diversity norm – with this applying to the school subjects as well as the teacher education subjects. One possible way of doing this is to put greater focus on raising language awareness by using all of the languages spoken in the classroom to thereby prepare children for negotiating linguistic and cultural differences and viewing diversity as a resource. For teacher education, this implies that questions of diversity, equality and social justice need to be addressed in discussions both on how to choose teaching content and how to work on different ways to transform content to learning in the classrooms. Michael Young's concept of powerful knowledge might be a fruitful entry point for discussions on these topics. Student teachers need to build awareness of their future roles as curricula-makers in everyday practice (Lambert 2014).

One way of making the discussions both theory-based and practically oriented is to analyse teaching aids like textbooks. Analysis of the selection of the content of different books, what is there and what is missing, leads to reflections on both powerful knowledge and the epistemic quality of the choices made by the textbook authors (cf. Hudson 2019). As shown in this article, looking at assignments can also shed light on transformation processes. Which roles are school children invited to enter, which functions do these roles have, and in which ways do they contribute to quality education and school children's establishment of powerful knowledge? One strength of teacher education is that student teachers also practise teaching under supervision. This permits the possibility of not only discussing different examples of how content can be transformed through textbooks but also trying out different transformation processes in classrooms and later critically reflecting on them.

Student teachers of today are preparing for work in societies undergoing rapid changes. Cummins and Early (2011: 155) stress the importance of making teachers aware of their important roles as powerful agents of change in the classroom, by letting them 'articulate and reflect critically on the instructional choices that we make on a routine daily basis and to examine alternative possibilities'. Teachers and student teachers need to open their eyes to diversity. Thus, the advice given by Cummins and Early, which we endorse, is to put on multilingual lenses.

References

Anly, I., E. Lissner and S. Nome (2015), *Kaleido 5. Grunnbok B*, Oslo: Cappelen Damm.
Bjerke, K. K. and Pedersen, M. O. (2017), *SALTO 7B Elevbok*, Oslo: Gyldendal.

Bjørndal, A., Eide, M., A. and Elvebakk, L. (2016), *SALTO 6B Elevbok*, Oslo: Gyldendal.
Bransford, J., Darling-Hammond, L. and LePage, P. (2005), 'Introduction', in L. Darling-Hammond and J. Bransford (eds), *Preparing Teachers for a Changing World*, 1–39, San Francisco: Jossey-Bass.
Cummins, J. and Early, M., eds (2011), *Identity Texts. The Collaborative Creation of Power in Multilingual Schools*, Stoke on Trent: Trentham Books.
Darling-Hammond, L. and Lieberman, A. (2012), 'Teacher Education around the World. What Can We Learn from International Practice?', in L. Darling-Hammond and A. Lieberman (eds), *Teacher Education around the World. Changing Policies and Practices*, 151–69, London: Routledge.
Eriksson, M. and Sahlin, P. (2017), *Klara svenskan åk 6. Språklära*, Stockholm: Natur och Kultur.
Følgjegruppa (2015), *Grunnskulelærarutdanningane etter fem år. Status, utfordringar og vegar vidare Rapport 5*, Stavanger: University of Stavanger.
Gericke, N., Hudson, B., Olin-Scheller, C. and Stolare, M. (2018), 'Powerful Knowledge, Transformations and the Need for Empirical Studies across School Subjects', *London Review of Education*, 16 (3): 428–44. doi.org/10.18546/LRE.16.3.06.
Gilje, Ø., Ingulfsen, L., Dolonen, J. A., Furberg, A., Rasmussen, I., Kluge, A., Knain, E., Mørch, A., Naalsund, M. and Skarpaas, Kaja G. (2016), *Med ARK and APP. Bruk av læremidler og ressurser for læring på tvers av arbeidsformer*, Oslo: Universitet i Oslo. Available online: https://www.uv.uio.no/iped/forskning/prosjekter/ark-app/arkapp_syntese_endelig_til_trykk.pdf (accessed 12 September 2020).
Gogolin, I. (2008), *Der monolinguale Habitus der multilingualen Schule*, Münster: Waxmann.
Haug, P. (2012), 'Aktivitetane i klasserommet', in P. Haug (ed.), *Kvalitet i opplæringa. Arbeid i grunnskulen observert og vurdert*, 58–76, Oslo: Samlaget.
Hélot, C. (2012), 'Linguistic Diversity and Education', in M. Martin-Jones, A. Blackledge and A. Creese (eds), *The Routledge Handbook of Multilingualism*, 214–31, London: Routledge.
Hudson, B. (2019) 'Epistemic Quality for Equitable Access to Quality Education in School Mathematics', *Journal of Curriculum Studies*, 51 (4): 437–56. https://doi.org/10.1080/00220272.2019.1618917
James, C. and Garrett, P. (1991), 'The Scope of Language Awareness', in C. James and P. Garrett (eds), *Language Awareness in the Classroom*, 3–20, London: Longman.
Kulbrandstad, L.A. (2001), 'Samfunnsvirkelighet og lærebokvirkelighet – nye former for språkvariasjon i samfunnet og i lærebøkene', in S. Selander and D. Skjelbred (eds), *Fokus på pedagogiske tekster 3*, 67–84, Tønsberg: Høgskolen i Vestfold.
Kulbrandstad, L. A. (2018), 'Increased Linguistic Diversity in Norway. Attitudes and Reflections', in L.A. Kulbrandstad, T.O. Engen and S. Lied (eds), *Norwegian Perspectives on Education and Cultural Diversity*, 142–59, Newcastle: Cambridge Scholars Publishing.
Kulbrandstad, L. A. and Ljung Egeland, B. (2019), 'Kraftfull kunnskap – en studie av temaet språk og migrasjon i svenske og norske lærebøker på mellomtrinnet', in

B. Ljung Egeland, T. Roberts, E. Sandlund Og P. Sundqvist (eds), *Klassrumsforskning och språk(ande): Rapport från ASLA-symposiet i Karlstad, 12–13 april, 2018. ASLAs skriftserie 27*, 137–60, Karlstad: Karlstad University Press. Available online http://kau.diva-portal.org/smash/record.jsf?pid=diva2%3A1319360anddswid=-1050 (accessed 12 September 2020)

Kulbrandstad L.I. (2019), 'Å se norskfaget med andrespråksbriller. En studie av læremidler for 5. -7. Trinn', *NOA*, 35 (2): 7–40. http://ojs.novus.no/index.php/NOA/article/view/1771.

Lambert, D. (2014), 'Subject Teachers in Knowledge-led Schools', in M. Young, D. Lambert, C. Roberts and M. Roberts (eds), *Knowledge and the Future School: Curriculum and Social Justice*, 159–87, London: Bloomsbury Academic.

Lärarutbildningskonventet (2018), *Tidigare lärarstudenters syn på lärarutbildningen. Analys av Lärarutbildningskonventets alumnienkäter 2017, 2015, 2013 och 2011*. Available online http://www.lararutbildningskonventet.se/wp-content/uploads/2018/11/Rapport-alumnenk%C3%A4t_LUK_2018.pdf (accessed September 12 2020).

Liberg, C., Edling, A., Folkeryd, J. W. and Af Geijerstam, Å. (2001), 'Analys- och tolkningsramar för elevers möte med skolans textvärldar', in L.I. Kulbrandstad and G. Sjølie (eds), På Hamar med norsk. Høgskolen i Hedmark rapport 11, 21–32, Innlandet, Norway. Available online: http://hdl.handle.net/11250/133972 (accessed 12 September 2020).

Lindberg, I. (2009), 'I det nya mångspråkiga Sverige', *Utbildning and Demokrati*, 18 (2): 9–37.

Loftsdóttir, K. (2009), 'The Diversified Iceland. Identity and Multicultural Society in Icelandic School Books', in S. Selander and B. Aamotsbakken (eds), *Nordic Identities in Transition – As Reflected in Pedagogic Texts and Cultural Contexts*, 239–60, Oslo: Novus.

Maude, A. (2016), 'What Might Powerful Geographical Knowledge Look Like?', *Geography*, 101 (2): 70–6.

McLean Davis, L. and Sawyer, W. (2018), '(K)now You See It, (K)now You Don't: Literary Knowledge in the Australian Curriculum: English', *Journal of Curriculum Studies*, 50 (6), 836–49, doi:10.1080/00220272.2018.1499807.

Medway, P. (2010), 'English and Enlightenment', *Changing English*, 17 (1), 3–12.

Niehaus, I. (2018), 'How Diverse Are Our Textbooks? Research Findings in International Perspective', in E. Fuchs and A. Bock (eds), *The Palgrave Handbook of Textbook Studies*, 329–43, New York: Palgrave Macmillian.

Otnes, H. (2015), 'Tildelte skriveroller og posisjoner I skriveoppgaver på mellomtrinnet', in H. Otnes (ed.), *Å invitere elever til skriving. Ulike perspektiver på skriveoppgaver*, 243–59, Bergen: Fagbokforlaget.

Pujata, G. (2018), 'Multilingualism for Life – Language Awareness As Key Element in Educational Training: Insights from an Intervention Study in Germany', *Language Awareness*, 27 (3): 259–76. doi:10.1080/09658416.2018.1492583.

SCB (2020), 'Sveriges befolkning efter födelseland/-region, medborgarskap och bakgrund, 31 december 2019'. Available online: https://www.scb.se/ (accessed September 12 2020).

Skolinspektionen (2017), *Arbetsformer och lärarstöd i grundskolan. Resultat efter Skolinspektionens oanmälda besök på 60 grundskolor den 18 oktober 2016*, Granskningsrapport. Stockholm: Skolinspektionen.

Skolverket (2018), *Curriculum for the compulsory school, preschool classes and school-age educare*. Available online https://www.skolverket.se/andra-sprak-other-languages/english-engelska (accessed 12 September 2020).

SSB (2020), 'Innvandrere og norskfødte med innvandrerforeldre'. Available online https://www.ssb.no/innvbef (accessed 12 September 2020).

Utdanningsdirektoratet (2017), *Core Curriculum – Values and Principles for Primary and Secondary Education*. Available online https://www.udir.no/lk20/overordnet-del/?lang=eng (accessed 12 September 2020).

Vertotec, S., (2007), 'Super-diversity and Its Implications', *Ethnic and Racial Studies*, 30 (6): 1024–54. doi:10.1080/01419870701599465.

Vertotec, S. (2019), 'Talking Around Super-diversity', *Ethnic and Racial Studies*, 42 (1): 125–39. doi:10.1080/01419870.2017.1406128.

Vinde, R., ed. (2018), *Den nya läromedelsdebatten*, Svenska läromedel.

Young, A. S. (2018), 'Language Awareness, Language Diversity and Migrant Languages in the Primary School', in P. Garrett and J. M. Cots (eds), *The Routledge Handbook of Language Awareness*, 23–39, New York: Routledge.

Young, M. (2009/2016), 'What Are Schools For?', in M. Young and J. Muller (eds), *Curriculum and the Specialization of Knowledge. Studies in the Sociology of Education*, 105–14, New York: Routledge.

Young, M. (2013), 'Overcoming the Crisis in Curriculum Theory: A Knowledge-based Approach', *Journal of Curriculum Studies*, 45 (2): 101–18. http://www.tandfonline.com/doi/full/10.1080/00220272.2013.764505

Powerful Reading and Epistemic Quality in first Language and Literature Education

Satu Grünthal, Pirjo Hiidenmaa and Liisa Tainio

Introduction

This article aims to present and discuss the role of literature education in Finnish primary and lower secondary education in the framework of powerful knowledge and epistemic quality. We focus on first language and literature ('L1') teachers' perceptions of their own work as literature educators, namely, which kinds of teaching methods they use, and which methods in their opinion arouse motivation among pupils.[1] In addition, we look at literature education in other school subjects. Our data come from large surveys of primary and lower secondary school teachers between 2017 and 2019. The data give us information on teachers' reasoning on classroom practices and their views on literature education.

According to reading research, engagement and intrinsic motivation enhance reading, and good reading literacy and fiction reading, in turn, correlate with good school achievement in all academic subjects (e.g. Guthrie and Wigfield 2000; Harjunen and Rautopuro 2015). Therefore, we discuss the following questions in the light of our data: How do teachers in Finland promote motivation and reading engagement? How do they enhance reading literacy skills? What can be defined as powerful knowledge and high epistemic quality in literature education?

School subjects that focus on first language and literature are highly sensitive to local contexts in different countries (Holmberg et al. 2019). In Finland, the L1 subject is called mother tongue and literature in the national curriculum, and, in contrast to many other countries, it includes both language and literature

---

[1] Throughout this article, we use the term 'pupil' for school children and youngsters in age groups from 7 to 15.

studies. The emphasis is on language, whereas the role of literature is smaller. In the latest curriculum for primary and lower secondary education (NC 2016),[2] literature covers both fiction and nonfiction (factual prose).[3] The integration of different subjects and co-operation between them are also emphasized, as well as language awareness and multiliteracy in all subjects. Since fiction and nonfiction are a suitable and adaptive tool for cross-subject education, literature education is also relevant in subjects other than L1.[4]

Theoretical background: Powerful knowledge and reading literacy

The concept of powerful knowledge was introduced by Young (2009) and later developed by many other scholars in different fields of education in order to 're-establish the importance of knowledge in teaching and curriculum development', as Gericke et al. (2018: 428) point out (also see e.g. Young 2013; Young and Muller 2014; Hudson et al. 2015; Lambert 2017; Hudson 2018).

Powerful knowledge is subject-specific and differs in a significant way from non-specialized knowledge. It is not acquired or produced informally as part of people's everyday lives, problems and themes: it is differentiated from everyday thinking and produced with conceptual language with specific approaches (Young 2013; Young and Muller 2014: 43, 50). The ultimate aim of powerful knowledge is to take pupils beyond their existing experiences into the 'unknown', into the previously unlearned (Ormond 2014: 166). It challenges pupils to surpass their comfort zones and to thereby improve their thinking, grow in expertise and gain mastery in knowledge and skills that would otherwise be unknown to them.

The concept of powerful knowledge is intimately tied with epistemic quality. In epistemology, a distinction is made between three types of knowledge: knowledge by acquaintance (*knowing who or what*), propositional knowledge (*knowing that*) and procedural knowledge (*knowing how*) (Winch 2012). Knowledge by acquaintance is a primary mode of knowledge, gained through the

---

[2] The latest Finnish National Curriculum for primary and lower secondary education was launched in 2014. In this article, we use the English translation from 2016.
[3] Factual prose covers several genres that may be described as subject-oriented and having non-imaginative content. These include, for instance, books of popular science, biographies and essays.
[4] In Finland, all teachers in primary and secondary education have a master's degree and pedagogical training. The difference is that in primary schools teachers have an MA in pedagogy and are qualified to teach all school subjects, whereas in secondary schools the subject teachers have an MA in their teaching subject. Primary school (grades 1–6) covers age groups from seven to twelve and lower secondary school (grades 7–9) age groups from thirteen to fifteen. Upper secondary school (grades 10–12, age groups sixteen to eighteen) is not discussed in this article.

senses: we recognize a scent or a person, for example. The second stage, *knowing that*, is a propositional and conceptual type of knowledge which can be expressed with declarative sentences, whereas the third stage of knowledge is procedural: *knowing how* refers to skills and knowing how to do something (Winch 2012). It must also be pointed out that *knowing that* and *knowing how* are closely conjoined because before grasping the *knowing how* stage in a certain field the learner must acquire propositional, conceptual knowledge about it (Winch 2012, 2015; Muller 2016; Hudson 2018). Following Hudson's (2018) reasoning, we also use *knowing how* in two additional senses: *inferential knowing how* refers to understanding how conceptual knowledge hangs together and *procedural knowing how* refers to the search for new knowledge or application of knowledge.

Knowledge that is procedural, empowering and inferential is of high epistemic quality (*knowing how*), whereas knowledge that is concerned with singular facts without a frame of reference and a vision of how the knowledge can be applied (*knowing that*) is of low epistemic quality (Hudson 2018). High epistemic quality promotes critical thinking, creative reasoning, the generation of multiple solutions and of learning from errors and mistakes, and powerful knowledge is reliable, community-specific and has a clear focus and object of study (Hudson 2018).

All subjects, both practical and academic, require all three types of knowledge (Winch 2012). However, different subjects have different knowledge traditions and diverse epistemologies, which are decisive in teaching and learning them (Gericke et al. 2018: 441). Understanding and mastering these traditions and epistemologies is a constant challenge for teachers and teacher educators.

Language and literature education comprises a strong emancipatory and empowering aspect since one of the goals in the Finnish National Curriculum (2016) is to encourage pupils to become active readers and to understand the meaning-making processes in textual and oral interaction. Reading and writing literacy, in today's terminology multiliteracy, includes the capability to master multimodal textual, visual and digital environments (Cope and Kalantzis 2009). As in other disciplines, the conceptual content lies in the core of the L1 discipline, and the complexity of this content increases when texts and oeuvres are read in different contexts. The discipline is of *high epistemic quality* since the object of the study – language and literature in their diversity and endlessly changing contexts – needs to be understood in their relevant framework and as essential elements in multifaceted human interaction. There are no clear rules to interpret a poem or to understand politeness in interaction. That is why the accurate use of discipline-bound concepts and the ability to develop and express one's opinions clearly about multimodal texts and textual environments are especially important.

Literacy skills are crucial for the development of critical thinking and powerful knowledge in any subject, and they enhance high epistemic quality in all academic fields. According to Maton (2014: 181–2), subject-specific powerful knowledge comprises not just one kind of knowledge but a mastery of knowing how different approaches are brought together. Because critical thinking promotes multiliteracy and vice versa, these are also elementary for emancipatory ambitions of education, which Hudson (2018) connects with powerful knowledge. Therefore, powerful knowledge is a relevant concept not only in individual subjects but also in interdisciplinary topics and projects in school (Gericke et al. 2018). Multiliteracy is one of the key concepts in the present Finnish National Curriculum for primary and upper secondary education (2016, e.g. 301–302), and is of particular importance in literature education.

Transaction theory (Rosenblatt 1978: 24–9) gives a useful starting point for conceptualizing reading and its processes. Rosenblatt distinguishes between aesthetic and efferent reading. In efferent reading, the focus is on facts and the content of the text, which the reader can pick up and carry along (*efferre* Lat. 'to carry away'). According to Rosenblatt, efferent reading refers to a cognitive way of reading, where the reader is engaged with narrative facts, plots, statements, characters and other empirical aspects of the text. Opposed to this stance is aesthetic reading, which involves the reader's emotions, affects and experiences in the meaning-making processes of the text. These two stances do not characterize texts themselves but readers' ways of reading and their strategies to understand what they read, and are often intertwined in individual reading processes. The meaning of the text is always created in a transaction between the text and the reader.

Smith (2012: 63–5) elaborated on Rosenblatt's dichotomy by adding a third stance, 'deferent reading' whereby readers narrow their reading and try to find one 'correct' meaning. This stance leads to reading where readers try to find the correct interpretation or predetermined meanings in the text, instead of seeing themselves as active producers of meaning who can create and negotiate the meanings and interpretations of texts both with the texts themselves and with other readers.

When we read literature – fictional or factual – we are first captured by the *knowing that* parts of the text: in fiction, we start with the plot, the characters and the overall impressions of the book, and in factual literature, we look for the facts and statements as the main issues of the text. The efferent stance of reading is foregrounded and readers are aware of it. To elaborate reading skills, pupils in school need to be taught how to develop the *knowing how* analytical skills in order to distance themselves from pure-content-based impressions. They also need to reach an understanding of how meanings are created: What are the narrative structures of the text and how is the whole fictional world of representation created? How are the statements and their relevance presented in factual prose, and how are these interconnected in their context? Besides these aspects, aesthetic reading must be taken into account. The task of a literature teacher is to bridge the gap between aesthetic and efferent readings of a text and give the pupils tools and concepts to analyse, interpret and discuss their reading experiences. Teachers need to strengthen their pupils' awareness of understanding the meaning-making processes and the diversity of interpretations, instead of looking for only one solution, which is a common approach in everyday thinking. The awareness of different aspects and stances of texts and the ability to discuss these using skilfully justified arguments can be described as high epistemic understanding.

It can be assumed that teachers of L1 and literature gain more insights into teaching reading strategies and multiliteracy skills during their university studies than teachers of other subjects. However, and in line with the new Finnish National Curriculum, reading fiction and factual texts should be promoted in all subjects. Therefore, all subject teachers should pay increasing attention to teaching subject-correlated literacy in their own disciplines and make their pupils aware of the epistemic quality – not only the content but the interpretations – of the texts they read. Teaching subject-specific literacy is also a process of transformation in which content knowledge is taught and learned (Gericke et al. 2018).

Empirical aspects of teaching powerful reading

The data on which our article is based comes from an encompassing reading motivation project in Finland called the Reading Clan.[5] It consists of results

---

[5] Our study is based on a large reading motivation project organized by a non-profit cultural organization, the Finnish Cultural Foundation, between 2017 and 2020. The core of the project was to donate books together with teachers' manuals to all primary and lower secondary schools in Finland (grades 1–9, age groups from seven to fifteen years) and to organize in-practice schooling for teachers. To support the project's core aims, there was also a need for research-based knowledge about literature education in schools. Our research team organized two rounds of encompassing research surveys, which were sent out to all primary and lower secondary schools in Finland (Lukuklaani 'Reading Clan', see Grünthal et al., 2019; https://blogs.helsinki.fi/lukuklaani/). In the first round, the research questionnaire (2017–2018) covered areas of teaching methods in L1, the number of books read, genre variation, favourite books at different grade levels, and the reading habits of teachers themselves, among other things. Concerning lower secondary schools, we were also interested in investigating the role of reading fiction and factual prose in other school subjects. We received 884 responses from primary schools and 1,018 responses from lower secondary schools (including 407 responses from L1 teachers). The second-round survey was the follow-up questionnaire, sent to teachers one to two years later.

from large teacher surveys, which included closed questions, analysed with statistical tools, as well as answers to open questions, analysed by qualitative content and text analysis. The qualitative data were thematized and analysed through the content analysis. In the following, we focus on teachers' answers as to the teaching methods they find motivating in literature education.

In earlier research, collaborative methods of reading have been regarded as the most motivating for students (e.g. Shelton-Strong 2012). They are also effective in an epistemological sense since they make the stances of the reading process visible and enhance literary understanding. Despite this, our survey results show that in Finland individually oriented methods in literature teaching prevail throughout: primary and lower secondary schools at present very much emphasize individual reading tasks rather than interactional, collaborative methods (Aaltonen 2020).

The most frequent literature teaching methods reported by primary school teachers are so-called book tippings, book diplomas, book snakes and other equivalents, drama methods, and book circles. In lower secondary schools, the list is almost the same: book tippings are the most commonly used method also there, followed by drama methods and book circles; only book diplomas were much less common than in primary schools (Aaltonen 2020). The most common teaching methods in our survey are listed below: teachers answered whether they had used these methods during the last school year or not.[6] The first percentage shows the answers from primary and the second from lower secondary school teachers.

- Book tippings (used by 91 per cent/87 per cent of teachers). Short presentations about the book with the aim to raise interest in reading it: the main characters and settings are presented, followed by an interesting extract from the book (preferably with a cliff-hanger). In schools, book tippings are carried out by professional book tippers from public libraries, by pupils themselves or by teachers.
- Book diplomas (84 per cent/34 per cent of teachers). Several templates for book diplomas are available on the Internet, made by the Finnish National Agency for Education, public libraries and the schools themselves. Book diplomas include book suggestions for different school grades, followed by writing tasks and other assignments. Pupils make their choices of books

---

[6] The teachers chose one option for 'I have used this method' between 'every day – every month – every semester – every school year – more rarely than a school year – never'. Due to the need to save space, the percentages shown here include the answers from 'every day' to 'every school year'.

and also decide whether they want to accomplish the diploma at a high or a moderate level.
- Book trees, book snakes and other methods make the number of books read in class visible. They are used by 65 per cent of teachers in the primary schools.[7] This method emphasizes the joint effort of the class because everybody adds a leaf or equivalent to the class wall after finishing a book. This method is sometimes used to compete with other classes: Which class reads the most books or pages during a certain time period?
- Drama methods (60 per cent/57 per cent of teachers). There is a very large variety in these, ranging from small improvisations and exercises to short dramatized sections from novels.
- Book circles (56 per cent/47 per cent of teachers).[8] As a pedagogical tool, book circles follow a certain basic method (see, e.g. Shelton-Strong 2012). Pupils are divided into small groups, and each group reads the same book in shorter sections agreed upon by the group. Each member completes a different task as the reading process goes on, and sections are discussed together on the basis of the tasks and the readers' roles. Different tasks are aimed at giving the pupils multiple viewpoints and ideas for joint discussions.

Overall, three of the five most popular methods in primary schools involve the social sharing of books and reading experiences (book tipping, drama and book circles). Book snakes or trees can also be included in social activities because they involve the whole reading community in a joint task. Although teachers reported the frequent use of such interactive methods, there was a lot of variation in their daily practices, and individual methods like diplomas were also very common (Grünthal et al. 2019). This is also true about the lower secondary schools. Although drama methods were reported as quite popular, the majority of teachers used them either seldom or not at all, and more than one-third of the teachers answered that they had never carried out a book circle in their class (Aaltonen 2020).

Yet, it is precisely the book circle method which deserves closer attention. One of the main goals of the Reading Clan Project for primary schools was to introduce the book circle method because of its positive impacts and its

---

[7] The surveys for primary and lower secondary school teachers were slightly different. The 'book snake' option was not available in the lower secondary school questionnaire because it was thought to be too childish for teenagers.
[8] In guide books and research, book circles are also called literature circles or reading clubs.

interactive, discussion-promoting role (Aaltonen 2020). Clearly, book discussions with peers and the need to argue for one's interpretations and understandings develop pupils' epistemic skills. The need to increase collaborative methods in L1 literature education is apparent in the light of both our results and those of the latest PIRLS survey (2016). According to PIRLS, Finnish ten-year-old pupils were behind their peers in discussing literary works and their qualities (Leino et al. 2017).

There was a relatively clear rise in using book circles in the primary schools after the Reading Clan Project had been launched and one specific type of book circle introduced to teachers. After the books were donated to schools, together with the introductory manuals, there was a change in the pupils' overall reading motivation, evidenced in the results of a follow-up survey: 65 per cent of the primary school teachers had used book circles, and their response overall was positive. Teachers agreed fully or mostly with the following statements: book circles have developed pupils' abilities to discuss the books they have read (85 per cent), book circles had motivated all types of pupils (75 per cent) and helped pupils to understand and evaluate the books they have read (73 per cent). Even more importantly, 80 per cent of teachers agreed fully or mostly with the statement that book circles had succeeded in motivating un-motivated pupils to read books (Aaltonen 2020).[9]

Altogether, there seems to be quite small emphasis on the reading process, supported by social sharing of ideas and interpretations, at school: the heaviest stress is on producing an individually written text (sometimes a visual product) about the book after finishing it. This might partly explain why a large number of pupils do not finish the books they are supposed to read: 62 per cent of L1 teachers in the lower secondary school answered that not everyone in their class finished the book they were reading last. At the same time, we know that the motivation of pupils today to read is declining heavily (see, for example, PISA 2018 and Leino et al. 2019), and there is a constant concern in the educational and societal arenas about the poor reading motivation of the young. It is evident that the powerful disciplinary knowledge of both primary school teachers and secondary school teachers of L1 needs to be enlarged towards interactional, group-oriented methods of teaching literature.

The choice of literature read at school is also an essential factor in motivating pupils to read and in promoting the interactive sharing of reading experiences,

---

[9] The preliminary results from lower secondary school teachers concerning the success of book circles are in line with these numbers (Aaltonen 2020).

and is an indicator of the teacher's powerful disciplinary knowledge. In this respect, our data provides us with some interesting viewpoints on book choices in primary and lower secondary schools (also see Tainio et al. 2019). As stated earlier, primary school teachers have a multidisciplinary expertise from the university with no or little emphasis on literature education, whereas lower secondary school teachers have specialized in language and literature studies and have a subject teacher qualification in teaching Finnish language and literature.

The didactic process of teaching and learning has often been described as a triangle or triad, with an equal emphasis on teacher, student and content/knowledge as well as the interaction between them (e.g. Frieden and Osguthorpe 2018; Hudson 2019). In literature education, the core content is literature; it provides the basis for the knowledge to be gained from reading. Since the first, and probably thus the most important, aim stated in the national curriculum for literature education in school is to encourage pupils in independent reading (NC 2016, e.g. 123), teachers constantly seek inspiring reading for pupils. In addition, according to the national curriculum, they should provide literature that binds the students to their own culture and broadens their knowledge of other cultures (NC 2016, e.g. 315, 499). Thus, the variety of books provided for pupils in literature education should not only offer them opportunities to gain 'enjoyment and fulfilment', which is one of the characteristics of high epistemic quality teaching (cf. Hudson 2019: 443), but also help pupils to obtain and share experiences, deepen their cultural knowledge, support their ethical growth, and enrich their language and imagination (NC 2016, e.g. 974–975; cf. Hudson 2019).

The Finnish National Curricula do not name any books to be read at school or give any recommended book lists; the choice of books is left up to teachers and is influenced by the books named in the textbooks on one hand, and by the books available in the school library on the other. According to our data, there are certain differences between the book choices of primary school teachers and L1 subject teachers. Primary school teachers very much rely on contemporary bestsellers, mostly Finnish ones but also some international ones, when they give reading tasks to their pupils (also see Cremin 2014). Lower secondary school teachers in L1 report, in certain respects, a greater variety of book choices. This might be due to their more profound university studies in literature and, therefore, provide proof of their better expertise in literature and disciplinary knowledge. However, as far as literature translated from other languages is concerned, for example, the selection of different cultural traditions and areas is not as wide as the national curriculum would indicate (see Tainio et al. 2019).

Reading fiction and factual prose in other subjects

We were also interested in finding out to what extent teachers other than L1 teachers use literature, both fiction and non-fiction, in their own disciplines in lower secondary school, and we received 611 answers to our questionnaire. Although the results are not statistically valid, they give us some insights into using literature outside of L1 lessons.

Overall, reading or using literature in other disciplines is very rare: more than 70 per cent of the respondents answered they use literature less than once a year. One teacher in ten makes the pupils read one fiction or non-fiction book a year. It is not surprising that teachers report using factual books more than fiction, and over half the teachers see factual books as more important in their own disciplines.

The minority of teachers who use literature (30 per cent) see the value of fiction and use at least one book or book chapter a year in their teaching. However, 42 per cent of the respondents reported that they neither read fiction themselves nor saw it as useful in their teaching. With regard to factual prose, 60 per cent of teachers use books or book chapters at least once a year with their pupils, the majority of them every semester, while 20 per cent do not use literature in their teaching at all.

However, the teachers who use literature, both fiction and factual prose, emphasize its value as a source of additional knowledge from which their pupils can profit. Most of these positive answers define reading fiction and factual prose as 'additional information' or 'a supplement to textbooks'. Extra reading is seen as valuable for 'good pupils' or 'for leisure time'. It is obvious that in these teachers' eyes, reading is meaningful in the sense of *knowing that*, that is, obtaining information and learning facts. According to these answers, teachers stress the content of the books read, not the aspects of critical reading skills nor the importance of understanding facts and knowledge in their specific contexts. Therefore, the *knowing how* aspects of reading could clearly be improved and work remains to be done in order to see fiction and factual prose as relevant sources for developing the epistemic quality of all subjects. As Judith Langer (2010) points out, literature provides the reader with a horizon of unlimited possibilities and promotes creative thinking. Therefore, it is a suitable tool for use in the education of all subjects.

Mathematics and natural sciences teachers answered our survey more diligently than teachers of foreign languages or, for example, history, which came as a slight surprise. One reason might be that mathematics teachers clearly see the interrelation between mathematical and literacy skills, especially in solving written textual assignments, and they stress the importance of good reading skills in their disciplines.

Some teachers mentioned that they use biographies of famous scientists and popular science books about contemporary topics, like climate change, in their teaching. In history and religion, fiction is sometimes read alongside the textbooks. Teachers stress the contrast between fact-based textbooks and fiction: by reading novels about wars and different cultures pupils gain a deeper understanding of individual emotions and experiences during historical events, processes and periods, and they obtain a sense of living in different religious and cultural contexts. Besides these ethical and mental goals in reading, students need to be trained to develop their analytical reading skills in different genres. Textual strategies and discursive choices need to be understood and discussed with pupils, not only the factual content of books: in reading literature, the *knowing that* is not enough, pupils must also develop their skills in *knowing how*. This means learning to analyse and understand the textual strategies with which the factual content in texts is created, and also the aims for which this content is created.

Implications for teacher education

The results of our surveys suggest that certain steps must be taken to develop the epistemic quality of Finnish teacher education in the fields of reading literacy and literature education. First, primary school teachers would profit from a stronger stress on disciplinary competencies: better command of children's and young adult literature would enlarge their own powerful knowledge, improve the epistemic quality of their literature teaching and widen their selection of books for pupils (also see Cremin 2014).

Second, despite their more in-depth university studies in literature, L1 and literature subject teachers seem to lack either the tools or the courage to adapt their knowledge to the full in practical classroom situations. The selection of books they use in their teaching is sometimes quite narrow, and their command of young adult literature could also be improved (also see Tainio et al. 2021).

Third, both primary school and L1 secondary school teachers should be able to adopt collaborative and interactive methods (e.g. drama) in literature education to a greater extent. The emphasis in both teacher groups on individual-oriented teaching methods is not in line with the research-proven benefits of collaborative methods. Also, teachers of other subjects should receive more training in teaching subject-specific literacy in their own disciplines. In addition, innovative ways and practices of using literature, both fiction and non-fiction, in all subjects should be developed.

However, one implication should be emphasized in particular. Both primary school and secondary school teachers should acquire stronger competencies in scaffolding the whole reading process and teaching levels of literary understanding, which is relevant in all subjects. Phases of literary understanding could be compared to the three dimensions of knowledge: the first and basic level is that of immediate personal response (knowledge by acquaintance), the second can be defined as propositional because it can be attained by answering WH-questions (propositional knowledge), and the highest level is the procedural one, where the reader makes connections and contextualizes the reading experience meaningfully (procedural knowledge). It is the teacher's task to improve the reading literacy of the pupils and, simultaneously, the epistemic quality of their reading skills. Such teaching has a transformational and emancipatory impact on the pupils. Low epistemic quality means only propositional knowledge about literature, and teachers' questions strengthen such views by asking only WH-type questions about the texts.

Literary discussions (like book circles) are a good way of developing the epistemic quality of literature education in schools. As Chevallard (2007: 132) notes, knowledge is encapsulated in situations and in those situations pupils can learn. Through discussing and sharing literature, pupils can improve their powerful knowledge about it. Moreover, they come to understand how their own transaction with texts (Rosenblatt 1978) enhances motivation, reading engagement and personal empowerment through literature.

Conclusion

To conclude, we crystallize the answers to, and new issues emerging from, our research questions: How do teachers in Finland promote motivation and reading engagement? How do they enhance reading literacy skills?

Promoting motivation and reading engagement

Teaching methods are central to promoting reading motivation and engagement. Our results show very little difference between the methods that primary school teachers and lower secondary school teachers use: in both cases, individual written tasks prevail and group-oriented, interactive methods are rarer. Secondary school teachers' wider university studies in language and literature and their stronger theoretical competence clearly do not affect their command of teaching methods. On the contrary, secondary school teachers' metacognitive competence to evaluate the effectiveness and popularity of their teaching methods seem to be weaker than that of primary school teachers, and their comments about the success of their teaching methods are partly contradictory. Eighty per cent of teachers evaluate that the latest literature task they gave to pupils caused considerable difficulties for some of them, but at the same time 90 per cent of teachers say that the same literature task was a success.

Secondary school teachers do not use interactive methods systematically or to a large extent: one may ask whether this is a question of a lack of competence or of confidence. It must also be kept in mind that teenagers in the lower secondary school are a challenging group to teach, making the importance of well-adapted powerful knowledge and good methodological skills in classroom situations even more important.

However, the book circles promoted by the Reading Clan project proved to be a successful way of engaging pupils and motivating them to read. We also gained evidence that teachers who read more themselves are more ardent literature teachers (also see Cremin 2014).

Enhancing reading literacy skills

Results from adult book circles indicate that book circles (book clubs) hold the potential to promote increased enjoyment of books which, in turn, enhances reading motivation (Dail et al. 2009). According to our data, book circles also increase motivation and reading engagement among reluctant readers in schools. In addition, they promote literature discussions and enhance pupils' abilities to talk about literature which, as discussed earlier in this article, are skills that clearly need to be developed in Finnish literature education. Good, interactive discussions about books that have been read promote high epistemic quality in literature teaching.

All in all, it is evident that there is still much emphasis on the *knowing what* elements of fiction and factual texts, and less emphasis on the *knowing how* part. Primary school teachers, L1 subject teachers and subject teachers of other disciplines should gain better competencies in knowing how to teach and use literature in a way that makes use of more integrative, interactional and motivating ways and that improves the pupils' epistemic abilities to read. Moreover, all teachers would profit from deeper and wider knowledge of fiction and non-fiction for their pupils.

Powerful knowledge and epistemic quality in literature education

Powerful knowledge presupposes surpassing one's previous limits of understanding, creating new contexts for that being learned, and finding the knowledge meaningful and empowering for oneself. In our data, we found many examples of teachers promoting powerful knowledge with high epistemic quality: they gave examples of teaching methods that were motivating and successful, and they created interdisciplinary projects. However, the data as a whole also raise concerns about the low epistemic quality of literature teaching in many respects: the variety of books teachers make their pupils read is often narrow and predictable, and too little effort is made to use interactional, group-oriented teaching methods. There are also hints that teachers' knowledge about children's and young adult literature is often insufficient.

It is clear that interactional and social methods improve reading literacy since they encourage pupils to express their interpretations of and ideas about the texts. In group discussions and in social interaction around texts, they gain an opportunity to see differences between interpretations made by their peers, compare them and ask about the premises and processes of interpretations. This leads to better awareness of the language and text, which in turn improves the understanding of the content.

We see pupils' engagement and motivation for reading as one of the most important aspects of high epistemic quality (Hudson 2018: 443) in teaching literature, namely, getting pupils to both enjoy reading literature and, at the same time, to develop critical and creative thinking as well as gaining factual knowledge through reading in all school subjects. These may all be considered aspects of powerful knowledge (Young 2009; Lambert 2017) that can be achieved through literature education.

Acknowledgements

We thank the Finnish Cultural Foundation for funding the Reading Clan research project, and for its support and collaboration.

References

Aaltonen, L.-S. (2020), *Lukuklaani-tutkimus. Ala- ja yläkoulujen alkukartoitusten koosteet, analyysi ja tiedottaminen. Tutkimusraportti 2017–2019*, Helsinki: Suomen Kulttuurirahasto.

Chevallard, Y. (2007), 'Readjusting Didactics to a Changing Epistemology', *European Educational Research Journal*, 6 (2): 131–4.

Cope, B. and Kalantzis, M. (2015), 'The Things You Do to Know: An Introduction to the Pedagogy of Multiliteracies: Learning by Design', in B. Cope and M. Kalantzis (eds), *A Pedagogy of Multiliteracies*, 1–36, London: Palgrave Macmillan.

Cremin, T. (2014), 'Reading Teachers: Teachers Who Read and Readers Who Teach', in T. Cremin, M. Mottram, S. Powell, R. Collins and K. Safford (eds), *Building Communities of Engaged Readers: Reading for Pleasure*, 67–88, London: Routledge.

Dail, A. R., McGee, L. M. and Edwards, P. A. (2009), 'The Role of Community Book Club in Changing Literacy Practices', *Literacy Teaching and Learning*, 13 (1–2): 25–56.

Friesen, N. and Osguthorpe, R. (2018), 'Tact and the Pedagogical Triangle: The Authenticity of Teachers in Relation', *Teaching and Teacher Education*, 70: 255–64. https://doi.org/10.1016/j.tate.2017.11.023

Gericke, N., Hudson, B., Olin-Scheller, C. and Stolare, M. (2018), 'Powerful Knowledge, Transformations and the Need for Empirical Studies across School Subjects', *London Review of Education*, 16 (3): 428–44. https://doi.org/10.18546/LRE.16.3.06

Grünthal, S., Hiidenmaa, P., Routarinne, S., Satokangas, H., and Tainio, L. (2019), 'Alakoulun kirjallisuuskasvatusta kartoittamassa: Lukuklaanin opettajakyselyn tuloksia', in M. Tarnanen, and M. Rautiainen (eds), *Tutkimuksesta luokkahuonekontekstiin*, 161–81, Jyväskylä: Suomen ainedidaktinen tutkimusseura.

Guthrie, J. T. and Wigfield, A. (2000), 'Engagement and Motivation in Reading', in M. L. Kamil, P. B. Mosenthal, P. D. Pearson and R. Barr (eds), *Handbook of Reading Research*, 403–22, Mahwah, NJ: Lawrence Erlbaum Associates Publishers.

Harjunen, E. and Rautopuro, J. (2015), *Kielenkäytön ajattelemista ja ajattelun kielentämistä*. Helsinki: Koulutuksen arviointikeskus.

Holmberg, P., Krogh, E., Nordenstam, A., Penne, S., Skarstein, D., Karlskog Skyggebjerg, A., Tainio, L. and Heilä-Ylikallio, R. (2019), 'On the Emergence of the L1 Research Field: A Comparative Study of PhD Abstracts in the Nordic Countries 2000–2017', *L1 – Language and Literature*, 19 (5): 1–27. DOI:10.17239/L1ESLL-2019.19.01.05

Hudson, B. (2018), 'Powerful Knowledge and Epistemic Quality in School Mathematics', *London Review of Education*, 16 (3): 384–97.

Hudson, B. (2019) 'Epistemic Quality for Equitable Access to Quality Education in School Mathematics', *Journal of Curriculum Studies*, 51 (4): 437–56. https://doi.org/10.1080/00220272.2019.1618917

Hudson, B., Henderson, S. and Hudson, A. (2015), 'Developing Mathematical Thinking in the Primary Classroom: Liberating Teachers and Students as Learners of Mathematics', *Journal of Curriculum Studies*, 47 (3): 374–98.

Lambert, D. (2017), 'Powerful Disciplinary Knowledge and Curriculum Futures', in N. Pyyry, L. Tainio, K. Juuti, R. Vasquez and M. Paananen (eds), *Changing Subjects, Changing Pedagogies: Diversities in School and Education*, 14–33, Helsinki: Finnish Research Association for Subject Didactics.

Langer, J. (2010), *Envisioning Literature: Literary Understanding and Literature Instruction*, 2nd ed., New York and London: Teachers College, Columbia University.

Leino, K., Ahonen, A. K., Hienonen, N., Hiltunen, J., Lintuvuori, M., Lähteinen, S., Lämsä, J., Nissinen, K., Nissinen, V., Puhakka, E., Pulkkinen, J., Rautopuro, J., Sirén, M., Vainikainen, M-P. and Vettenranta, J. (2019), *PISA 2018. Ensituloksia*, Helsinki: Opetus- ja kulttuuriministeriön julkaisuja.

Leino, K., Nissinen, K., Puhakka, E. and Rautopuro, J. (2017), *PIRLS 2016. Lukutaito luodaan yhdessä*, Jyväskylä: Koulutuksen tutkimuslaitos.

Maton, K. (2014), 'Building Powerful Knowledge: The Significance of Semantic Waves', in B. Barrett and E. Rata (eds), *Knowledge and the Future of the Curriculum: International Studies in Social Realism*, 181–97, London: Palgrave Macmillan Limited.

Muller, J. (2016), 'Knowledge and the Curriculum in the Sociology of Knowledge', in D. Wyse, L. Hayward and J. Pandya (eds), *SAGE Handbook of Curriculum, Pedagogy and Assessment*, 92–106, London: Sage Publications.

National Core Curriculum for Basic Education 2014 (English translation) (2016), Helsinki: Finnish National Board of Education.

Ormond, B. (2014), 'Powerful Knowledge in History: Disciplinary Strength or Weakened Episteme?', in B. Barrett and E. Rata (eds), *Knowledge and the Future of the Curriculum: International Studies in Social Realism*, 153–66, London: Palgrave Macmillan Limited.

Rosenblatt, L. (1978), *The Reader, the Text, the Poem. The Transactional Theory of the Literary Work*, Carbondale, IL: Southern Illinois University Press.

Shelton-Strong, S. J. (2012), 'Literature Circles in ELT', *ELT Journal*, 66 (2): 214–23. doi:10.1093/elt/ccr049

Smith, C. H. (2012), 'Interrogating Texts: From Deferent to Efferent and Aesthetic Reading Practices', *Journal of Basic Writing*, 4: 59–79.

Tainio, L., Aaltonen, L.-S. and Leksis, S. (2021), 'Harry Potter vai Anna Liisa? Sukupuoli ja opettajien lukusuositukset perusopetuksen äidinkieli ja kirjallisuus -oppiaineessa'. Ainedidaktiikan symposium 2020. Suomen ainedidaktinen tutkimusseura.

Tainio, L., Grünthal, S., Routarinne, S., Satokangas, H. and Hiidenmaa, P. (2019), 'Primary school pupils' literary landscapes: What do Finnish- and Swedish-speaking Pupils Read at School?', in H. Höglund, S. Jusslin, M. Ståhl and A. Westerlund (eds), *Genom texter och världar: Svenska och litteratur med didaktisk inriktning – festskrift till Ria Heilä-Ylikallio*, 217–33, Vaasa: Åbo Akademi University Press.

Winch, C. (2012), 'Curriculum Design and Epistemic Ascent', *Journal of Philosophy of Education*, 47 (1): 128–46.

Young, M. (2009), 'Education, Globalisation and the "Voice of Knowledge"', *Journal of Education and Work*, 22 (3): 193–204.

Young, M. (2013), 'Overcoming the Crisis in Curriculum Theory: A Knowledge-based Approach', *Journal of Curriculum Studies*, 45 (2): 101–18.

Young, M. and Muller, J. (2014), 'On the Powers of Powerful Knowledge', in B. Barrett and E. Rata (eds), *Knowledge and the Future of the Curriculum: International Studies in Social Realism*, 41–64, London: Palgrave Macmillan Limited.

Teaching Practices in Transformation in Connected Social Science Swedish Classrooms

Marie Nilsberth, Christina Olin-Scheller and
Martin Kristiansson

Introduction

Through a wide range of international and national policies (cf. Redecker 2017; Unesco 2018), education in Sweden and many other countries today faces strong demands to become digitalized. Hence, teachers are under pressure to implement digital resources in instruction (Player-Koro, Bergviken Rensfeldt and Selwyn 2017). This has been shown to profoundly reframe the classroom as a learning space. A general change that the digitalization of the school seems to contribute to is a movement from collective forms of work to a greater individualization (Selwyn 2016). While 'one-to-one' approaches that equip each student with digital resources seem to provide many practical benefits for teaching, the school is less able to prepare students to participate in a more critical approach to the digitalized society (Davies 2017). New technologies are often subordinated to traditional classroom teaching practices and negotiated away when the new teaching structures conflict with the institutional need for control, overview and safety (Tanner, Olin-Scheller and Pérez Prieto 2019; Blikstad-Balas and Klette 2020). Studies also reveal the risk that the use of digital devices might overshadow the subject content and that the technical aspects will become the main focus of teaching activities (Selwyn, Nemorin, Bulfin and Johnson 2017; Willermark 2018; Kjellsdotter 2020).

Moreover, the introduction of new digital media is affecting the media ecology in classrooms, in turn altering both the spatial and visual conditions for teacher–student interaction (Lum 2006; Sahlström, Tanner and Olin-Scheller 2019). In this chapter, we discuss from a Swedish educational perspective the changing teaching practices that digitalization entails with a specific focus on the intersection of teachers' subject knowledge and educational knowledge in a particular subject –

social science. We address subject-specific issues relating to the subject content of law and order, a fundamental societal issue rarely in the focus of research (Tväråna 2019). As discussed in Gericke, Hudson, Olin-Scheller and Stolare (2018), we view the curriculum question 'what to teach' and the pedagogy question 'how to teach' as being interrelated and inseparable in education research. Thus, a key issue in this study concerns how the classroom interaction pattern between teachers and students is significant for learning processes and the quality of education (Edwards and Mercer 1987; Grossman, Loeb, Cohen and Wyckoff 2013; Gericke, Hudson, Olin-Scheller and Stolare 2018).

School subjects are closely related to academic disciplines. However, disciplinary knowledge is always transformed when applied in new educational contexts. In line with Gericke, Hudson, Olin-Scheller and Stolare (2018), we understand transformation as an integrative process through which specialized knowledge, developed in subject disciplines, is reshaped and re-presented in educational environments by way of various transformation processes. Since different school subjects are embedded to various degrees in digital media (Sutherland et al. 2004) and the technology challenges the 'grammar' and tradition of the subjects in different ways (Erixon 2016), it is interesting to study how subject content is transformed in digitalized classrooms. It is also of interest to address epistemic issues of school subjects relating to the corresponding academic disciplines and different forms of knowledge in digital teaching practices. Social science in the Swedish context is cross-disciplinary, relying foremost on the academic disciplines of political science, economics, sociology and law. Earlier research on this subject discerns tensions between the reproduction of facts and critical thinking (Odenstad 2010; Tväråna 2019), which makes issues of transforming specialized knowledge in digital teaching and learning practices a particular interest. Taking as an example a lesson in social science about the work of courts of law, the aim of this chapter is to deepen knowledge on *what* and *how* content is represented in a digitalized classroom and discuss how transformation processes can enable knowledge of high epistemic quality.

Theoretical framework

When teachers teach, they use the knowledge available to them in a specific context. Everything ranging from subject history and subject theory through to steering documents, sociology, pedagogical philosophy and cognitive science form the basis for a transformation process, in the sense of Ongstad's (2004) term 'Omstilling'. In terms of 'Omstilling', transformation in classrooms means that school subjects are shaped and reshaped when new elements affect the definition of the subject, such as the strong demands on teaching to become digitalized. When discussing the transformation processes of teaching different school subjects, we focus in our chapter on what Marsh and Willis (2007) call the enacted curriculum. The enacted curriculum, Marsh (2009: 4) states, 'deals with professional judgements about the type of curriculum to be implemented and evaluated'. Thus, the enacted curriculum refers to the actual curricular content that students engage with in the classroom. Here teachers make judgements about what pedagogical methods to use and make a selection in relation to subject content.

In this chapter, we are interested in transformation of the content in a certain classroom where both the teacher and the students are using digital resources. Our point of departure is that the students' and teachers' engagement with texts in the classroom may be understood as literacy practices based on questions of how, why and with whom people communicate and interact through different kinds of texts (Street 1984; Barton 2007; Gee 2010). 'Text' in this perspective is to be understood broadly, including letters of the alphabet and numbers as well as images, sounds, films, talk and so on. This perspective means a social understanding of literacy where questions regarding the relationship between power and language are brought to the fore, as particularly emphasized in studies on critical literacy (Janks 2012; Luke 2012; Comber 2015).

Students' academic achievement strongly relates to literacy aspects of instruction and, in order to study issues of content and transformation processes in a digitalized classroom, we use the framework of literacy engagement and achievement (Cummins and Early 2015) in our analysis. In relation to literacy aspects, Cummins and Early state that effective instruction is characterized by components such as scaffolding meaning as well as activating and building on students' background knowledge. Moreover, teaching must also include explicit instruction in order to extend students' knowledge of academic language as well as provide challenging tasks. This model highlights students' access to print (that is, letters and alphabetical figures) material as well as students' engagement in literacy as a direct determinant of developing literacy. In our study, we are specifically interested in students' access to and achievement of literacy in relation to the content part of the school subject social science.

Method and material

The example we explore in this paper comes from a larger data set in the project *Challenges in the connected classroom,* namely, the Swedish part of the Nordic collaboration *Connected Classroom Nordic (CCN).* It is a video ethnographic study where we are looking at teaching quality in all Nordic countries in the subjects of L1, mathematics and social sciences over 3 years. Four consecutive lessons in each subject are recorded with three cameras directed at the teacher, a focus student and the focus student's screen. The same class is followed over 3 years, and the data we draw on here come from year 7 in the first of two classrooms we are following in the Swedish school. The selected school had a digital profile in which all students were equipped with personal laptops, and the teachers were encouraged to use digital materials in their teaching. The three recordings are edited into a single compiled video where the three camera angles are shown simultaneously. This enables us to follow the teaching from the teacher's perspective through the interaction between the focus student and his/her peers, and in terms of what is happening on the computer screen. The video recordings may therefore be described as a combination of a setting-centred, a person-centred and a content-centred approach (Rusk, Pörn, Sahlström and Slotte-Lüttge 2014). In the first step of the analysis, all video data are coded using the qualitative software NVIVO, with a coding manual developed within CCN, focusing on different aspects of teaching quality such as the organization of teaching, student participation, use of digital resources and language use.

Guided by this initial analysis, we identified the example used in this paper as interesting for further analysis. It is an example where the teacher has planned and is enacting teaching largely involving digital resources and the students are using their personal laptops during the whole lesson. As mentioned, we use the literacy engagement framework (Cummins and Early 2015) as an analytical lens where we especially focus on the interaction patterns formed in the teaching with regard to collective and individual aspects as well as transformation processes in relation to the epistemic quality (Hudson 2018) of the school subject social science. In the analysis, we concentrate on the following questions about how the teaching contributes to:

- *Activating students' background knowledge*: what are the opportunities for the students to connect the teaching to previous understandings?
- *Providing explicit instruction*: how does the teacher represent the subject-specific content?

- *Scaffolding meaning*: how does the teacher scaffold the students' understanding and use of academic language in relation to the subject-specific content?
- *Challenging assignments*: how does the teaching challenge the students' thinking in terms of the subject-specific content?

Results

Law and order – digitally mediated literacy practices in the social science classroom

Our analysis focuses on part of a lesson in the subject of social science. It is a segment of 31 minutes in year 7 in the area of 'Law and order' dealing explicitly with the different professional roles in a courtroom. As support for his lecture, the teacher uses a Prezi, digital software for making multimodal presentations. In Prezi, he has collected short written texts about each professional role, some images and embedded YouTube clips featuring various professionals presenting their work and role. The written texts consist of short summarized facts, certain parts written in black and other parts in blue. The students have their laptops open and are instructed to copy at least the blue text in *OneNote*. The lesson in focus follows on from a previous occasion that started on this work. The segment we analyse can be divided into three phases: first, an introduction (20:00–21:15) where the teacher instructs the students on what to do; second, the teacher's lecture supported by Prezi (21:15–32:40); and third, seat work in pairs/small groups (32:40–51:05). The terms and concepts we consider to be central for subject-specific academic language are underlined in the transcriptions.

Phase one: Introduction, 20:00–21:15

We start our analysis as the teacher begins his lecture and opens his Prezi presentation that is also projected onto the whiteboard. The focus student Stina has her personal laptop open in front of her, with an open Word document and is ready to take notes. Her peers also have their laptops open, ready to take notes (Figure 7.1). The students look towards the teacher, who begins to instruct the students:

- *Remember that you write down the blue text. We will not have such a long talk today, because I also want you to come to a new assignment that we will do together. But first we have to finish this thing about persons in the <u>courtroom</u>.*

Figure 7.1 The teacher's introduction.

The teacher moves the pointer around different images in Prezi, enlarging them one at a time, and repeats what they had already been talking about:

- *We have talked about <u>the prosecutor</u>. We have talked about <u>the injured party</u> (moves again) <u>the accused</u> (moves again) and <u>the prosecutor</u>. Remind me, did we listen to the woman that told us about her job as a prosecutor? Yes, okay. Then we come to <u>the counsel for the defence</u>, and that is the first thing that we write down today, right?*

Analysis phase one

In the introduction, Prezi, with its possibility to smoothly navigate between and focus on the images, works to remind the students about what they talked about before. In terms of literacy engagement (Cummins and Early 2015), this may be understood as a way to activate the students' prior knowledge about the subject area they are focusing on. It also works as a way of creating common ground as they are about to commence the new activity. The teacher's talk infers that they are in the middle of a process that follows a commonly known routine as they focus on one role at a time. The students are given access to two different texts that are put into play in the introduction in relation to each other. First, the teacher uses the Prezi presentation, consisting of images, film clips and print text, which the teacher controls from his computer. Second, the students are supposed to copy all of the blue text in the Prezi presentation, that is, text the teacher has selected in advance as being the most important parts. Thus far, there is not much scaffolding in relation to use of academic language beyond labelling the different parties in the courtroom. The students are asked to confirm what they had been talking about earlier, but there is no orientation to how they have understood the different terms. The teacher frames the lecture as something they should carry out quite rapidly, and the content is presented as a linear trajectory with a supposed beginning and end. In short, the introduction only briefly connects to the students' experiences, understandings or awareness of the academic language in this specific area of content, and thus far does not stand out as intellectually challenging for the students.

Phase 2: Teacher lecture, 21:15–32:40

The second phase of the activity consists of the teacher's lecture about the new content that follows from the prior session. The instruction follows a pattern where the teacher first shows a text about one of the professional roles in the courtroom for the students to copy, followed by a short video clip on the same role. In his lecture, the teacher mainly focuses the content in relation to three roles: the prosecutor, the counsel for the claimant and the judge.

The teacher shows a text about the prosecutor and gives a lecture about what his/her role is (Figure 7.2).

Figure 7.2 Stina is copying the blue text from Prezi.

- *The prosecutor is the one who tries to prove that the suspect is guilty. He represents the state and tries to convict the suspect, the suspect is called the accused. However, the counsel for the defence helps the accused, tries to prove the accused person's innocence or, if he has admitted guilt, to get the most lenient punishment possible. Sometimes the accused has pleaded guilty, and then the counsel tries to get the most mild sanction, that is punishment, possible. And you see here the blue text, the counsel helps the accused ((the student raises her hand, but does not get an opportunity to talk)).*

While the teacher is talking, the focus student starts to copy the text in Prezi. The teacher points out what is written in blue.

It is good if you keep track of that, the fact that the counsel for the defence tries to get the most lenient punishment possible. We will listen to a short clip where counsel for the defence tells us about this. ... there will be some difficult words in these films, but I think it is valuable that you get a chance to listen to these people that have these jobs for real.

By now, our focus student Stina has finished writing and is waiting for a moment while the teacher prepares the film clip since there is some problem with the browser. Together, the class watches the short film clip (1 minute 15 seconds), where a female lawyer talks about her work as counsel for the defence. Stina is looking up at the clip, and her notes are displayed on the screen (Figure 7.3).

Figure 7.3 Watching the YouTube clip about the counsel for the defence.

After the clip, the teacher comments:

- *She said something important there, that not only the police and prosecutor can look for evidence but also the counsel for the defence can collect evidence ... then ((moving to another text in Prezi)) I did not mark this in blue ... Ahmed?*

The teacher is interrupted by Ahmed, a student in the class who has not lived in Sweden very long, who asks a question about the economic aspects of obtaining legal support:

- *I heard many times lawyer, lawyer, lawyer ... who pays, is it Sweden that pays or is it the people themselves who pay?*

The teacher answers:

- *Well it is like this in Sweden, that if you don't have the economic resources you can get a counsel for defence for free if you are the suspect of a crime. And the lawyer, that means a person that is educated in law, and is there to help you ... eh, the counsel for the claimant party*

During the teacher's explanation, Stina starts to write the next text, about the counsel for the injured party, on her laptop. In this case, all of the text is black, and she copies it all. After answering Ahmed's question, the teacher continues to introduce the next clip about the claimant's counsel.

- *And what was a claimant now, do you remember? Raise your hands! Anna?*
- *The one who has been a victim of a crime*
- *Yes, normally the one who has been a victim of a crime, and the counsellor helps and explains to that person how this prosecution is going to take place.*

This film is also a little longer than 1 minute. In the film, a lawyer talks about what it means to be counsel for the claimant for about 1 minute (Figure 7.4). At one point, the lawyer says the claimant does not have to pay for the help, but that the accused person or persons might have to, thus touching on the topic that Ahmed brought up earlier. Stina has finished writing and is now listening, yet is also playing with her laptop and writing and erasing long lines with the letters h and g. When the clip finishes, the teacher concludes:

Figure 7.4 Watching the YouTube clip about the counsel for the claimant.

- *Yes, that was <u>the counsel for the claimant</u>. We have a few more persons to look at, it is <u>the chair</u> and <u>the lay persons</u>. Here is <u>the chair, the judge</u>, who is the one leading the discussion. He alone is not solely responsible for the court to reach <u>a verdict</u> but he has help from <u>the lay persons</u>. If you have watched American movies, you might have seen <u>a jury</u>. It is not exactly the same here in Sweden. The <u>lay persons</u> do not have to be educated in law, they are assigned by <u>politicians in the community</u> and it should not be only men or only women, not only rich and not only poor, but they should represent the whole of <u>society</u>.*

The teacher concludes that the laypersons and the judge listen to all parties before they reach a verdict and decide on what kind of punishment is appropriate. During this talk, he also shows a text about the judge and the laypersons, some of it in black and some in blue. The focus student rapidly writes on her laptop during the teacher's talk (Figure 7.5).

After this, the teacher shows yet another clip where the judge is talking about his work (not shown in Figure 7.5). During this clip, the focus student is listening and looking at the film for a while, but also reading on her screen. The teacher comments on the last clip:

- *They are good to listen to these people who have this as their real jobs, but it is a bit slow. We are going to talk about <u>the lay persons</u> but not now, I had planned that we should also have time to do something else.*

Figure 7.5 Stina writes the blue text down in OneNote.

This rounds up the lecture in which the teacher took about 11 minutes to talk and show film clips about persons in the courtroom, as organized through the Prezi presentation. He tells the students he also wants them to be more active, and thus they are now going to change to another activity.

Analysis phase 2

The different people presented during the lecture are all roles needed to fulfil the institutionalized processes of the courtroom. As shown in the transcripts (see the underlined words and phrases), the teacher's lecture is quite dense with subject-specific terms tied to the subject area of Law and order. These terms are not primarily connected to a scientific disciplinary language, but in this case are more related to a professional language and aspects of citizenship tied to an institution. The lecture is organized around the Prezi presentation, which is a multimodal text where different resources such as print text, colours, images and the video clips help the teacher scaffold meaning and develop the students' understanding in relation to the content. However, besides what the various legal professionals mention in the videos, there are few examples of how they are related to each other or what would happen if certain roles were removed from the context. Hence, in terms of explicit instruction and scaffolding meaning, this lecture and the digital resources chiefly help the students obtain a picture and overview of what the courtroom looks like but provide little support for them to understand the inner structure or relations between different actors.

Looking at other aspects of the literacy engagement framework, such as the activation of background knowledge and challenging assignments, these are less prominent. At one stage, a student raises an authentic question about the economic issues of obtaining legal counsel. In relation to the planned content, *understanding law and order in Swedish society*, this question holds the potential to connect the content to societal issues and aspects of being a citizen in a democratic society in ways that could increase the epistemic quality of their dialogue. However, the teacher only gives a short response to the question, and does not at this time take the opportunity to develop this aspect of the content further, or to enter into dialogue with the student about what experiences or concerns led him to pose the question. Instead, it seems like the teacher prioritizes sticking to his planned lecture without allowing the time that elaboration on the student's question would require. The students' assignment is basically to listen to the teacher, watch the videos and copy the blue text. Even if this is able to help them obtain a general picture, these tasks are predominantly rote and routine. The challenge for the students seems more to be how to keep pace with taking notes during the short time that the text is shown before moving on to the video. Otherwise, they are not expected to engage in more complex analysis or dialogue about how to understand the different roles in relation to each other or how this content is important for their future lives. The teacher's comment about how juries work in movies and TV series, that most students are assumed to have knowledge of, could be an opening to their background knowledge. Yet, the students are not given any opportunity to respond to this reference and, besides one short question about what is meant by 'claimant', the students are not asked to give an account of their own understanding of the content and whether this has changed as a result of the teaching.

Phase 3: Seat work in pairs/small groups. 32:40–51:05

At this stage of the lesson, the teacher introduces a new assignment that he wants the students to work on individually. He holds up a piece of paper and says:

- *You know that this is what it is about! This is a list of concepts, difficult words from <u>probation</u> to <u>prosecutor</u>. These we should all be well acquainted with. For the rest of this lesson you should study these and I will show you where you can find them.*

The task for the students is to repeat and rehearse the concepts through a digital memory game, tiny cards, which the teacher has prepared. He demonstrates on his own computer where in the learning platform they can find the link to the tiny cards (Figure 7.6). At first, Stina looks a little confused and cannot find the tiny cards, which probably has to do with the fact that they have to refresh their screen view as they are working online and the game has just been recently uploaded. The students help each other find the link, and Stina opens it. The game consists of small virtual cards that can be flipped around by touching the screen, where the concept is on one side, and the definition is on the other. At first, the students are uncertain of what the point is, and the teacher clarifies that it is like a memory game where they first look at the concept and try to remember what it is, and then flip the card to see if they were right.

Britta, sitting next to Stina, understands it and exclaims:

- *Ah, you are supposed to quiz your own brain?*

Stina looks at how Britta is going with the game and then tries herself. The students can pick the cards in any order, and Stina starts testing herself on some of the terms: rule, norm and law. The game starts by showing a definition for which she is supposed to pick the right term among three terms. Stina reads the definition aloud and chooses the alternative 'law', which was correct. She then continues to work with the cards by herself, without talking, focusing on her own screen while her peers are talking to each other.

Figure 7.6 'Tiny cards', a game about concepts and terms related to Law and Order.

The teacher is moving around the classroom and helping the students at their desks to get started with the game. It is the teacher who has constructed the game himself, which is shown in the pictures where he has used himself and certain teacher colleagues as picture models. Stina laughs and points at the screen when she suddenly recognizes one of the teachers.

After 10 minutes of individual work with the game, some students are finished and the teacher tells them they should do it once again, to exercise more.

- *If you think this is childishly easy, that is good, because this is what you are supposed to know when you get the test.*

Stina responds and asks when are they having the test, and the teacher answers that he has not yet decided on a date but will let them know 10 days ahead. She continues working by herself, but after a few minutes she finds something interesting that she wants to comment on to her peers related to the term life sentence.

- *Is eighteen years a <u>life-time sentence</u>! That is not <u>life</u> for me, I thought it was at least twenty-four!*

Her peers do not respond to this, meaning there is no further dialogue. The teacher instructs the class that they can go on with some other questions if they are finished with the game. Yet, our focus student continues with the cards, appearing to be focused.

At 46:50, Stina closes the game and goes back to the notes from the lecture where she has written about all the persons and then finds the questions the teacher has instructed them to do next. She had already started on this before and now continues where she ended. The questions are mainly about explaining different terms and concepts, one at a time, and the student writes her answer in the same document as the questions. One question is to explain the term perjury (Swe. *mened*), and Stina searches for this on Google (Figure 7.7). At the top of the Google search list an excerpt from Wikipedia is shown, and she reads the explanation verbatim.

Stina sits quietly for a while and then asks Britta to explain the word. Britta points to her own screen and Stina recognizes the same explanation from Wikipedia.

- *You have copied it, right?*

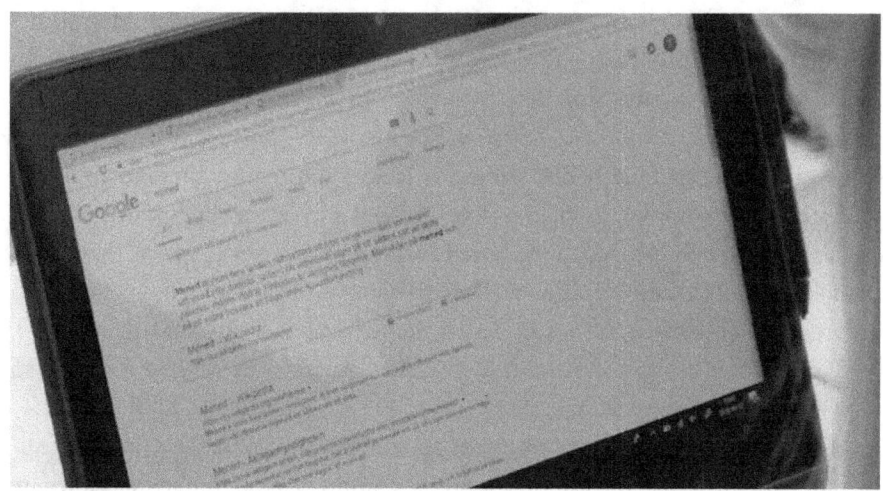

Figure 7.7 Searching for concepts with Google.

No further discussion takes place between the students, and Stina uses the phrase from Wikipedia to solve the task. During her writing, the teacher interrupts their individual work and wants to move on with a lecture and clip about the last legal role they still have left to talk about, the laypersons.

Analysis phase 3

In his introduction to this task, the teacher frames it as more active compared to the previous lecture, which is thus represented as more passive from the students' point of view. During this phase, the students are given an explicit opportunity to engage individually with and meet challenges in relation to texts and academic language concerning the planned content. The assignment is focused on a list of subject-specific terms and concepts the students are supposed to acquire. Memorizing explanations and definitions of concepts is a common strategy in social science teaching, but also something that could be problematized since it sets the focus on knowledge as a multitude of separate parts rather than on scaffolding contextualization and understanding of the relationships between the different terms. It is also interesting how both the teacher and the focus student primarily connect the task to the test that is coming up, rather than framing it as important knowledge in relation to citizenship.

The assignment the students are working in involves multimodal digital resources. In the game, they have an opportunity to engage with the concepts through multimodal texts involving colours, different fonts, images and animations that together help to make the assignment more interesting. Through this multimodal game, the students gain access to the concepts in new and engaging ways that may help them memorize the terms highlighted in previous work. As for the degree of the challenge, however, the game does not seem to be particularly demanding as it does not require them to apply the terms to more complex problems. The questions they are supposed to answer are also very much focused on recalling and explaining terms, rather than more complex use of academic language. Here they use Google and Wikipedia, which are frequent online sources for student-initiated searches (Blikstad-Balas 2016), as digital resources to solve the task and are content with finding a phrase to copy that works as an answer.

However, other potential ways exist to connect the content to the students' lives during this task. One example is Stina's comment about life sentence, where she clearly refers to her own background understanding. The task about perjury also raises questions that could have been developed and connected to previous instructions had the teacher noticed them. Yet, as the teacher moves around the classroom there are few opportunities to discuss these questions, and during this lesson there is no time given to ask questions the teacher could use as a point of departure to deepen the students' understanding and meaning-making.

Discussion

In this chapter, we took as an example a lesson in social science where a multitude of digital resources are being used. The teacher and the students in the example have access to a wide range of texts, almost exclusively mediated through digital technology such as the teacher's pre-planned Prezi presentation as well as learning platforms and programs on their personal laptops.

With use of digital technology, the students are given opportunities to engage with subject-specific language that may help them build potentially powerful knowledge about Law and order important for being a knowledgeable citizen in contemporary society. Our analysis shows that the content represented in this specific teaching situation is closely related to the academic subjects which the school subject social science relies on in Sweden. Hence, in terms of literacy engagement (Cummins and Early 2015), the teacher provides explicit instruction to represent subject-specific content with a strong focus on concepts. The students are expected to copy readymade explanations from the teacher's presentation, and later on they play a game to memorize the meaning of the subject-related concepts. The teacher uses authentic material, such as the videos, and the students work with the tiny cards showing examples of known persons. Here, digitalization offers the teacher an opportunity to be creative and to make a great many different resources available in his teaching. The digital devices also offer the teacher the possibility to transform the academic subject content in order for it to be accessible to the students as well as a chance to stick to the pre-planned teaching trajectory without being interrupted. Thus, in terms of access to knowledge, the potential to develop the students' awareness of and control over academic language and let the students engage in, understand and use academic language is present.

However, drawing further on the literacy engagement framework, high quality in teaching also depends on a student's acquisition of knowledge through engagement with content. This dimension points to the need to further discuss the role of digital technology when it comes to activating students' background knowledge, scaffolding meaning-making and providing challenging assignments. The fact that the students' participation is largely limited to copying and memorizing, that also functions well with the predominant test discourse they are oriented to, means that their engagement mainly focuses on separate parts, whereas a more holistic approach to how the parts could be related and ordered in relation to each other is less visible in this example. There are some instances that might have provided openings to a more holistic approach; for instance, the question from Ahmed, the reference to the jury in American movies, or Stina's reflection on the duration of a life sentence. These are instances that open up to make connections with the students' background knowledge, but here they are not picked up and further developed. This could be partly due to the constraints of the digital media, as the pace of the lesson mainly follows the pre-planned trajectory represented in the Prezi presentation and the game. The teacher even comments on the pace, noting that the videos might be too slow and that he wants the students to have time for the game he has planned (see end of second example). During the students' individual work, it is also very difficult for the teacher to have an overview of all of the students' screen activities, which makes it hard to pick up Stina's reflection about life sentence. Hence, in this example, the digital resources seem to constrain possibilities to engage with the students' background knowledge due to the lesson's pace and the lack of overview of the students' screen activities that are taking place 'under the teacher's radar' (Asplund, Olin-Scheller and Tanner 2018).

To conclude, in spite of the creative use of digital resources that the lesson discussed in this article exemplifies, the students' opportunities for literacy engagement are limited. The students' transformation processes of the subject content may be described as reproducing definitions of concepts, which makes for a restricted literacy engagement. Regarding epistemic quality, our example shows that on one hand the digital devices offer the teacher a possibility to be creative and have full control over the enacted curriculum. This gives students access to subject-specific content in more varied and possibly more inspiring ways. On the other hand, the students' literacy engagement in the analysed sequence may be described as restricted in many respects as it follows a prepared track with few possibilities to pick up the students' questions and ideas. In this example, it seems as if the teacher's literacy engagement with the digital texts is richer than that of the students, which points to the challenge of teaching to develop practices that are more engaging also for the students.

References

Asplund, S., Olin-Scheller, C. and Tanner, M. (2018), 'Under the Teacher's Radar: Literacy Practices in Task-Related Smartphone Use in the Connected Classroom', *L1 Educational Studies in Language and Literature*, 18: 1–26. doi:10.17239/L1ESLL-2018.18.01.03

Barton, D. (2007), *Literacy: An Introduction to the Ecology of Written Language*, 2nd ed., Malden, MA: Blackwell Publishing.

Blikstad-Balas, M. (2016), '"You Get What You Need". Students' Attitudes towards Using Wikipedia When Doing School Assignments', *Scandinavian Journal of Educational Research*, 60 (6): 594–608. https://doi:10.1080/00313831.2015.1066428

Blikstad-Balas, M. and Klette, K. (2020), 'Still a Long Way to Go. Narrow and Transmissive Use of Technology in the Classroom', *Nordic Journal of Digital Literacy*, 15 (1): 56–60. doi:10.18261/issn.1891-943x-2020-01-05

Comber, B. (2015), 'Critical Literacy and Social Justice', *Journal of Adolescent & Adult Literacy*, 58 (5): 362–67. https://doi.org/10.1002/jaal.370

Cummins, J. and Early, M. (2015), *Big Ideas for Expanding Minds: Teaching English Language Learners Across the Curriculum*, Toronto: Rubicon Press/Pearson Canada.

Davies, C. (2017), 'Putting Technology in the Hands of Learners: Perspectives on Formal Education's Initiatives Around One-To-One Digital Technologies', *Oxford Review of Education*, 43 (3): 255–60. doi: 10.1080/03054985.2017.1304919

Edwards, D. and Mercer, N. (1987), *Common Knowledge: The Development of Understanding in the Classroom*, London, UK: Methuen.

Erixon, P-O. (2016), 'Punctuated Equilibrium: Digital Technology in Schools' Teaching of The Mother Tongue (Swedish)', *Scandinavian Journal of Educational Research*, 60 (3): 337–58. doi:10.1080/00313831.2015.1066425

Gee, J. P. (2010), 'A Situated-Sociocultural Approach to Literacy and Technology', in E. Baker (ed.), *The New Literacies: Multiple Perspectives on Research and Practice*, 165–93, Kindle Edition.

Gericke, N., Hudson, B., Olin-Scheller, C. and Stolare, M. (2018), 'Powerful Knowledge, Transformations and the Need for Empirical Studies across School Subjects', *London Review of Education*, 16 (3): 428–44. doi.org/10.18546/LRE.16.3.06.

Grossman, P., Loeb, S., Cohen, J. and Wyckoff, J. (2013), 'Measure for Measure: The Relationship between Measures of Instructional Practice in Middle School English Language Arts and Teachers' Value-Added Scores', *American Journal of Education*, 119 (3): 445–70. doi:10.1086/669901

Hudson, B. (2018), 'Powerful Knowledge and Epistemic Quality in School Mathematics', *London Review of Education: Special Issue on Knowledge and Subject Specialist Teaching*, 16 (3): 384–97.

Janks, H. (2013), 'Critical Literacy in Teaching and Research', *Education Inquiry*, 4 (2): 225–42.

Kjellsdotter, A. (2020), 'What Matter(s)? A Didactical Analysis of Primary School Teachers' ICT Integration', *Journal of Curriculum Studies* (published online). doi: 10.1080/00220272.2020.1759144

Lum, C. (ed.) (2006), *Perspectives on Culture, Technology and Communication: The Media Ecology Tradition*, Cresskill, NJ: Hampton Press Inc.

Luke, A. (2012), 'Critical Literacy: Foundational Notes', *Theory into Practice*, 51: 4–11. doi:10.1080/00405841.2012.636324

Marsh, C.J. (2009), *Key Concepts for Understanding Curriculum*, 4th ed., London and New York: Routledge.

Marsh, C. J. and Willis, G. (2007), *Curriculum: Alternative Approaches, Ongoing Issues*, 4th ed., Columbus, OH: Pearson Merrill Prentice Hall.

Odenstad, C. (2010), *Prov och bedömning i samhällskunskap. En analys av gymnasielärares skriftliga prov*, Karlstad: Karlstad universitet.

Rusk, F., Sahlström, F., Pörn, M. and Slotte-Lüttge, A. (2014), 'Perspectives on Using Video Recordings in Conversation Analytical Studies on Learning in Interaction', *International Journal of Research & Method in Education*, 38 (1): 39–55. doi:10.1080/1743727X.2014.903918

Sahlström, F., Tanner, M. and Olin-Scheller, C. eds (2019), 'Introduction: Smartphones in Classrooms: Reading, Writing and Talking in Rapidly Changing Educational Spaces', Special Issue of *Learning, Culture and Social Interaction*, 1–5.

Selwyn, N. (2016), *Is Technology Good for Education?* Chichester: Wiley

Selwyn, N., Nemorin, S., Bulfin, S. and Johnson, N.F. (2017), 'Left to Their Own Devices: The Everyday Realities of One-To-One Classrooms', *Oxford Review of Education*, 43 (3): 289–310. doi:10.1080/03054985.2017.1305047.

Street, B. (1984), *Literacy in Theory and Practice* (Vol. 9), Cambridge University Press.

Sutherland, R., Armstrong, V., Barnes, S., Brawn, R., Breeze, N., Gall, M., Matthewman, S., Olivero, F., Taylor, A., Triggs, P., Wishart, J. and John, P. (2004), 'Transforming

Teaching and Learning: Embedding ICT into Everyday Classroom Practices', *Journal of Computer Assisted Learning*, 20: 413–25. doi: 10.1111/j.1365-2729.2004.00104.x

Tväråna, M. (2019), *Kritiskt omdöme i samhällskunskap. Undervisningsutvecklande studier av samhällsanalytiskt resonerande i rättvisefrågor*, Stockholm: Stockholms universitet.

Player-Koro, C., Bergviken Rensfeldt, A. and Selwyn, N. (2017), 'Selling Tech to Teachers: Education Trade Shows as Policy Events', *Journal of Education Policy*: 628–703. doi:10.1080/02680939.2017.1380232

Redecker, C. (2017), 'European Framework for the Digital Competence of Educators: DigCompEdu', in Y. Punie (ed.), EUR 28775 EN. Publications Office of the European Union, Luxembourg. Retrieved 20180926 from https://ec.europa.eu/jrc/en/digcompedu

Tanner, M., Olin-Scheller, C. and Pérez Prieto, H. (2019), *Classrooms under Pressure. Ed-tech and Teachers' Positions in a Digitally Rich Upper Secondary School*, paper presented at NERA, 6–8 March, Uppsala, Sweden.

UNESCO (2018), ICT Competency Framework for Teachers. Retrieved 20200624 from https://unesdoc.unesco.org/ark:/48223/pf0000265721

Willermark, S. (2018), *Digital Didaktisk Design: Att utveckla undervisning i och för en digitaliserad skola*, Trollhättan: Högskolan Väst.

8

Epistemic Quality in the Intended Mathematics Curriculum and Implications for Policy

Jennie Golding

Introduction

The discussion in this chapter is in the context of the English school mathematics curriculum and addresses the characterization of epistemic quality in school mathematics: what is it, why does it matter, and what might it look like in a classroom? I develop my arguments by considering which epistemic values are being communicated in official curriculum documents and in the related curriculum and assessment materials used by teachers. I ask how the consequent received curriculum is impinged on by Gericke et al.'s (2018) 'transformation' of knowledge in the classroom, and what impact the related epistemic communications appear to have on the epistemic quality available to students. Within the characterization of epistemic quality, I argue in particular for the valuing of *epistemological*, as well as general *epistemic, ascent* (Winch 2013) in mathematics curriculum planning. I draw on a recent large, longitudinal classroom-close study to explore what that might mean, to what extent each of epistemic and epistemological ascent is being achieved, and how those might be enhanced. Finally, I discuss the implications for curriculum system policy (Schmidt and Prawat 2006), including in relation to curriculum materials, assessments and teacher initial and continuing education.

'Curriculum' itself has been a contested term in the education literature: I use the word to signify the *range* of experiences associated with education institutions, whether *intended, enacted, experienced* or *achieved* (Mullis and Martin 2015). For many jurisdictions in recent years, including England, the *intended curriculum* has been developed as a 'national curriculum' for ages 5 to 16, that in some form embodies centralized intentions for school-associated learning experiences. In England, teachers enjoy a high degree of autonomy in how curriculum is enacted but work with high-stakes student assessments at ages 11, 16 and 18. The English curriculum structure is largely subject-based: arguably, the focus issues are even more central in a thematically or 'problem-based' structure, where the role of disciplines is itself contested.

I draw on work that explored the enactment of the 2014 mathematics curriculum in England, which arguably aligns rather better than its predecessor with the epistemological priorities of the parent discipline. The focus curriculum aims to promote students' mathematical conceptual fluency, reasoning and problem-solving in mathematics. Internationally, such aspirational goals are widely valued but have not been achieved at scale.

I engage with the *epistemic quality* – discussed by Hudson (2018) and understood to be the quality of the syntactical and substantive mathematics – made available to learn in the classroom, and in particular the quality of *epistemology*: the theory of the disciplinary knowledge, especially with regard to its methods, validity and scope, and the approaches to establishing new knowledge as justified belief. I discuss later 'which' mathematics discipline should be the target of school mathematics. I use empirical data to explore how curriculum transformation processes can be constrained by curriculum communication, and by teacher capacity – their knowledge, skills and beliefs (Golding 2017). I discuss the mathematical epistemic quality evidenced in classrooms, and identify valued aspects that appear to be harder to achieve, at least with the curriculum texts being used. Finally, I suggest developments in the analysed curriculum system which might better support widely valued outcomes.

Empirical work drawn on

Between 2016 and 2022, (between 2016 and 2022) I have led a group of ten researchers exploring curriculum enactment: in particular, the ways teachers and students drew on, and were impacted by, related curriculum materials and assessments ('curriculum texts'). We asked 'How is the new curriculum being enacted in classrooms? What curriculum and assessment materials are teachers and students drawing on, and how? What is the impact on teachers and on students?'

The study sampled classes of students aged 5–18, the latter pursuing a calculus-rich pre-university course, and followed classes over at least two years. It drew on the voices of ~400 teachers, ~4,100 students, nearly 200 schools/

colleges, full-lesson observations of ~350 classes, and longitudinal attainment data for those classes. The samples used were representative in terms of several features known to affect teaching and learning in England, such as school size, location and socio-economic intake, assessed inspection quality and typical student attainment. All classes were using curriculum materials and/or high-stakes assessments provided by the market leading mathematics education publisher in England, which also funded the study. Each year, for each class, we observed complete lessons featuring newly emphasized aspects of the intended curriculum, and talked with focus groups of students. We either interviewed or surveyed class teachers and school/college mathematics leads termly and surveyed all students in secondary study classes. We also drew on curriculum, curriculum material and assessment-related documentary analysis, and progression data for students in study classes.

The research data collection and all non-routine analyses were undertaken by phase- and subject-specific specialist researchers. Further details of the approach taken, including the approach to analysis, and some key outcomes, are given in Golding (2021). Studies of this nature, large-scale and longitudinal but close to the intended objects of curriculum policy, namely teachers and students in classrooms, are unusual, and the institutional ethnographic approach adopted (Smith 2005) allowed distinctive affordances of cross-phase and longitudinal lenses, comparison of teacher with student response, and theorization of student as policy-player. In this chapter, I focus on epistemic characteristics of the data.

Epistemic quality

Hudson (2018) exemplifies high/low epistemic quality in primary school mathematics with brief descriptions of widely contrasting transformations of the intended curriculum; our data suggested a range of quality between those two extremes, varying over time within a single classroom, but also across parallel classrooms and schools, and to some extent across phases. Epistemic quality is judged in relation to the knowledge valued in mathematics learning – which depends on who is doing the valuing, and for what purposes, for whom. I shall show that there is significant overlap between what appears to be communicated as valued in the focus national curriculum, in the target curriculum materials, and in the related assessment criteria, and what is claimed as valued by much of the mathematics education community – and apparently, by policymakers. In school mathematics, I contend that the related range of documentation suggests that 'high epistemic quality' includes access to

- knowledge that is discovered *or* created by the person engaging with it, including
- utilitarian knowledge for everyday purposes
- socially and economically empowering knowledge that enables appreciation and harnessing of the world
- creative know-how that delights and affirms
- knowledge of the syntax and epistemology of school mathematics as a discipline closely related to (but different from) the parent discipline (Golding 2018)
- appreciation of the beauty, power and satisfaction of working with such knowledge as an intellectual endeavour
- over an appropriate range of substantive mathematical content *and processes*.

This is a broader and more detailed characterization of high epistemic quality in school mathematics than found in Hudson (2018). The related knowledge might be explicit, implicit or tacit (Tirosh 1994). By *mathematical epistemology* within school mathematics, I reiterate that I mean the **mathematical scope, methods including communication, ways of knowing and of coming to know**, that are valued in the parent discipline, suitably transformed for access by the target group of students. I argue that one goal of school mathematics should be to induct school students into such valued knowledge and practices, at a level accessible to current student capacities but increasingly aligned with those of the parent discipline, as well as, when appropriate in application, of related disciplines – because it is only thus that young people have access to the potential of mathematics for their own, and society's, purposes. Morrow (2008: 72) reminds us that access involves not only exposure to opportunity to learn but active agency – commitment and effort – on the part of the student, towards that learning.

For students aiming to transition to higher education courses that are mathematically intense, there is a range of evidence that similar values are also held by those in higher education (Rach and Heinze 2016). For these students, there is a need for support into a university community with a different, and increased, expectation of organization for learning, quite different forms and purposes of curriculum, pedagogy and assessment, and a higher level of rigour, formalization and abstractedness of the espoused epistemology (Gueudet 2008). Although such disjunctures with typical school mathematics provision are widespread globally, they differ in profile across jurisdictions and also between different mathematics-intensive courses and universities within jurisdictions (Gueudet op. cit.). In Bernstein's (2000) terms, students need to acquire the recognition rules in order to recognize the speciality, and hence the potential, of the discourse, yet in terms of epistemic education in schools, I argue the appropriate needs vary.

For young people whose school mathematics is intended to provide an epistemic basis for less mathematically intense pathways, many of which place a significant demand on mathematical literacy, there is across much of the western world a mismatch between accounts of employer and further education needs and what is perceived to be widely achieved, in terms of confidence and competence in mathematical functioning appropriate to a range of occupational, personal and social needs (e.g. Eurypides 2011). For these different purposes, the epistemic quality of mathematics that is valued would appear to include most of the above characteristics but the target knowledge of syntax and of epistemology, as of substantive knowledge, and the nature of the epistemic *transformation* from parent purpose to classroom, might vary. A key question for curriculum players at all levels is, therefore, what mathematics epistemic provision is appropriate for which young people, at which stage (and who decides)?

I argue in Golding (2018), that school mathematics per se takes place in a constrained context, with novice mathematicians, so that the appropriate epistemic approach should be closely, and increasingly, related to that of the parent discipline – but is necessarily different from it. Within *applications* of school mathematics there are other considerations that serve perhaps to further constrain the alignment of an epistemic approach in order to accommodate the epistemic values of the field of application – a variety of 'rhetorical norms' (Kitcher 1991). I refer above to the challenges associated with then moving to the epistemic values associated with, for example, those of mathematically intensive courses at university, although Golding (2020) shows such challenges are not insuperable.

Yet, even within those, there are significant differences about what is valued epistemically across mathematics-intensive courses. I have vivid recollections of my first term at university, when those following mathematics, physics and engineering courses encountered partial differential equations for the first time. For mathematicians, the epistemic goal was to establish whether there existed at least one solution to a given *class* of PDEs and, if so, whether that was unique, and the nature and asymptotic behaviour of such solution(s); the physicists sought specific (preferably closed) form(s) of solution(s) to a *particular* equation when modelling a particular situation, from which they might explore the physical nature of those solutions, and the engineers wanted a possibly numerical *approximation* to a single solution to a particular equation that modelled a physical situation within a given range of the variables, but also and importantly, to know how stable that approximation was, and within what error bounds. These were all making intensive use of mathematics but for different purposes. One might argue that all experienced a high quality of epistemic access, but the nature of that differed across interest groups. There are therefore choices to be made in relation to the purposes of any intended curriculum and, within that, the characterization of high-quality epistemic access might vary.

Epistemic quality communicated in curriculum texts

The 'Purpose Statement' in the target 2014 curriculum states (DfE p 1),

> Mathematics is a creative and highly inter-connected discipline that has been developed over centuries, providing the solution to some of history's most intriguing problems. It is essential to everyday life, critical to science, technology and engineering, and necessary for financial literacy and most forms of employment. A high-quality mathematics education … provides a foundation for understanding the world, the ability to reason mathematically, an appreciation of the beauty and power of mathematics, and a sense of enjoyment and curiosity about the subject.

This constitutes an aspiration for *expansive* (Engestrom 1987) mathematics learning, well-aligned with the characterization of high epistemic quality suggested above.

The document delineating the intended curriculum continues: 'The national curriculum for mathematics aims to ensure that all pupils:

- become **fluent** in the fundamentals of mathematics, including through varied and frequent practice with increasingly complex problems over time, so that pupils develop conceptual understanding and the ability to recall and apply knowledge rapidly and accurately … Mathematics is an interconnected subject in which pupils need to be able to move fluently between representations of mathematical ideas.

- **reason mathematically** by following a line of enquiry, conjecturing relationships and generalizations, and developing an argument, justification or proof using mathematical language.
- can **solve problems** by applying their mathematics to a variety of routine and non-routine problems with increasing sophistication, including breaking down problems into a series of simpler steps and persevering in seeking solutions'.

Similarly, the focus of the pre-university A-Level specification, first taught from September 2017, was developed to provide a continued coherent pathway from the 11–16 curriculum. The key aspirations for deep conceptual fluency, accompanied by mathematical reasoning and problem-solving, represent processes included in previous A-Level specification documents, but the latter two especially enjoy renewed emphases in the current specification. These are well aligned with disciplinary values.

The national curriculum 'programme of study' follows its 'purpose' statement with a list of target content, arranged largely within two-year blocks, within which these process aspirations are intended to be worked out. On analysis, the intentions communicated are to provide foundations for content progression within mathematics, working also towards a grasp of the foundations for the disciplinary epistemology and distinctive mathematics cultural appreciation, together with mathematical literacy for personal, social and occupational purposes. Progression within knowledge of mathematical content is present but not detailed in that document, supported by a strong mathematical hierarchy. There is some indication of intended progression within key processes, and also of epistemological learning.

For example, in the primary curriculum we read 'explore and make conjectures about … ', 'develop their skills of rounding and estimating as a means of predicting and checking the order of magnitude of their answers', 'checking the reasonableness of their answers' …. (DfE 2013, Primary: 4, non-statutory guidance) and then, in secondary mathematics, 'move freely between different representations', 'make and test conjectures', 'look for proofs and counterexamples', 'explore what can and cannot be inferred … ', 'begin to model situations mathematically and express the results using a range of formal mathematical representations' (DfE 2013: 3, Key Stage 3 programme of study, 'working mathematically'). Then for older students (DfE 2013: 3, Key Stage 4 programme of study), the curriculum suggests use mathematical language and properties precisely; make and test conjectures about the generalisations that underlie patterns and relationships; look for proofs or counter-examples; begin to ... reason deductively in geometry, number and algebra; ... assess the validity of an argument and the accuracy of a given way of presenting information; ... use mathematical language and properties precisely; ... model situations mathematically and express the results using a range of formal mathematical representations, reflecting on ... any modelling assumptions.

Within these excerpts, we see a clear progression in what is expected of students in terms of coming to know, and harness for their own use, valued ways of working mathematically, as they go through their compulsory schooling. There is, then, some clear intention of epistemic, including epistemological, *ascent* (Winch 2013).

There remains, though, a deficit in other aspects of what is valued by those who practise mathematics in a range of fields, which relates to, for example, overt appreciation of the choices mathematicians make in definitions, for example, of a^0, notions of elegance or comparative strengths of different approaches, the search for a fundamental cross-situation or generalized structure that lends power to representations and transformations, the overt valuing of exposure to mathematics as potentially fallible – and I discuss this further below.

The above 'programmes of study' for ages 5–16 (DfE 2013) were developed by a mathematics education 'expert group', moderated by ministers, and initially received a cautious welcome from both the mathematics and mathematics education communities, although aspirations for the years to the end of primary education (typically, age 11 in England) were widely thought to be overly aspirational. I have shown they include knowledge of procedures and processes, of flexible fluency, communication, problem-solving and reasoning, thus mathematical 'know-that' and procedural 'know-how' (Ryle 1946), yet feature little explicit syntactic know-how. The pre-university study focused on a curriculum developed by university mathematics experts in an otherwise parallel process so that some stage-specific 'transformation' of the appropriate epistemic substance was integral to the genesis of the studied curricula.

In the focus studies, similar epistemic analysis was undertaken of the sets of curriculum materials under scrutiny and assessment materials produced to support preparation for high-stakes examinations at ages 16 and 18. We found that the mathematics epistemic quality represented in any one set of the target materials was at least moderately well-aligned with curriculum intentions, representing key processes in discipline-coherent ways largely appropriate to the target students. Support for developing a robust and flexible fluency was well represented, and opportunities for students to build up progression in mathematical reasoning and problem-solving were usually explicitly identified. Explicit exposure to epistemological approaches was well-aligned with that expressed in the programme of study, although sometimes conservative in extent.

In parallel, teacher support materials typically offered lesson plans, identification of likely misconceptions and barriers to student success, tools for probing student thinking around given tasks, ways to build up confidence in approaching the more demanding of those and of supporting resilience in that approach …. Such materials are described as 'teacher educative' by Davis and Krajcik (2005) since they hold the potential to expand and enrich teachers' grasp of subject and subject pedagogic knowledge key to effective teaching. A comparative weakness, in general, though, was the low level of overt communication of mathematical *epistemology* in either teacher or student materials: for example, what was being accepted as validity of approach or argument, and valued ways of communicating that, and of mathematical exploration, remained largely implicit.

We also analysed high-stakes assessments taken by most students at ages 11 and 16 ('GCSE') and by some at 18 ('A-Level'). The curriculum was introduced without significant piloting, meaning exemplar such assessments usually post-dated curriculum materials and first teaching. However, our analysis showed that test materials for eleven-year-olds, nominally focused on 'arithmetic' and 'reasoning', usually featured an interpretation of 'reasoning' less ambitious than that adopted in the related curriculum materials, or arguably, intended in the curriculum, and tended to marginalize measurement, geometry and data handling. At GCSE, early assessment-related materials appeared coherent with both curriculum intentions and with the focus curriculum materials but, over time, targeted levels of reasoning and of problem-solving appeared to decrease. A-Level assessments followed a similar pattern, albeit remaining more aspirational than corresponding curriculum materials.

What we see, then, is that to discipline-informed readers, the focus intended curriculum, most curriculum resources, and early assessment materials communicated epistemic values moderately well aligned one with another, although with clear limitations in relation to alignment with disciplinary values, especially in relation to epistemological aspects of those.

Impact of curriculum texts on quality of epistemic access

The early teacher interviews *and* classroom observations across our studies showed that teachers' interpretation of key processes such as mathematical fluency, reasoning and problem-solving showed significant variation: for example, some talked about 'fluency' as meaning rapid rote reproduction, others as the flexible, efficient and reliable use of appropriate facts and procedures. Some identified problem-solving with 'task presented in words' and others as 'successful, sometimes sustained, application to complete an unfamiliar (to the target students), sometimes semi-structured or unstructured, task'. The nature of teachers' *interpretation* of the available curriculum documents, and hence their epistemic aims, therefore varied, and this naturally resulted in students having access to opportunities of variable epistemic quality.

For any one phase in the study, all study classes were using the same set of curriculum materials, designed to be highly teacher-educative (Davis and Krajcik 2005), so this variation is in some ways surprising. Within a single school, the mathematics teacher community sometimes developed a distinctive and apparently influential curriculum discourse which, in common with Smith (2005), we interpreted as curriculum text. However, we also found schools where different teachers interpreted curriculum intentions in very different ways.

Early curriculum enactment, then, appeared very variable in terms of key processes and classroom communication also of mathematics epistemology, even though all study teachers and students were using materials moderately well-aligned with curriculum intentions. As assessment-related materials became available, a clear intertextual hierarchy (Smith 2005) emerged. It was unusual to talk with a teacher who had read the official intended curriculum: almost all relied on curriculum materials or on the school's related 'schemes of work' for their initial interpretation. Within that, there was selection as teachers imposed their own prejudices in relation to the communicated intentions. It was common, for example, across age groups, to find teachers who 'saved' problem-solving or reasoning for their 'quick finishers' or who selected only the most accessible of related questions: '*These students don't do problem-solving*' (Year 11 teacher, Spring 2017). As assessment materials became available, those acquired immediate interpretational authority. In some early cases, this privileging of assessment materials focused teachers' attention on aspirations for problem-solving and reasoning for all students but, in others, as assessment aspirations appeared to dilute over time, teachers analysed that and their practice soon reflected it. Sadly, as teachers became more confident with emergent assessments, there emerged practices which offered students attaining weakly at either 'tier' of GCSE entry an impoverished and sometimes mathematically incoherent experience. Students sometimes talked about teaching directed at strategic approaches that would gain the relatively small number of marks needed for key 'gatekeeper' grades, especially through their examination year: *'We practise spotting where we can get one of the marks in a question, so we're quite good at that'* (Year 11 student, Spring 2018). In each phase of the study, though, there were also teachers who developed an approach that was epistemically of high quality, as characterized above, including in its epistemological communication, and who were able to maintain that.

In classrooms, then, coherence of intended curriculum, curriculum texts and, to some extent, assessments did not always support enactment aligned with those. Over time, incoherence of enacted curriculum with intentions often emerged, supported by high-stakes assessments not fully aligned with epistemic intentions.

How is the enactment of such potential constrained by the quality of the teacher's own knowledge?

In England, most teachers of learners aged 5–13 are not subject specialists, and many beyond that have limited specialist knowledge. For non-subject-specialists, particularly for primary teachers teaching across the curriculum, the typical English one-year initial teacher preparation is likely to be insufficient to inculcate a deeply epistemic, and especially epistemological, grasp of school mathematics from a teacherly perspective. Even as a subject specialist, in a performativity system examination performance pressures mean that as an end, attainment is frequently privileged over depth of subject grasp, arguably, though perhaps fallaciously, consistent with a moral purpose of optimizing the range of pathways subsequently open to young people.

Furthermore, teaching for the expansive learning envisaged in the intended curriculum requires wide and deep subject-specialist (including pedagogical and here, I argue, epistemological) knowledge (Eurydice 2011), sophisticated skills and positive affect, including beliefs (Golding 2017). Our study showed that teachers of all ages, whatever their mathematical background, usually lacked initial capacity to enact the focus curriculum as intended, though a minority had already developed, or were developing, with the support of either externally provided 'courses' or teacher-educative curriculum materials, curriculum-coherent ways of working. Such development required a significant investment of time and effort and, usually, the support of internal or external colleagues as teachers wrestled with unfamiliar mathematical approaches and the related pedagogy. If epistemic, or especially, epistemological, aspects of curriculum intentions were not explicitly exemplified in such development support, then certainly non-specialist teachers, but often specialists also, remained unaware of them. Examples evidenced included teacher uncertainty about the role of dynamic demonstration in proof, teacher confusion as to whether a square is a rectangle or a cylinder a prism, and teacher unwillingness to engage with alternative arguments presented by learners. Deep, sustained and often collaborative, teacher professional development coherent with curriculum intentions, supported by external expertise perhaps from high-quality teacher-educative resources, was generally needed before teachers could make significant progress towards high-quality epistemic access. Without that, we frequently observed, and teachers reported, lessons where the epistemic quality was apparently limited by teacher capacity: *'I wasn't quite sure I could cope with where they might take that discussion, so I shut it down'* (Year 5 teacher, Spring 2018).

Epistemic quality achieved in the enacted curriculum

High-quality epistemic access then depends on teacher capacity and commitment, curriculum interpretation and on the adopted textual hierarchy (together contributing to Gericke et al.'s (2018) 'transformation'). In our studies, interpretation was usually initially led by teacher-educative resources, sometimes heavily edited with the result of reducing epistemic aspiration. Interpretation later became dominated by high-stakes assessment texts, which for some came to threaten epistemic quality achieved. For others, though, these served to enhance aspirations, particularly for more highly attaining students, since teachers began to acknowledge that, without enactment rather better aligned with emerging assessments, students would under-achieve.

Epistemic and epistemological ascent

Bernstein (2000) theorizes an epistemic quality of *verticality* within a knowledge structure, that is, the hierarchical, cumulative development of knowledge within a discipline, and mathematics represents the archetypal such field. Winch (2013) discusses the relationships needed between (school) subject knowledge, inferential ability within that body of knowledge, and ability to validate and establish new (to student) truths if, as argued, one goal of school curriculum is to support a move from disciplinary novice towards expert. He goes on (128) to argue that 'a (consequent) key feature of good curriculum design is the ability to manage the different types of knowledge in a sequence that matches not just the needs of the (discipline-related) subject but also that of the student, so that the different kinds of disciplinary knowledge are introduced in such a way that the development of expertise is not compromised'. This reminds us that curriculum transformation aimed at achieving high epistemic quality in the classroom is student-, context- and time-dependent.

Within that argument, the clearest instantiations of such *epistemic ascent* might be expected in those school subjects stemming from vertically structured disciplines. The best mathematics curriculum resources, then, support an appropriate enacted epistemic ascent for all learners. Our data suggested that the focus curriculum resources were largely structured to support such ascent, at least in terms of mathematical content and processes. Teachers, though, selected from materials in ways which did not always reflect such structure, such that, for example, they might edit out some aspects of the intended progression. They usually reported this to be because, as in Winch above, they felt that at least some of their students did not at that time have the foundations on which to make such ascent. However, as above and on other occasions, emerging assessments served to restrict access to the epistemic progression reflected in curriculum materials. Overall, though, we observed over time some nascent and widespread classroom growth in the mathematical process progression made available to students.

Importantly, we searched in particular for evidence of access to *epistemological ascent*, without which learners cannot fully participate in, or appreciate, the powerful culture of the discipline, and it is to this that I now turn.

Quality of epistemology available in the classroom

Expanding on the initial definition of epistemology adopted, I suggest *high* epistemological quality features opportunity to learn about, for example,

- the nature(s) of mathematical knowledge, contested though that might be: for example, its relationship to sensed – and intrinsically

fallible – knowledge deriving from the world around us; its intrinsic interconnectedness and structure;
- the scope of mathematics study, and aspects of mathematical thinking that are of particular interest to different users;
- justification for new(-to-learner) knowledge, whether created or discovered, explicit, implicit or tacit (Ryle 1946);
- foundations for, and validity of, mathematical belief;
- the authority for new mathematical knowledge as residing within the subject itself, its substance and syntax – rather than with the teacher or the curriculum materials …

and, *for epistemological ascent,* that these should develop over time so that students' ways of mathematical working and being are increasingly aligned with those of mathematics practitioners in different fields.

In the classrooms in our studies, we found access to high-quality appropriate epistemology was unusual, and the typicality for England of our findings is reflected in, for example, Ofsted (2012). We did, though, observe positive examples in all phases from ages 5 to 18, with some primary classes showing a high value for clearly articulated reasoning about classification, about the enumeration of all possibilities, about the comparative strengths of different arguments that the sum of two odd integers must be even …. We observed 11-year-olds wrestling with Goldbach's conjecture that any even number greater than two is the sum of two prime numbers, exploring ways in which this might be proved or disproved – and a delight that the conjecture remains unproved: 'That's what maths is about, really, isn't it?' (Year 7 teacher, Spring 2018, in response to a student saying 'So no one knows? Really? That's so cool ….'). 15-year-olds with relatively poor prior attainment were seen using spreadsheets to explore the effect different football scoring systems would have had on last year's teams' league positions, and trying to develop a convincing scoring system that would have resulted in a different champion – but then analysing the effect that such alternative scoring systems would likely have had on teams' tactics. We saw a pre-university class persist with grappling with the nature and location of complex roots of a quartic equation, trying to understand their nature by comparing different representations of the related function and 'playing' with complex approximations and function transformations in order to make better links between those – and then evaluating the relative elegance and power of the different approaches they had explored.

These classroom experiences all brought with them a deep satisfaction for students and, not infrequently, an element of surprise or of a frustration supported and eventually worked through. We consider that in different ways each of the described experiences represented access to high-quality mathematical epistemology, but they were unusual. Each in its own way drew on highly skilled teaching, deeply knowledgeable not only about the mathematics and the epistemology but about the students and their learning of mathematics at that point in time.

Our analysis of the intended mathematics national curriculum is that such opportunities are supported at a high level and are clear to subject-specialist teacher educators but are not presented in detail, applied to individual delineations of target content, so that it is easy for the busy classroom teacher to lose sight of them. Teacher guidance in curriculum documents was generally epistemologically sound, but it often lacked depth and detail, and was sometimes limited in scope: many aspects of widely valued mathematical epistemology are not easy to codify, and so perhaps, to begin to make accessible especially to non-specialist teachers, let alone to students.

As above, though, given that for teachers and even more so for students, curriculum materials and, especially, assessment-related materials are privileged over programmes of study for interpretation of the intended curriculum, the key documents to analyse are assessments. Epistemological grasp at school-appropriate levels is typically not easy to assess in timed written papers and so, in a performativity system, is likely to be marginalized unless teachers have other, compelling, reasons to privilege it. Further, as suggested above, successful development requires in-depth sensitivity to students, their learning and the mathematical opportunity. Identification and harnessing of epistemological potential for particular classroom contexts is therefore highly dependent on teacher capacity, including their awareness and valuing of epistemological ascent in students.

What might be missing?

There is clearly, however, *opportunity* to develop epistemological knowledge within the intended curriculum. Further, I have shown there is *epistemological ascent* embedded within the guidelines given, reflected, for example, in expectations of increasing rigour in communication of mathematical argument as students progress through compulsory schooling.

However, the nature of epistemological knowledge is of syntactical know-how which, unlike procedural know-how, is difficult to codify and so to represent effectively in curriculum materials or written teacher support and difficult, especially, then to structure for teaching. It includes, for example, as illustrated above but poorly represented in any of the documents analysed, that:

- some mathematics is contested or ill-defined
- there are easy-to-understand conjectures which are not resolved
- definitions of, for example, a^0 are for mathematicians to agree on – but different decisions bring different implications, including different links with, and potential for coherent working with, existing definitions
- there is frequently mathematical potential in asking 'what if not ... ?' ....

It is therefore unsurprising that a well-crafted and detailed approach to a mathematical epistemological ascent is not satisfactorily represented in the materials under study, but there is room for significant development. For example, although 'proof' is expected, the (insufficient) role of multiple examples or of dynamic demonstrations to constitute proof is not, nor their role in inductive thinking. Explicit notions of elegance, of infinity, of invariance or equivalence are missing, the sometimes-competing roles of sense and logic are implicit but not explicit. And the cultural and contextual embedding of mathematical meanings and practices is also hidden: are they global and shared, can they assimilate ethnomathematics, or do they have to change to accommodate that? Teaching for such considerations is highly demanding.

Conclusion

I have argued for particular characterizations of high epistemic quality in school mathematics and, within that, for an explicit characterization of high-quality mathematical epistemology. Our study shows that the quality of access to such epistemic, and especially such epistemological, engagement in the school classroom, and its ascent, varies enormously. For example, observed promoted mathematical authority varied from 'because the textbook says so' to deeply challenging student experiences developing and fully justifying new-to-them knowledge: we observed the range in each age phase. We found that even 'specialist' teachers often marginalized epistemological considerations in the classroom: teaching for high-quality epistemological learning, and its progression, appears to be *highly demanding* of teacher capacity. It is therefore unlikely to happen at scale unless there is sustained, explicit and detailed support for related teacher development, including in teacher-educative curriculum materials, but also in other curriculum texts – and a valuing of that in high-stakes assessments.

There are clear implications for curriculum system innovation. If young people are to learn that mathematics is a meaningful and empowering creative discipline that they can harness for multiple purposes, and communicate to others, requiring shared vocabulary and syntax, then I have argued we need, as a minimum:

- an intended curriculum that is developed by education and mathematics experts to reflect epistemic ascent(s) towards the quality of mathematics practice valued by the range of end-users
- and which overtly values the range of disciplinary epistemology, structured to support high-quality progression within that
- innovative teacher initial and continuing education that prepares teachers for the (demanding) transformation of those qualities for effective classroom use so that they 'know the mathematics' in epistemically and pedagogically powerful ways appropriate to their learners and contexts
- curriculum materials and learning assessments fully and explicitly coherent with those aspirations, developed in detail and depth.

Making progress towards such goals is challenging, but the work reported in this chapter suggests many aspects are at least moderately susceptible to development, and identification of goals is first step to their attainment. It is clear that sustained subject-specific teacher education, both pre- and in-service, is central, and that goal-coherent, teacher-educative curriculum materials and assessments can contribute to that. However, work is needed to develop codification of valued outcomes in detail and in depth, together with identification of those aspects which are necessarily implicit or tacit. In a world where many issues of importance rely on cross-disciplinary approaches, as identified by the OECD's 'Compass 2030' initiative (http://www.oecd.org/education/2030-project/), it is also important to identify which aspects of epistemic development benefit from subject-focused teaching and learning, and which can at least equally well be developed in cross-disciplinary contexts, under what conditions. We have ambitious aspirations for the learning of our young people in the twenty-first century: their flourishing merits investment in innovative teacher development to support those aspirations.

Acknowledgement

The study drawn on in this chapter was funded by Pearson UK. It focused on Pearson's mathematics curriculum resources and assessment-related materials.

References

Bernstein, B. (1996), *Pedagogy, Symbolic Control and Identity: Theory, Research, Critique*, rev. ed., Lanham, MA: Rowman & Littlefield.

Davis, E. A. and Krajcik, J. S. (2005), 'Designing Educative Curriculum Materials to Promote Teacher Learning', *Educational Researcher*, 34 (3): 3–14.

DfE (Department for Education) (2013), *National curriculum in England: Mathematics Programmes of Study*, available at https://www.gov.uk/government/publications/national-curriculum-in-england-mathematics-programmes-of-study

Engestrom, Y. (2001), 'Expansive Learning at Work: Toward an Activity Theoretical Reconceptualization', *Journal of Education and Work*, 14 (1): 133–55.

Eurydice (2011), *Mathematics Education in Europe: Common Challenges and National Policies*. EACEA (Education, Audiovisual and Culture Executive Agency), European Commission.

Golding, J. (2017), 'Mathematics Teacher Capacity for Change', *Oxford Review of Education*, 43 (1): 502–17.

Golding, J. (2018), 'Mathematics Education in the Spotlight: Its Purpose and Some Implications', *London Review of Education*, 16 (3): 460–73.

Golding, J. (2020), 'Transition to University: Contributions of a Specialist Mathematics School', *Teaching Mathematics and Its Applications*, 40(1): 40–55, https://doi.org/10.1093/teamat/hraa005

Golding, J. (2021, under review), Researching Curriculum Policy Enactment at Policy Actor Level: Approaches, Affordances and Challenges.

Gericke, N., Hudson, B., Olin-Scheller, C. and Stolare, M. (2018), 'Powerful Knowledge, Transformations and the Need for Empirical Studies across School Subjects', *London Review of Education*, 16 (3): 428–44.

Gueuedet, G. (2008), 'Investigating the Secondary–Tertiary Transition', *Educational Studies in Mathematics*, 67: 237–54.

Hudson, B. (2018), 'Powerful Knowledge and Epistemic Quality in School Mathematics', *London Review of Education*, 16 (3): 384–97.

Kitcher, P. (1991), 'Persuasion', in Pera, M. and Shea, W. R. (eds), *Persuading Science: The Art of Scientific Rhetoric*, 3–27, New York: Science History Publications.

Morrow, W. (2008), *Bounds of Democracy: Epistemological Access in Higher Education*, Pretoria: HSRC Press.

Ofsted (2012), *Mathematics Made to Measure*, London: HMSO.

Rach, S. and Heinze, A. (2016), 'The Transition from School to University in Mathematics: Which Influence Do School-Related Variables Have?', *International Journal of Science and Mathematics Education*, 15 (7): 1–21.

Ryle, G. (1946), 'Knowing How and Knowing That', in Gilbert Ryle (ed) *Collected Papers*, 212–25, New York: Barnes and Noble.

Schmidt, W. H. and Prawat, R. S. (2006), 'Curriculum Coherence and National Control of Education: Issue or Non-Issue?', *Journal of Curriculum Studies*, 38 (6): 641–58.

Smith, D. E. (2005), *Institutional Ethnography: A Sociology for People*, Walnut Creek, CA: AltaMira Press.

Tirosh, D., ed. (1994), *Implicit and Explicit Knowledge: An Educational Approach*, Norwood, NJ: Ablex Publishing Co.

Winch, C. (2012), 'Curriculum Design and Epistemic Ascent', *Journal of Philosophy of Education*, 47 (1): 128–46.

9

A Material-dialogic Perspective on Powerful Knowledge and Matter within a Science Classroom

Mark Hardman, John-Paul Riordan and Lindsay Hetherington

Introduction

'Powerful' disciplinary knowledge has the potential to enrich students' lives by providing access to understanding beyond everyday experience (Young 2011). Learning science or any other school subject requires understanding of the core body of content within an academic discipline. However, contemporary discussion of disciplinary knowledge remains at the sociological level, offering little clarity around how such knowledge manifests in the complex and unique contexts in which people learn. The framing of powerful knowledge inherits a dualist philosophical assumption that a curriculum concept is a universal phenomenon, acquired through a myriad of activities and applied in new situations, but nevertheless something which is acquired (or not) (Hardman 2019). The question then becomes how these universal concepts are acquired through the unique context of a specific classroom.

Gericke et al. (2018) begin to address this question by highlighting the *transformations* made as disciplinary knowledge is taught in schools. These transformations occur at the societal, institutional and classroom levels. The term 'transformation' is an umbrella term reflected in both the tradition of didactics, for example, 'didactic transposition' (Chevallard 2007), 'omstilling' (Ongstad 2006) and 'reconstruction' (Duit 2013), as well as within the curriculum tradition in Bernstein's (1973) notion of 're-contextualization'. As well as considering transformations, the term *epistemic quality* moves us towards conceptualizing how classroom activities have differing qualities in conveying the epistemology of disciplines (Hudson 2018). In this chapter, we focus on the classroom and seek to address the overarching question of:

How can the transformation processes related to powerful knowledge and epistemic quality be described?

Our contention is that the notions of transformation and epistemic quality hold the potential to frame the ways in which disciplinary knowledge and epistemology manifest in the classroom. However, as these notions are being developed, in this book and elsewhere, we wish to guard against any simplistic framing whereby idealized disciplinary understandings are in some way *represented* in classrooms. In our view, a learner does not receive a reduced, simplified form of some universal understanding. Understanding of a subject discipline, in terms of both knowledge and the epistemology of the discipline, emerges from the dynamic, messy and material contexts of classrooms. In this chapter, we consider how a *material-dialogic* frame (Hetherington et al. 2018; Hetherington and Wegerif 2018) might contribute to this discussion. We first briefly lay out the material-dialogic frame and our reasons for proposing it. After that, we use a case study of a science classroom to support the usefulness of the frame in considering transformations of disciplinary knowledge in classrooms.

Emergence over representation: The material-dialogic frame

Mollenhauer (1983) argues that in the sixteenth and seventeenth centuries children were first placed in classrooms and separated from the world they were to learn about. Since then, curricula have been developed aimed at providing children with the knowledge they will require in their adult lives. Education in most societies is concerned with representing the 'real world' in a way that allows students to learn about that world 'as it is' (Osberg and Biesta 2004). But, as Osberg, Biesta and Cilliers (2008) argue, such real-world representations do not account for meaning-making as an emergent process within classrooms. They advocate seeing:

> schooling as a practice which makes possible a dynamic, self-renewing and creative engagement with "content" or "curriculum" by means of which school-goers are able to respond, and hence bring forth new worlds.
>
> (Osberg, Biesta and Cilliers 2008: 225)

Therefore, while considering the transformations between academic disciplines and school subjects, we need to foreground the emergent nature of those understandings. Students do not simply receive an imperfect or reduced version of disciplinary knowledge in schooling. Likewise, disciplinary knowledge is not purely derived from everyday experience; this is Young's (2011) argument that powerful knowledge is that which takes students beyond their everyday experiences and opens up new ways of seeing the world. However, rather than simply argue against 'top-down' or 'bottom-up' accounts of transformations, we wish to argue against any stratification of disciplinary knowledge and school knowledge in how transformations might be characterized: they are not ontologically distinct. A teacher brings their own understandings of a subject discipline (or disciplines) into the classroom as they deploy resources and activities which they hope convey something of disciplinary knowledge, and the nature of that knowledge, to pupils. The teacher's disciplinary knowledge and pedagogy meet the experiences of the pupils and the material resources and context of the classroom. Rather than an imperfect conveying of knowledge and epistemology, framed as some ideal, we argue that transformations should be seen as emergent. Emergence involves the coming together of different influences in a dynamic and unpredictable way such that new meanings emerge. In Osberg, Biesta and Cilliers' (2008) terms, 'new worlds are brought forth' as disciplinary understandings, everyday understandings, resources and context come together.

To further this characterization, we draw on 'new materialist' perspectives which suggest that the material in classrooms itself has a role to play in agentic processes of meaning-making (Coole and Frost 2010). We develop this by focusing specifically on what we are calling a *material-dialogic* perspective, which we have already begun to develop in relation to science education (Hetherington et al. 2018; Hetherington and Wegerif 2018), although we feel it has potential to also shed light on other subject areas. The perspective begins to recognize some of the complexity of transformations by framing teacher, pupil and content as entangled within the material circumstances of classrooms.

The material-dialogic frame draws on the work of Karen Barad, who defines an onto-epistemological position she calls 'agential realism' (Barad 2007). This position is onto-epistemological in the sense that it challenges the separation of mind and matter implied in epistemologies where mind is seen as learning *about* matter. Rather, Barad draws on quantum physics to challenge the distinctions made between mind/body, known/knower and meaning/matter, which are instead all seen as entangled:

> To be entangled is not simply to be intertwined with another, as in the joining of separate entities, but to lack an independent, self-contained existence.
>
> (Barad 2007: 19)

In this way, 'matter matters' (Barad 2003: 803) in processes of meaning-making. However, in Barad's relational ontology, matter is not given separate agency (cf. Latour's Actor-Network Theory) but is an active participant within an entangled 'material-discursive process'. New materialism, therefore, challenges the focus upon a single aspect of teaching and learning: talk, gesture, models, values and identity cannot be separated out within research, nor divorced from the physical and historical contexts in which they are situated.

As well as Barad's agential realism, the perspective we propose draws on dialogic theories of learning and teaching (Wegerif 2011; Mercer and Howe 2012) in order to consider the role of materials in the processes of learning science. Dialogic theories draw from Bakhtin, who notes that: 'I hear voices in everything, and dialogic relations among them' (Bakhtin et al. 1986: 169). Through a review of both science education literature and research on dialogic education, we make the case that Barad's ideas have the capacity to develop both and provide a way to better understand the role of the material in science classrooms (Hetherington et al. 2018). We see practical materials, whiteboards, videos, diagrams, computers and any other artefact as having a *voice* in the classroom, along with the verbal, gestural and narrative voices which inhabit the 'dialogic space'.

While we will not rehearse our arguments in full, it is useful here to foreground a couple of theoretical elements of this frame, before delving into its relation to transformations through a case study. We already mentioned the importance of entanglements in Barad's work, and to this we add the notion of *intra-action*, as opposed to *interaction*. Whereas an interaction sees separate, pre-existing entities coming together in some way, Barad's intra-action refers to the entangled co-emergence of a *phenomenon* which cannot be separated into constituent parts or ascribed simple causal processes. In Barad's terms, a *phenomenon* is therefore the unit of analysis rather than the separate elements which have a voice within the classroom, be they people, diagrams, equipment, gestures, etc. Barad (2007) explains how phenomena emerge within specific historical and social contexts through the intra-actions of humans and non-humans.

Gericke et al. (2018) make a compelling case for transformations as a viable area of research in relating powerful disciplinary knowledge to classroom practices and suggest that:

An initial transformation is made in the planning phase, when the teacher draws up the lesson plans, selects the teaching content and considers how it should be represented in such a way that it will be possible for the students to grasp. A second part takes place in the actual teaching situation, when teachers and students are confronted with the representations of content. In this way, the transformation can be described as a process of continuous reconstruction.

(Gericke et al. 2018: 437)

This account recognizes the continuous reconstruction of disciplinary knowledge into content and then into the material through which content is "represented" in the classroom, as well as the ways it is enacted and perceived. Gericke et al. draw on the *didaktik* tradition in which the situational aspects of teachers' disciplinary and pedagogic knowledge, students' prior knowledge and material contexts are all considered. As such, their formulation of the notion of a transformation recognizes that representation is not a simple process of mapping from a discipline. Barad's framework also implies a rejection of representationalism (Milne and Scantlebury 2019) in favour of the continuous (re)emergence (not reconstruction) of phenomena from their material-discursive context. This matters because this perspective foregrounds the co-implication of the teacher's disciplinary and pedagogic knowledge, pupils' prior knowledge and understanding, and material contexts in which learning is taking place. Disciplinary knowledge, transformed into teaching content and materials, is not static representations but evolving material-discursive phenomena. Barad's frame therefore echoes the rejection of simple representation when considering transformations but goes further in suggesting that the meaning and matter cannot be separated; both emerge from the dynamic interplay of influences within a setting.

Barad's frame thus brings into relief any implicit characterization of transformations as 'top down', in which disciplinary knowledge and epistemology are represented in content, which is itself represented in students' minds. A materialist frame denies the presence in a classroom of disciplinary knowledge as abstract universals which are represented only in imperfect form. Instead, the teacher, pupils, materials and environment constitute all there is, and disciplinary knowledge involves the entanglement of these. However, such a frame does not assume that a pupil's understanding emerges 'bottom up' from experience either. The teacher has their own disciplinary understandings which are brought into the dialogic space alongside the pupils' ideas; disciplinary knowledge also exists within resources, materials and activities. The intra-action among all these elements, human and other-than-human, means that all enact agency in the processes of teaching and learning. Therefore, disciplinary knowledge itself enacts agency in the teaching and learning taking place, meaning that knowledge matters, and is materialized, in a way that is neither simply representational *nor* simply emergent. Knowledge is transformative, and transformed as learning takes place in a material-dialogic space.

This shift in focus afforded by a material-dialogic frame suggests to us two interrelated things which are in line with the notion of transformations: first, disciplinary understandings cannot be considered in isolation but must be considered as entangled within the phenomena of classrooms. Second, the understandings of teachers and pupils around school subjects are not 'representations' of academic disciplines in the sense that there is a simple mapping of one to the other. In considering the importance of powerful disciplinary knowledge and epistemic quality in education, we recognize that the phenomena of a classroom differ from the phenomena of a scientific research laboratory, for example. The transformations of scientific understandings from one to the other involve fully recognizing the entanglements of matter and meaning within each. We think that this framing allows the full complexity of teaching and learning to be acknowledged, without losing sight of the importance of engaging young people in developing understandings which relate to subject disciplines. In order to further this view, we now draw upon a case study of a science classroom.

An empirical test case

The case study in question is drawn from a research project exploring instructional strategies to promote conceptual change (Riordan 2014, 2020). Figure 9.1 summarizes the research design, although a more detailed account can be found elsewhere (Riordan et al. 2021). From the outset of this project, we recognized the material influences upon the teacher, learners and classroom, as well as discussions throughout the project, included the material dimension. Therefore, alongside coding of the data to respond to the project's wider research questions, the data set was further analysed using the material-dialogic frame in order to identify what, if anything, this theoretical frame can add to considerations of classroom transformations and their role in practice.

The case focuses on three lessons on chromatography taught by an experienced science teacher: David. Chromatography is the process by which chemicals are separated according to their different properties. In a simplistic guise in early secondary education, this often takes the form of a thin strip of paper suspended in a beaker so that it just touches some water (the solvent in this case). Dots of ink from pens are made towards the bottom of the paper, and as the water migrates up the paper the different inks within the pen (solutes) are deposited at different distances up the paper. The pattern made on the paper (the chromatogram) reveals the different inks and their solubility (how easily they dissolve). The lessons took place in a large comprehensive school in London and were taught to a group of high-attaining Year 8 students (twelve- to thirteen-year-olds). David was asked to plan and teach the lessons as he would normally within the sequence determined by the science department.

a) Lesson video analysis (1 hour x 3)

b) Teacher verbal protocols (2 hours x 3)

c) Pupil group verbal protocols (1 hour x 3)

d) Researcher group interviews (1 hour x 3)

Figure 9.1 Research design.

Three one-hour lessons were video recorded from three angles; the teacher had a lapel microphone and other microphones were positioned on desks in the centre of the room. Two researchers (Riordan and Hardman) observed the lessons and took field notes. Following the lessons, and over a period of several weeks, the teacher was engaged in three sessions of *teacher verbal protocols*, in which he watched the videos of the lessons and commented upon what was happening, without input from the researchers. This process was also videoed. Retrospective debrief interviews then allowed further discussion with the teacher, which was also videoed. The complementary use of video protocols and retrospective debriefing follows Taylor and Dionne (2000) and allowed us to include teacher commentary on their thinking and actions. In order to also obtain the perspective of pupils, clips were selected which were of interest to the two researchers. These were then shown to a self-selecting group of six pupils who undertook *pupil verbal protocols* – commenting upon the videos with minimal input from the researchers. They were then asked questions to prompt further discussion. Three of these were conducted: one for each recorded lesson.

To analyse the rich data we had gathered, two researchers coded the videos related to the first lesson separately, including the video of the lesson itself, of the verbal protocol with the teacher, the retrospective debrief with teacher, and the protocols and debrief with students. The teacher also coded the lesson himself. The researchers and teacher then met to discuss their initial coding. The teacher and researchers then coded all of the videos relating to each of the two subsequent lessons (videos of the lessons, of teacher verbal protocol and pupil verbal protocols). There was a further meeting once all of the coding had been completed (which was also video recorded).

The layering of verbal protocols in which teachers and pupils retrospectively analyse the classroom phenomena, videos of which are then also analysed, can in itself be seen as a material-discursive process in which meaning is made by the teachers, pupils, researchers and the video of the classroom intra-acting with each other across these multiple layers. Our understanding of the transformation of knowledge about chromatography as a material-dialogic practice thus emerged through a *diffractive* process in which data, theory and emerging insights are read and re-read through one another (Mazzei 2014). We do not have space here to lay out the full implications of new materialist frames for research methodology. Suffice to say that we see the outcomes as emergent from the processes of research, rather than as a simple representation of the case we explored.

Our consideration of a material-dialogic frame within this case study fits within the broader question outlined at the start of this chapter (and elsewhere in this book): how can the transformation processes related to powerful knowledge and epistemic quality be described? The frame suggests that greater attention must be paid to how disciplinary knowledge and epistemic quality actually manifest in a classroom via material-discursive intra-action, and how this leads to new understandings. We therefore take up this question by focusing on how the concept of chromatography was manifested in the classroom through intra-actions between the teacher, pupils and materials.

Transformations of disciplinary knowledge through 'Non-Human' materials

One finding of relevance to supporting a material-dialogic interpretation is our coding of David being in dialogue with 'non-human means'. While there is much to be debated about the utility of enumerating the interactions with specific aspects of the classroom, we coded 308 such intra-actions over the three lessons. While this number is of course a product of our research process, it highlights the role of classroom resources and context in transformation processes. The most frequent engagement with material was the Interactive Whiteboard, used to project images to the class, but also to make notes, show images of the experimental setup, and to agree definitions of key terms. Mini whiteboards were used by pupils to generate models of the process of chromatography, and the teacher continually refers to these within the teaching. The mini whiteboards are also used in nonconventional ways – sometimes displaying a 'covert message' to another class member, but even at one point being bent by a pupil to demonstrate the curvature of the chromatograph (the paper on which ink flows upwards when dipped in a liquid). Pupil exercise books contain drawings and descriptions of the process of chromatography. Here we see that the materials of the classroom are intra-acting with the understandings of the teacher and the pupils.

Our suggestion that the material within a classroom is important in learning will not be controversial to readers, however, we contend that this has not received a great deal of attention in relation to transformations. This is not to say that every material intra-action in our data becomes meaningful. For example, the blinds blow in the wind, a mobile phone goes off, there is noise outside the classroom. Here the dialogic space is open to the broader world, but the teacher and class downplay the significance of some incidents like this within observed intra-actions (or absence thereof).

In order to exemplify the role of material in transformations of disciplinary knowledge in classrooms, take the observation that some pupils developed the misunderstanding that the lighter colours travel further up the paper. This initially emerges within the dialogic space as pupils intra-act with the experimental findings (the ink and the paper). Figure 9.2 shows example chromatograms which David displayed on the interactive whiteboard during discussion. During the first lesson we recorded, David asks for ideas about what might be influencing how far the inks travel up the paper. Figure 9.3 shows that pupils suggest 'Dark vs Light' as one factor they believe to be important. In the second lesson we recorded, a pupil writes an account of chromatography (examples of which are seen in Figure 9.4) on a mini whiteboard:

> Water attracts most particles, so inks which are lighter colour have less pigment and go further.

The pupil verbal protocols show that this idea persists for some of the pupils after the lessons. During teacher verbal protocols, David watches back video of the discussion he has with a pupil at the time, and reflects on this, saying:

> [pupil] says "I meant pigment", and I didn't give them the word at all. They, they picked up that word from somewhere at the, in the first lesson, where they started doing the actual experiment. And I'm, I'm bugged by that word, because I think it's got in the way of ever such a lot because they keep going back to this thing about pigment.

By deploying a material-dialogic frame, we can draw attention to the nuance of this situation. The original experimental results combined with the everyday understanding of pupils around ink pigments lead to the emergence of a new understanding. This enters the dialogic space and is crystallized on the whiteboard during discussion. When the pupils come to then express their ideas on mini whiteboards, these materials – the chromatogram, the classroom whiteboard and the mini whiteboards – influence the understandings that some pupils have.

It is through material-dialogue between the teacher, pupils and materials that a misconception emerges. Our data therefore suggest that considering transformations involves recognizing the agency of material aspects of the classroom. Pupil prior knowledge (here about pigments) intra-acts with the class experimental results during dialogue. Here we have what diSessa (2006: 265)

Material-Dialogic Perspective in Science Classroom 167

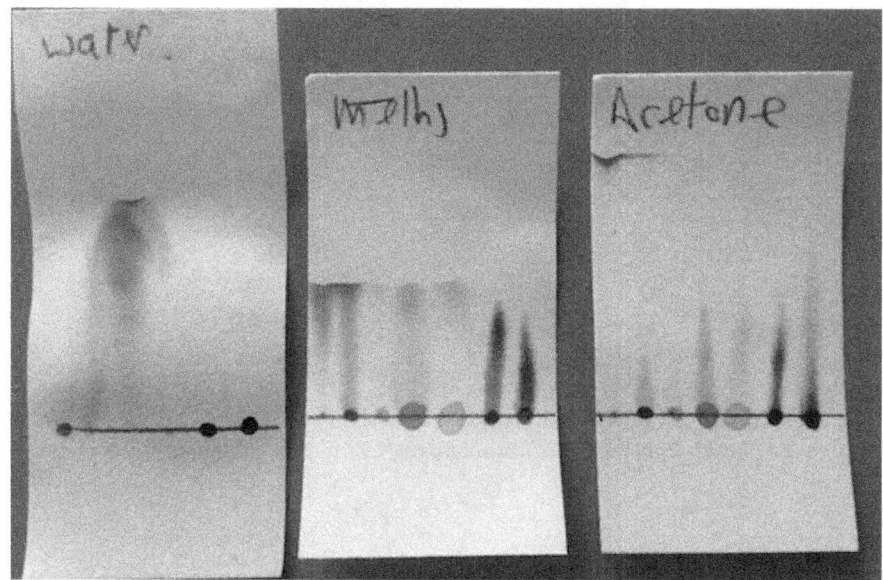

Figure 9.2 The chromatograms engaged with over the lessons.

Figure 9.3 The classroom whiteboard: a dialogic space.

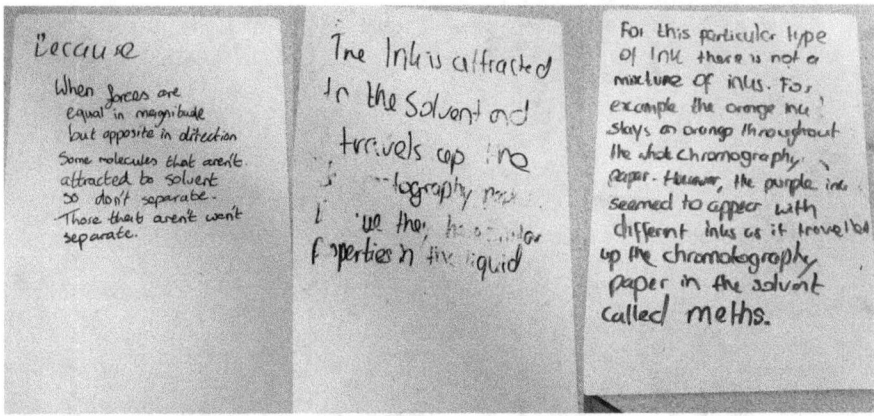

Figure 9.4 Pupil explanations of chromatography on mini whiteboards.

called the primary difficulty, 'students must build new ideas in the context of old ones'. The pigment idea is expressed in writing on a mini whiteboard which then learners and teacher engage with further. Prior knowledge can, in other circumstances, be generative of new ideas in a more positive way, but in this case an idea emerges and persists, which is counter to established scientific understanding.

A material-dialogic frame allows us to ask questions of what it is that the teacher and pupil are actually in dialogue with, and how meaning emerges from this. This role of material resources is often overlooked in attempts to describe how intended content is enacted and learned in relation to school subjects.

Models, matter and phenomena

Beyond the foregrounding of matter, we believe a material-dialogic frame offers other affordances in considering transformations. We found that in synthesizing the material and the dialogic it becomes fruitful to frame 'phenomena', in Barad's (2007) terms, as involving entanglements between people and the models of chromatography present within the classroom. Throughout the lesson physical, mathematical and schematic models are presented, developed and discussed. Indeed, the repeated dialogue with interactive and mini whiteboards occurs when the teacher is asking pupils to develop and explore models, and on occasions these individual models are 'amplified' as they are discussed with the whole class. There are also gestural models which have significance to the teacher and the pupils, and which are repeated several weeks after the original lessons – for example, gestures around the movement of particles. The experimental results have meaning and are mentioned several times. While not strictly 'models', they are signifiers of findings within the experiment.

In considering how powerful disciplinary knowledge is transformed in classrooms, the material-dialogic frame allows us to see that teacher and pupils are in dialogue with the physical manifestations of a scientific concept; in this case, chromatography. The concept is not present in the room as some universal, ontologically distinct ideal but is present in the models which have a material presence in the classroom. These models are physical, mathematical and diagrammatic but also manifest in gestures, verbal descriptions, written definitions, videos and animations.

This realization fits with a philosophical shift in how models are characterized in both science and science education. Gilbert and Justi (2016) reflect on the development of model-based learning over the last few decades and are explicit in their shift away from seeing models as simply representations which denote and support acquisition of universal concepts. Instead, they chart a move towards seeing models as 'artefacts' which are developed in classrooms and through which people reason. This approach corresponds with a shift in the philosophy of science to seeing models as artefacts (e.g. Knuuttila 2011) and positions models not just as things which are reasoned about, but as artefacts which are integral to reasoning in science, and in learning science (Hardman 2017). Similarly, Tytler et al. (2013) chart the development of research into drawings, diagrams and visual representation in science education, and detail their position that students reason through the representations which they generate as part of learning science. We suggest that the material-dialogic frame furthers this literature by seeing models and drawings as emergent from the material-dialogue of classrooms. It also allows us to see such phenomena as involved in the transformation of powerful disciplinary knowledge and epistemological understandings within processes of teaching and learning. In our data, we found that models and diagrams, as artefacts within the classroom, were central to the processes of teaching and learning. In this sense, we might go as far as proposing that disciplinary knowledge is transformed as these models emerge within classrooms.

Yet, the focus on materials within a material-dialogic space is not just confined to the considering of models. Embodied cognition (e.g. Barsalou 2008) is another research area which highlights the need to reconsider learning as involving material aspects of the classroom; the role of the body and its actions in how we come to understand the world is being better understood, although it remains in its infancy. Related to this is the role of gestures in science education and the growing understanding of the role these play in learning (Callinan 2014; Carlson et al. 2014; Johnson-Glenberg and Megowan-Romanowicz 2017). Even how a science teacher demonstrates a scientific technique may be affected by the relative position of students in the room: Jackson, Meltzoff and Decety (2006) found that observing actions from a first-person perspective is more tightly coupled to the sensory-motor system than from a third-person perspective, which requires observers to also process visuospatial information. Bringing these existing accounts of the material aspects of classrooms together with the material-dialogic frame suggests to us that powerful disciplinary knowledge is manifest in classrooms within the models that teachers and pupils are entangled with, but also in the gestures, demonstrations, equipment and even phrases that are deployed. In thinking about transformations, this shows us that the disciplinary knowledge and pedagogic knowledge of the teacher are intra-acting continuously within a dynamic context involving pupils' ideas and material resources.

Much of the teacher verbal protocols and interviews with David involved him evaluating how different actions, approaches and narratives have evolved in his practice and emerged in the studied classroom. For example, when reviewing the first lesson during teacher verbal protocols, he says:

> Then we got these lovely A4-sized ones [mini whiteboards] and it has revolutionized my classroom, because I can go round, and read ... I'm not a great believer of putting long ideas into an exercise book, because they are really attached to them once they are there. ... I think that they feel far more, um, free to explore their ideas on these mini whiteboards.

David has an understanding of chromatography, which is brought together with the repertoire of strategies he uses in the classroom. This case study shows that David considers chromatography as a topic which lends itself to empirical demonstration/experiment, and then pupils working in small groups to discuss, and using mini whiteboards to generate explanations of how chromatography works at a microscopic level. The pupils experience and come to understand chromatography through experimental results, dialogue involving whiteboards, gestures and embodied understandings within a material-dialogic space. The transformation of disciplinary knowledge into classroom learning emerges from teacher understandings and pedagogical strategies meeting with pupil understandings and the materials of classrooms.

Transformations and the phenomena of classrooms

As discussed at the start of this chapter, Gericke et al. (2018) develop the notion of transformations as a way of considering how powerful disciplinary knowledge is brought to the classroom. In this chapter, we added a different theoretical lens, drawing on a material-dialogic account from the work of Barad and Bakhtin. This lens, we believe, further develops a focus upon the specifics of how knowledge manifests within the classroom; how concepts within a curriculum are enacted and learned. We suggest that the role of materials has been underplayed in the discussion to date, but we hope that our case study goes some way to showing that the resources, models and dialogue which emerge within the classroom are indeed the actual stuff of teaching and learning, not some imperfect representation of idealized knowledge.

We therefore propose that a material-dialogic perspective frames disciplinary knowledge as bound within the phenomena of classrooms. Teacher, pupils and materials all play an agentic role as they intra-act, and all bring disciplinary knowledge into play. As a teacher brings their own understandings into the classroom, and their planning unfolds in activities and resources, these become entangled with the embodied understandings of pupils, and the materials within that context. Our case study suggests that powerful, disciplinary knowledge is manifest in the models and dialogue which emerge in the classroom, and which support student understanding. We also suggest that entanglement with models and pedagogical strategies such as generating hypotheses may contribute to pupil understandings of the epistemology of science. We hope the frame and analysis might be extended to other school subjects.

The entanglements of matter and meaning within classrooms are the site of teaching and learning. Each professional scientist may have different understandings, and be entangled with different people, materials and context – different phenomena. In labelling a transformation between understandings in the professional discipline of science and the science classroom in schools, we draw on patterns and resemblances that we believe link the two. However, this is not a simple case of correspondence, nor is school science a representation of professional science in the sense of being a reduced or simplified version. While our analysis still speaks to the transformations between disciplinary knowledge and school subjects, we contend that a material-dialogic frame challenges the sense in which a re-contextualization, transposition or reconstruction of knowledge might be framed as there being something ideal or universal which is maintained between settings. The phenomena of a scientific workplace and the phenomena of a classroom are different, as every context is different. Teacher understandings, curricula and resources are always entangled with pupils and material contexts in new phenomena.

Recognizing this entanglement matters when we think about teaching and learning because the details of how disciplinary knowledge is transformed into classrooms influence pupil learning. We suggest that pupils, initially at least, come to understand a topic like chromatography through the specific models they generate and enter into dialogue with. These models come about as teacher understandings meet pupil understandings and the resources in the classroom. We have seen that in our case study the experimental results, classroom whiteboards and mini whiteboards were all important in the generation of understanding (and sometimes misunderstanding). The material-dialogic frame suggests that teachers and researchers should pay attention to not just the knowledge or 'content' to be taught but also to the material resources within the dialogic space. We believe that a material-dialogic perspective foregrounds the importance of matter, shifts attention to the phenomena of classrooms in teaching and learning, and guards against simple accounts of representation. It therefore speaks to the messy and emergent nature of teaching, learning and research within school subjects.

Our consideration of a material-dialogic frame has begun to raise further questions for us as well: to what extent are various classrooms (indeed, different material-dialogic spaces) different from each other, and what impact do these differences make to emerging understandings within that space? How do specific activities, contexts and resources condition the disciplinary knowledge and epistemological understandings that pupils develop? We hope to continue exploring these issues. In relation to how we can describe the transformation processes related to powerful knowledge and epistemic quality though, we suggest that the material-dialogic frame already highlights the need to move past representational accounts. Instead, it allows us to consider how pupils learn through being entangled within phenomena, which emerge from teacher intentions, understandings, pedagogical strategies and the materials within specific classrooms.

References

Bakhtin, M. M., Holquist, M. and Emerson, C. (1986), *Speech Genres and Other Late Essays*, Texas: University of Texas Press.
Barad, K. (2003), 'Posthumanist Performativity: Toward an Understanding of How Matter Comes to Matter', *Signs: Journal of Women in Culture and Society*, 28 (3): 801–31. https://doi.org/10.1086/345321

Barad, K. (2007), *Meeting the Universe Halfway–Quantum Physics and The Entanglement of Matter and Meaning*. London: Duke University Press.
Barsalou, L. W. (2008), 'Grounded Cognition', *Annual Review of Psychology*, 59: 617–45.
Bernstein, B. (1973), *On the Classification and Framing of Educational Knowledge*, London: Tavistock.
Billingsley, B. and Hardman, M. A. (2017), 'Epistemic Insight: Teaching and Learning about the Nature of Science in Real-World and Multidisciplinary Arenas', *School Science Review*, 98 (365): 57–8.
Callinan, C. (2014), *Constructing Scientific Knowledge in the Classroom: A Multimodal Analysis of Conceptual Change and the Significance of Gesture* (unpublished PhD), University of Leicester.
Carlson, C., Jacobs, S. A., Perry, M. and Church, R. B. (2014), 'The Effect of Gestured Instruction on the Learning of Physical Causality Problems', *Gesture*, 14 (1): 26–45. https://doi.org/10.1075/gest.14.1.02car
Chevallard, Y. (2007), 'Readjusting Didactics to a Changing Epistemology', *European Educational Research Journal*, 6 (2): 131–4. https://doi.org/10.2304/eerj.2007.6.2.131
Coole, D. and Frost, S., eds (2010), *New Materialisms–Ontology, Agency, and Politics*, London: Duke University Press.
diSessa, A. (2006), 'A History of Conceptual Change Research: Threads and Fault Lines', in K. Sawyer (ed.), *The Cambridge Handbook of the Learning Sciences*, 265–82, Cambridge: Cambridge University Press.
Duit, R. (2013), 'Model of Educational Reconstruction', in R. Gunstone (ed.), *Encyclopedia of Science Education*, 1–3, Netherlands: Springer. https://doi.org/10.1007/978-94-007-6165-0_157-1
Gericke, N., Hudson, B., Olin-Scheller, C. and Stolare, M. (2018), 'Powerful Knowledge, Transformations and the Need for Empirical Studies across School Subjects', *London Review of Education*, 16 (3): 428–44. https://doi.org/10.18546/LRE.16.3.06
Gilbert, J. and Justi, R. (2016), *Modelling-based Teaching in Science Education*, New York: Springer.
Hardman, M. A. (2017), 'Models, Matter and Truth in Doing and Learning Science', *School Science Review*, 98 (365): 91–8.
Hardman, M. A. (2019), 'Ghosts in the Curriculum–Reframing Concepts as Multiplicities', *Journal of Philosophy of Education*, 53 (2): 273–92. https://doi.org/10.1111/1467-9752.12339
Hetherington, L. and Wegerif, R. (2018), 'Developing a Material-Dialogic Approach to Pedagogy to Guide Science Teacher Education', *Journal of Education for Teaching*, 44 (1): 27–43. https://doi.org/10.1080/02607476.2018.1422611
Hetherington, L., Hardman, M., Noakes, J. and Wegerif, R. (2018), 'Making the Case for a Material-Dialogic Approach to Science Education', *Studies in Science Education*, 54 (2): 141–76. https://doi.org/10.1080/03057267.2019.1598036
Hudson, B. (2018), 'Powerful Knowledge and Epistemic Quality in School Mathematics', *London Review of Education*, 16 (3): 384–97. https://doi.org/10.18546/LRE.16.3.03

Hudson, B. (2019) 'Epistemic Quality for Equitable Access to Quality Education in School Mathematics', *Journal of Curriculum Studies*, 51 (4): 437–56. https://doi.org/10.1080/00220272.2019.1618917

Jackson, P. L., Meltzoff, A. N. and Decety, J. (2006), 'Neural Circuits Involved in Imitation and Perspective-Taking', *NeuroImage*, 31: 429–39.

Johnson-Glenberg, M. C. and Megowan-Romanowicz, C. (2017), 'Embodied Science and Mixed Reality: How Gesture and Motion Capture Affect Physics Education', *Cognitive Research: Principles and Implications*, 2 (1). https://doi.org/10.1186/s41235-017-0060-9

Knuuttila, T. (2011), 'Modelling and Representing: An Artefactual Approach to Model-Based Representation', *Model-Based Representation in Scientific Practice*, 42 (2): 262–71. https://doi.org/10.1016/j.shpsa.2010.11.034

Mazzei, L. A. (2014), 'Beyond an Easy Sense: A Diffractive Analysis', *Qualitative Inquiry*, 20 (6): 742–6. https://doi.org/10.1177/1077800414530257

Mercer, N. and Howe, C. (2012), 'Explaining the Dialogic Processes of Teaching and Learning: The Value and Potential of Sociocultural Theory', *Learning, Culture and Social Interaction*, 1 (1): 12–21. https://doi.org/10.1016/j.lcsi.2012.03.001

Milne, C. and Scantlebury, K. (2019), *Material Practice and Materiality: Too Long Ignored in Science Education*, London: Springer.

Mollenhauer, K. (1983), *Vergessene Zusammenhänge: Über Kultur und Erziehung*, München: Juventa.

Ongstad, S. (2006), *Fag og didaktikk i lærerutdanning: kunnskap i grenseland*, Oslo: Universitetsforlaget.

Osberg, D. and Biesta, G. J. J. (2004), 'Complexity, Knowledge and the Incalculable: Epistemological and Pedagogical Implications of "Strong Emergence"', *Proceedings of the 2004 Complexity Science and Educational Research Conference. 30 September – 3 October*, 207–27.

Osberg, D., Biesta, G. and Cilliers, P. (2008), 'From Representation to Emergence: Complexity's Challenge to the Epistemology of Schooling', *Educational Philosophy and Theory*, 40 (1): 213–27.

Osborne, J. F. (1996), 'Beyond Constructivism', *Science Education*, 80 (1): 53–82. https://doi.org/10.1002/(SICI)1098-237X(199601)80:1<53::AID-SCE4>3.0.CO;2-1

Riordan, J.-P. (2014), *Riordan J P 2014 Techniques, Tactics and Strategies for Conceptual Change in School Science*, PhD thesis, Canterbury Christ Church University.

Riordan, J.-P. (2020), 'A Method and Framework for Video-Based Pedagogy Analysis', *Research in Science and Technological Education*, 1–23. https://doi.org/10.1080/02635143.2020.1776243

Riordan, J.P., Hardman, M. & Cumbers, D. (2021) 'Pedagogy Analysis Framework: a video-based tool for combining teacher, pupil & researcher perspectives', *Research in Science & Technological Education*, doi:10.1080/02635143.2021.1972960

Taylor, K. L. and Dionne, J. P. (2000), 'Accessing Problem-Solving Strategy Knowledge: The Complementary Use of Concurrent Verbal Protocols and Retrospective Debriefing', *Journal of Educational Psychology*, 92 (3): 413–25.

Tytler, R., Prain, V. and Hubber, P., eds (2013), *Constructing Representations to Learn in Science*, Rotterdam: Sense Publications.

Wegerif, R. (2011), 'Towards a Dialogic Theory of How Children Learn to Think', *Thinking Skills and Creativity*, 6 (3): 179–90. https://doi.org/10.1016/j.tsc.2011.08.002

Young, M. (2011), 'The Return to Subjects: A Sociological Perspective on the UK Coalition Government's Approach to the 14–19 Curriculum', *The Curriculum Journal*, 22 (2): 265–78. https://doi.org/10.1080/09585176.2011.574994

10

Investigating the Nature of Powerful Knowledge and Epistemic Quality in Education for Sustainable Development

Per Sund and Niklas Gericke

Introduction

In this chapter, the concept of powerful knowledge is studied by using the concept of *transformation* as a key concept to describe the different characteristics of powerful knowledge in educational content relating to education for sustainable development (ESD). The concept of transformation takes the didactization of disciplinary subject area knowledge into consideration, that is, how it is transformed into something that is teachable in lower secondary school cross-curricular settings (Gericke et al. 2018).

This empirical study focuses on how the concept of powerful knowledge can be understood and characterized in the context of teachers' discussions from three different subject areas when addressing the same thematic topic of sustainable development (SD). As the content of SD draws from multiple disciplines addressing the environment, society and the economy, powerful knowledge covering this topic thus needs to be drawn from different disciplines. Based on teachers' descriptions of the possible contributions from their own school subjects in cross-curricular collaborations, the aim is to identify what constitutes transformed powerful knowledge of ESD. In the Swedish context, teachers of the three subject areas of science, social science and language often collaborate when it comes to ESD at the lower secondary school level and are therefore the target of this study in which we use empirical data gathered in an earlier study (Sund and Gericke 2020).

The general aim of the study is to explore what teacher teams can generate in terms of educational content related to ESD. More specifically, the study aims to identify the potential for generating powerful knowledge in such cross-curricular collaborations. The research question guiding the study is: *What are the specific educational content contributions of different subject areas, such as science, social science and language, when enacting the curriculum theme of ESD in cross-curricular settings?* The results of each subject's unique contributions are used to discuss the nature and transformation of powerful knowledge in ESD. The unique contributions from all three subject areas combined show the nature of the increase in epistemic quality for enhancing action competence. In this way, the study mainly addresses the second research question of the KOSS programme (see Chapter 1), that is, how can the transformation processes related to powerful knowledge and epistemic quality be described? But, the first KOSS programme question is also addressed: How can the nature of powerful knowledge and epistemic quality in different school subjects be characterized?

Background

Powerful knowledge

The notion of *powerful knowledge* relates to the conceptual knowledge to which the teaching should be oriented. The idea of powerful knowledge was introduced by Young (2009) as a curriculum principle. While discussing the question of which knowledge pupils are entitled to have access to, he argues that 'in all fields of enquiry, there is better knowledge, more reliable knowledge, knowledge nearer the truth about the world we live in and to what it is to be human' (Young 2013: 107). This knowledge is specialized in terms of the boundaries between disciplines and subjects that define their focus and objects of study. Powerful knowledge differentiates from the experiences that pupils bring to school or older learners bring to college or university. It is also stressed that this differentiation is expressed in the conceptual boundaries between school knowledge and everyday knowledge (Young 2015). Hence, Young's definition of powerful knowledge has a curriculum theory perspective and is viewed as a curriculum principle that ignores how it should be dealt with in the classroom, which Young considers as a pedagogic problem more than a curriculum-based problem (Young 2015: 97). From a European tradition of Didaktik theory, Gericke and colleagues (2018) argue against this dichotomization between curriculum and pedagogy and instead emphasize the need to relate to teaching and learning. Many of the outcomes of teaching activities not only depend on the knowledge that is taught and the teacher, but also on the learner, teacher groups, the school and society. Accordingly, since the relationships between content, teachers and pupils are central in the Didaktik tradition, curriculum principles from a Didaktik perspective therefore need to consider these aspects. As a consequence, Gericke et al. (2018) re-conceptualize powerful knowledge as being understood at three levels: societal, institutional and individual levels, as different versions of transformed powerful knowledge. In this study, we draw on this definition and investigate powerful knowledge at the individual level in relation to how teachers of different subject areas can teach powerful knowledge of ESD together in cross-curricular collaborations.

Epistemic quality

The term 'epistemic' is concerned with the knowledge that is involved in a teaching and learning situation. In turn, the concept *epistemic quality* has been developed by Brian Hudson in various articles and refers to the quality of what pupils learn, make sense of and are able to accomplish in the teaching and learning situation (e.g. Hudson 2016, 2019). The concept of epistemic quality, like that of 'transformation', has been developed in the European field of Didaktik research, albeit with a specific focus on mathematics education. Hudson describes epistemic quality as a way of distinguishing a notion of mathematics as fallible and as including aspects of creativity, uncertainty and reasoning that can generate multiple solutions, that is, being of high quality. This is in contrast to mathematical fundamentalism where knowledge is seen as infallible, authoritarian and dogmatic, that is, of low epistemic quality. In ESD, we claim that epistemic qualities show the complexity of these issues. There are rarely simple answers to sustainability issues such as climate change or the fair and equal distribution of natural resources. An increase in epistemic quality in this study is understood as an increase in pupils' qualitative possibilities to understand and work with complex sustainability issues. More and different qualitative aspects in teaching (content, context, values, methods, role of pupils, purposes) generate a higher epistemic quality in the educational content that pupils encounter in the classroom activities.

Transformation

Individual school subjects are not simple reductions of an overarching discipline. Educational content knowledge is always *transformed* to fit the educational purpose of teaching (Gericke et al. 2018). *Transformation* is defined as an integrative process in which disciplinary knowledge is transformed into knowledge that is taught in school. In Didaktik theory, *what, how* and *why* are integrative in the sense that they cannot stand alone in a teaching context. It is therefore a relational model that stresses the interdependence of the variables (Klafki 1995; see e.g. Bladh, Stolare and Kristiansson (2018) for a discussion about these matters). In this study, and in line with this tradition, we consider that together they generate what can be referred to as the *educational content* (Sund 2008) that pupils encounter in their activities at school. In this chapter, we study the concept of *powerful knowledge* empirically in the three given school subject areas in terms of its transformation from curriculum to pedagogy and address the *why* question ('why teach') in addition to the *what* and *how* questions.

The concept of powerful knowledge and the transformation processes of the educational content must be understood in a wider societal context. The compilers of curriculum often claim that it needs to address contemporary societal challenges. In such cases, transformation often relates to interdisciplinary topics like climate change or consumption. Questions which then emerge are: How should interdisciplinary topics such as ESD be taught and organized in school? What constitutes powerful knowledge in such topics? These questions are addressed later in the chapter.

Transformation is here understood as a process of forming educational knowledge as stated in the curriculum based on a collaborative teaching context. The transformation processes take place in the education system at the individual (teacher level), at the institutional level in teacher groups (school level) – both of which are affected by the changes and challenges on the societal level (Gericke et al. 2018). In contemporary schooling, teachers are strongly affected by different transformation pressures from the societal level, such as the media and global discussions about climate change (Sund, Gericke and Bladh 2020). Hence, the school subject and what is taught in school are not only a direct transformation of the discipline but also a result of other transformation processes. ESD, for example, is a topic that is highly influenced by the different transformation processes of various subject teachers. Transformation is therefore understood as part of an integrative, didactical process in school (Hudson 2016).

Interdisciplinary/multidisciplinary or cross-curricular (in compulsory school) issues like ESD are very important for society. This makes ESD a suitable context for empirical research on the concept of powerful knowledge, which aims to empower learners to become informed citizens. An important question to address is whether knowledge that is linked to different school subjects/ subject areas and relates to the same cross-curricula topic (e.g. sustainability) is powerful or not. If powerful knowledge relating to a theme differs greatly between different school subjects, it would provide strong support for the idea that powerful knowledge is specialized and discipline bound, and that teachers of different subjects with different educational content should work together in cross-curricular collaborative settings. Hence, it is important to have a comparative perspective when researching powerful knowledge, investigate the relationships between the content-specific and more generic features of teaching (the educational content) and see how they occur and differ in various subject areas. It is also important to explore how powerful knowledge is manifested in teachers' collaborations by using a research framework that takes account of the didactical questions of *what, how* and *why* in relation to ESD. To understand the concept of powerful knowledge empirically, the research should not only include curriculum principles but also focus on the role that teachers play in the transformation and enactment process towards ESD, as in the theory of Didaktik (Klafki 2000). We address this process here by studying the differences and similarities in the teachers' descriptions of the teaching dimensions of *what, how* and *why* in order to discern how their subject areas contribute to cross-curricular ESD teaching. These dimensions are widely recognized in European educational research relating to subject specialization (i.e. Hopmann 2007; Sjøberg 2009) and are outlined by Klafki as a way of discerning teachers' instructional approaches. In teaching practice they are inseparable (Klafki 1995), but in this chapter we investigate them separately as analytical units in teachers' discussions about ESD. The *what* dimension focuses on ESD-related subject matter and abilities, the *how* focuses on the methods and the collaborations and influences outside the local school context that are made use of in the teaching, while the *why* focuses on the teachers' starting points and long-term purposes for their ESD teaching.

Education for sustainable development and action competence

All teachers need to address sustainability in one way or another due to the contemporary global threats currently facing humankind (Wals and Kieft 2010). According to the Swedish curriculum (Education 2011) for the 9-year compulsory school (13–16 years), teachers in all subjects and subject areas are expected to teach and promote SD. This is often done by teachers individually, in accordance with the ESD approach that is stressed in UN policy documents (UNESCO 2017). From this policy perspective, SD is often understood as a concept embracing the environment, the economy and society. A Venn diagram is often used to represent SD (see Figure 10.1). This consists of three circles symbolizing the dimensions that overlap each other with a joint area in the centre, which is a suitable way of operationalizing SD as the work can easily be structured in each of the three areas (e.g. Gough 2002). However, the model has been criticized for many reasons. First, the equal size of the three circles does not generally represent real-life situations. Second, there is a risk that the dimensions will be viewed as separate and facilitate trade-offs between environmental, social and economic perspectives and priorities, thereby prioritizing one dimension at the expense of others (Giddings et al. 2002).

The overall aim of ESD is to support the development of *action competent* citizens (Jensen and Schnack 1997). This is to enable pupils to act in informed ways and participate in debates, discussions and decisions about developmental and future-oriented issues at both a private everyday level and a comprehensive societal level. From a curriculum perspective, it can be said that pupils should develop powerful knowledge that becomes the *powerful knowledge of the learner*, which means that the taught knowledge should empower pupils by providing knowledge of the powerful (Young 2015). Due to the multidisciplinary nature of the topic, this can be done through collaborative work in which all of the dimensions are addressed. Moreover, the teaching should enable pupils to participate in societal change in an informed way, that is, by creating *action competence*.

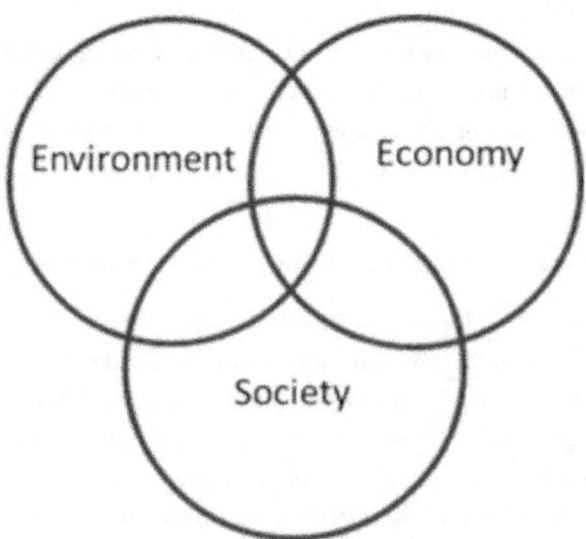

Figure 10.1 Venn diagram representation of SD and its dimensions.

Subject areas

Some school subjects form subject areas, such as science, social science and language, through which common aspects like perspectives, knowledge production or teaching methods enable one person to teach a group of specific subjects. In Sweden, it is common for secondary school teachers to teach between two and four school subjects in any of the major subject areas. For example, science teachers often teach biology, chemistry and mathematics, social science teachers teach civics, history, geography and religion, and language teachers often teach the Swedish language combined with English (second language) or a third language such as German, French or Spanish. This type of subject combination appears to facilitate cross-curricular work (Gericke et al. 2020), which means that, in a Swedish context, it is about collaboration between different subject areas where teachers from different disciplines are expected to work together on complex thematic issues, such as sustainability.

One important starting point for this study concerning powerful knowledge is that different subject areas have different *educational content*. For example, social science teachers have been found to use class discussions more often than science teachers (Oulton, Day, Dillon and Grace 2004). They also tend to use more group discussions, interactive lectures, group research projects, interdisciplinary work and class debates than science and language teachers (Borg, Gericke, Höglund and Bergman 2012). These studies imply that teachers of different subject areas address the didactical questions of what, why and how differently, that is, they tend to pursue different teaching traditions. This was also confirmed in a large-scale study of upper secondary school teachers in Sweden (Borg et al. 2012). In this study, we pursue the issue further by investigating what kind of educational content science, social science and language teachers contribute to the curriculum theme of ESD.

Work in cross-curricular settings

The practical cross-curricular work (MacMath 2011) between these three groups may be understood as *co-operation, collaboration* and *overlapping collaboration*. We visualize them in the different Venn diagrams shown in Figure 10.2. In the first, three subject areas cooperate on a common theme, SD, but through their educational content offer pupils specific knowledge, teaching methods and perspectives. In this way, the teachers contribute their respective disciplinary content, perspectives, methods and skills to provide a broad and holistic educational content that is suitable for ESD. However, as the content does not overlap, it is difficult for pupils to relate the subject-area perspectives to each other, and it is up to the individual pupil to fuse the perspectives together into a learning content. In a *collaboration*, some parts are common to all three subject areas (e.g. topics such as recycling and climate change), whereas others are specific subject-area-content contributions to ESD. This can be considered as an ideal model for cross-curricular work because the different subject areas complement each other holistically and at the same time address the commonalities in the content and methods to facilitate pupils' meaning making. In the third type, *overlapping collaboration*, all the subject areas cover the same ESD educational content in a similar way of teaching, which would be quite pointless. We therefore argue that collaboration has the potential to provide powerful knowledge of the highest epistemic quality because it creates a common ground for the learner while simultaneously providing unique and different disciplinary aspects of the different subject areas.

What, how and why – analysis of educational content

Subject content issues (*what*) in sustainability are often at the centre while describing the transformation processes. But what happens to the educational content if the teaching methods and purposes also change in the transformation process? In order to answer this question, a study of the taught content

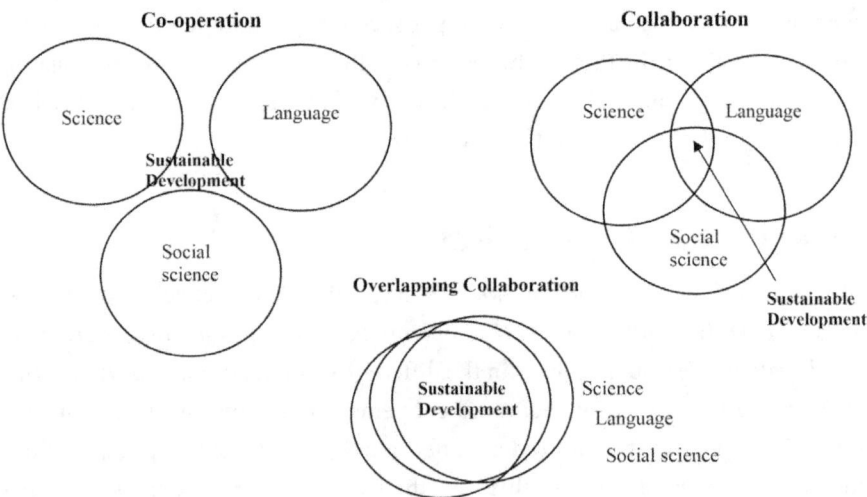

Figure 10.2 Different ways of organizing cross-curricular work.

knowledge also needs to include values and the abilities that are practised along with the content knowledge (Munby and Roberts 1998). For this purpose, a theoretical framework is required that considers how the various teaching and learning approaches used in cross-curricular settings could influence the overall *educational content* that pupils can be expected to encounter in ESD. The aspects of *what, how* and *why* are therefore used as analytical units to discern the educational content of ESD (Sund 2008).

The starting point for this study is that the knowledge traditions and epistemologies of different subjects are diverse and influence the ways content is both selected (the *what* and *why* questions) and taught (the *how* question). The overall purpose of this research is to study how powerful knowledge in cross-curricular settings is manifested in different subject areas. By making comparisons between the subject areas, it is possible to discern the uniqueness of each area's educational content contributions (powerful knowledge) to ESD in the classroom (Gericke et al. 2020).

In this study, we are interested in cross-curricular work of science, social science and language teachers in lower secondary school regarding ESD, which is why we study the specific contributions from each subject area. We also assume that *powerful knowledge* is the specific educational knowledge contribution from each area, while *epistemic quality* is formed by the combined unique contributions of each subject area together. In *collaborative* work, it seems to be possible for three subject areas to together create an educational content with additional quality that single subject areas cannot achieve alone. In this study, we call this additional combined quality *high epistemic quality* of the educational content that can help learners to become more powerful and ESD action competent.

Aim of the empirical exploratory study

The overall aim of the study is to understand the kind of educational content related to ESD that cross-curricular teacher teams can generate. Since cross-curricular ESD collaboration is stated in the curriculum as important, it is about finding the potential in the teachers' responses for generating powerful knowledge in cross-curricular collaborations.

The different characteristics of powerful knowledge that are generated in different subject areas is one focus. These characteristics are studied by the three didactical dimensions of what, how and why, which together show the transformation in each subject area into ESD educational content. Another focus is to compare the different characteristics of powerful knowledge and discern how they together can increase the overall epistemic quality of the educational content and enhance collaborative ESD work. The educational content of a collaborative ESD teaching approach could make it easier to develop competencies that support pupils' informed societal actions. The research question is:

What are the specific educational content contributions of different subject areas, such as science, social science and language, when enacting the curriculum theme of ESD in cross-curricular settings?

Methodology

In order to answer the research question, discussions about the possible contributions of science, social science and language to ESD were held with lower secondary school teachers (years 7–9) from five schools in two municipalities in mid-Sweden.

Selection of the teachers

Teacher groups from the subject areas of science (chemistry, biology and physics), social science (civics, history, geography and religion) and language (Swedish [mother tongue], second language [English] and third language [German, French and Spanish]) were contacted in the five secondary schools. We asked the principals to assess the availability of the teachers in the different subject areas. The teachers grouped themselves into 10 teacher groups according to school and subject area. The groups were quite homogenous in terms of teaching experience, professional background and knowledge about cross-curricular work.

Group discussion and procedure

The group discussions were guided by specific questions connected to the what, how and why dimensions (see below) and developed into more open discussions about the different aspects of collaborative work. The didactical dimensions of *what, how* and *why* were used to shed light on the transformation from curriculum to taught knowledge and educational content. The group discussions were filmed and fully transcribed before being analysed.

Phase 1

In this phase, the aim was to gather data from the individual teachers in each group before the group discussion started. After the introduction, the teachers were asked to individually, through silent reflection, write down their responses on post-it notes to the question: *How do you think that your science/social science/ language teaching contributes to the implementation of sustainable development in your school?*

Phase 2

The aim in this phase was to gather data from the teachers' discussions without any interference from the discussion leader. Here, the teachers discussed and categorized their written responses on post-it notes. Each group explained their responses to each other and stuck their post-it notes on the board.

Phase 3

In this phase, the aim was to gather data about how the teachers worked. This was done by asking them about their practices in relation to ESD, and how this had changed the educational content (in an overarching sense including *what* and *why*) in the last 10 years due to the latest curriculum reform of 2011 that included ESD and cross-curricula work.

Data analysis

The data relating to the teachers' arguments about their contributions to ESD in phases 1 and 2 constitute the data for the *what* dimension. The data from phase 3 were used to analyse the how-dimension. In both of these analyses, five analytical questions about important educational aspects of ESD were used (Sund 2008):

1) Why are environmental issues important?
2) What does the teaching aim to change?
3) What kind of inter-human relations are established?
4) How useful is school knowledge in environmental and development issues?
5) What role do pupils play in education and environmental work?

The data transcripts from all three *phases* constitute the data for the *why* dimension. Analytically, we identified the *why* dimension by looking for objects of responsibility (Sund and Wickman 2008). These form a coherent context for long-term purposes, which in this study is seen as an illustration of what the teacher group regarded as the most important reasons for enacting ESD. These results were first summarized for each teacher group and then for each subject area in order to answer the question: *What does this teacher group, in this specific subject area, really value together when discussing their ESD teaching?*

Results – didactical dimensions in three subject areas

For each subject area the result is presented together as a summary of *what*, *how* and *why* in order to form a common picture of the educational content contribution to ESD from each of the separate subject areas. For a more detailed analysis and extensive presentation of the results, see Sund and Gericke (2020).

The educational content of ESD in science

In the interviews with the four teacher groups in the subject area of science, their educational content contribution to ESD work mainly consisted of topics connected to the environmental dimension, such as eutrophication, radiation and global warming. The *what* aspect mainly consisted of ecological issues that reflected a lack of knowledge and could be solved by learning more science. The content focused on the subject knowledge, and the pedagogical task was to teach the pupils factual and conceptual knowledge that would enable them to take proper decisions and carry out the right actions. The *how* related to teacher-centred methods, which did not give pupils many opportunities to develop communicative abilities such as analysis or critical thinking. The *why*, or the purpose of ESD, was to offer pupils a scientifically factual foundation that would enable them to make good individual decisions.

The educational content of ESD in social science

In the interviews with the three teacher groups in the social science subject area, the teachers regarded ESD issues as conflicts between human interests, such as unfair global distribution of resources. Environmental problems and developmental challenges were more politically and morally oriented than just learning factual knowledge. This indicated that these were political issues. The *what* was value and ability oriented. Although social science includes the entire spectrum of ESD dimensions, in the interviews the ecological dimension was mentioned, but the focus was on the social dimension. The economic dimension was mentioned in relation to world trade, mainly in terms of economic growth being a threat to sustainability. Given that ESD is anthropocentrically oriented, human interests and developments were in focus. The politically based perspective of ESD emphasizes the importance of democracy in the classroom activity and *the how* aspect was covered by regular participation in group activities. Pupils were encouraged to develop their individual abilities, develop an action competence and engage in democratic discussions about the development of a more sustainable society or world. The *why* of education was to strengthen each pupil in relation to other people.

The educational content of ESD in language

Three teacher groups were interviewed in the subject area of language. The language teachers' contribution was to support the collaboration between science and social science regarding reading, writing and presenting. Here, the ESD-related content primarily concerned values, recycling and when people's lifestyles and their consequences were regarded as threats to the natural world. Scientific knowledge was regarded as prescriptive and used to indicate the best ways of living. This view resembled those communicated by the media and adopted by the pupils and included discussions about the economic dimension being important for achieving sustainability. The development of a more environmentally friendly society was unambiguous, in that it was thought that having the right knowledge would lead to people having better values and behaving in ecologically correct ways. The *what* was a mixture of language abilities, such as reading and writing, and normative value-laden statements from science and social science about how to live 'ecologically more right'. The methods, *the how*, were quite teacher centred. This was evident in their discussions about the threats and possibilities with digitalization, and the desire to regain teacher control. The *why*, the purpose, is students' identity-making and communication with other people.

Comparisons – discerning powerful knowledge and epistemic quality

In order to make the potential contributions of the educational content more visible in each subject area, we conducted a comparative analysis of the groups and of the common and specific contributions from each subject area. These are visually represented in Figure 10.3. The circles represent the contribution of educational content from the didactical dimensions for each subject area of ESD (*what, how* and *why*). The overlap of the circles represents commonalities, that is, where the different subject area teachers address similar issues, and represents possible starting points for collaboration in cross-curricular work. The areas where there is no overlap represent content that is only addressed in one subject area and is that area's unique ESD educational content contribution, that is, the *powerful knowledge* from that specific subject area.

Unique contributions from each subject area

The specific educational content from science was primarily scientific facts, a *what*, that were mainly related to the environmental dimension, such as the consequences of energy use and production, eutrophication, radiation and global warming (I) (Figure 10.3). The *how* was a transmissive type of teacher-centred teaching where science knowledge and abilities were the main aims. The purpose, the *why*, was to teach the pupils valuable content (what) that they would then automatically use to solve environmental problems such as climate change. Social science offered a *what* in the social perspective of ESD concerning social justice, international relations, politics, trade and peace. Social science specifically offered a *how* that differed from the teaching methods in science (II), for example, through critical investigation work and frequent group discussions about the consequences of climate change and social justice for other people and cultures. The language teachers did not have a disciplinary ESD-related content to offer, but often used common media content such as news and nature TV channels, a *what*, that was assumed to be close to the pupils' everyday lives. The *how* was teacher-centred, where ICT tools were important. The language teachers' main educational content contribution to ESD was driven by their long-term purpose, the *why*-dimension, concerning pupils' personal development, which enabled them to participate in the general development of society (III).

To summarize, the specific contributions and *character of powerful knowledge* from science is scientific knowledge, *a what* (I). Social science can contribute with social justice, international relations, politics and trade that is often manifested in the classroom as group discussions and reflections, *a what and a how* (II). Language contributes with an aim of making the educational content of ESD meaningful by identity making, self-esteem and personal development, *a why* (III). Accordingly, the three subject areas are seen to complement each other in the didactical dimensions of ESD.

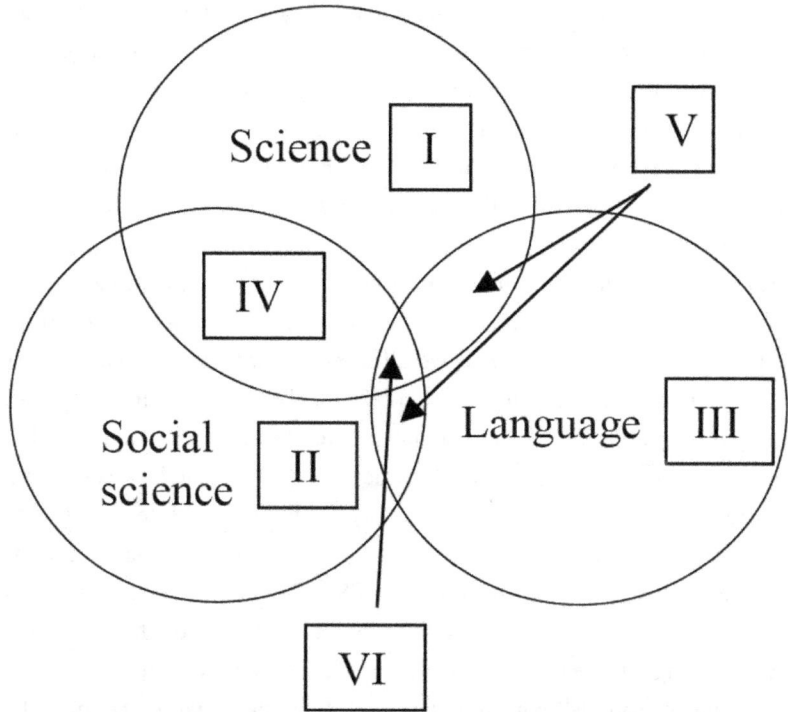

Figure 10.3 The representation shows the different subject areas' contributions of educational content to ESD.

Starting point for ESD collaboration – common contributions

The teachers from the science and social science subject areas could collaborate in ESD teaching by means of curricular commonalities and educational content since both of these areas focus on the use of natural resources, energy production and environmental degradation (segment IV) (Figure 10.3). As language teachers offer an everyday view of ESD content, such as recycling, healthy food and lifestyle issues, a common contribution in the subject area tradition could be reading and writing tools that enhance the ESD collaboration for all three subject areas (V). In segment (VI), there are some overall commonalities in ESD educational content, such as societal discussions about recycling, climate change, activism and organic food.

Discussion

The results show there is potential for *collaborations* between teachers from the three different subject areas in cross-curricular work on ESD. Science and social science teachers seem to be able to work closely together on relevant ESD content that is supported by the core content in the curriculum, and language teachers can offer important complementary media perspectives. There is some overlap (see Figures 10.1 and 10.3), mainly concerning the *what* dimension, which means there are good possibilities to establish collaborative cross-curricular work between teachers from the subject areas of science, social science and language.

The unique contributions of educational content – *powerful knowledge* – from the subject areas differ in character. Three unique contributions, one from each subject area, are connected to three different didactical dimensions. Science teachers primarily contribute scientific facts about things like biodiversity, toxicology and radiation (*what*). Social science teachers contribute with facts related to the social and economic dimension of SD such as social justice, international relations, politics and trade (*what*), but also with teaching methods like group discussions, analysis and debates (*how*) as a way of enhancing students' abilities regarding political discussions in ESD. This *how* creates a value-laden educational content for ESD related to social justice and global citizenship education. Language teachers (mainly second languages) contribute with the development of pupils' communications, their personal development and identity-making (*why*). The results show that the nature of powerful knowledge can have different characteristics in different subject areas and that collaboration can be a way of offering pupils powerful knowledge that embraces all three didactical dimensions. These results show that, besides being understood as a curriculum principle (Young 2015), powerful knowledge can also be used as a concept in empirical studies based on theoretical standpoints from the Didaktik tradition.

Language teachers' work on pupils' identity-making and self-esteem has not been identified in previous studies. Further, the findings are in line with two large-scale studies previously carried out with over 3,000 upper secondary school teachers (Borg, Gericke, Höglund and Bergman 2012, 2014), which showed that language teachers were more positive towards economic growth (Borg et al. 2014). This may be understood as language teachers being part of the discussions at a societal level through media coverage, where economic growth is part of the media discourse. Science and social science teachers are more directly connected to ESD through the core content in national curriculum. This curriculum content is more rooted in disciplinary critical traditions, which, for example, problematize economic growth (Munby and Roberts 1998).

Stables and Scott (2002) argue that only the most highly motivated teachers engage with ideas or frameworks outside their own disciplines. This might explain why closer collaborations between science and social science teachers are more likely to occur. Both subject areas are familiar with ESD from a knowledge perspective in their curricula, while language teachers do not really see themselves as an obvious part of this type of cross-curricular collaboration. In this study, the language teachers' sense of a lack of relevance to ESD gives the subject area a weak framing (Bernstein 1999) of the content through which a media view of SD can dominate and replace the subject tradition. This means that language offers a broader view of SD than science and social science, which might be more connected with what pupils encounter in the societal discourse around ESD. A weaker framing of the subject area in relation to ESD also means that language teachers can embrace all of the ESD dimensions simultaneously (environment, social and economic). On the other hand, science and social science teachers can offer deeper and more critical perspectives on the content knowledge, which from a pupil perspective may need to be complemented by a public media view of SD. In that way, language teachers could link different ESD perspectives to provide a link between the societal discourse through the media of ESD to more critical standpoints, such as those provided by the science and social science teachers. For example, Summers, Corney and Childs (2004) showed that science teachers have a relatively narrow understanding of ESD that is closely connected to the discipline. The weak framing allows the language teachers in this study to focus more on the boundary between school knowledge and everyday knowledge, whilst the science and social science groups reflect (in differing ways) on the boundary between disciplines and subjects. Language teachers can thereby make an important contribution to cross-curricular teaching.

The results of this study show that the different subject areas can complement each other in the cross-curricular work of ESD. They also indicate that the teachers of these subject areas transform ESD into a teaching practice differently, as hypothesized by Gericke and colleagues (2018). For example, the science and social science teachers seem to transform aspects of ESD according to their scholarly disciplinary traditions, that is, science teachers on science facts and social science teachers on the dichotomy between individual responsibility (action competence) and political responsibility. The transformation in science is quite limited and close to the discipline, and most of the facts are explicitly described in the national curriculum as core content. The social science teachers' transformation is more complex in that they transform the curriculum content concerning democracy and political issues by repoliticizing the policy level of ESD in the curricula into educational situations in which the pupils' roles and discussions are important, as discussed by Sund and Öhman (2018). Language teachers seem to transform ESD directly from the media, that is, from a non-disciplinary discourse. However, language may also transform the general values in the curriculum into a teaching purpose of meaningfulness and personal development.

One way of understanding the nature of powerful knowledge in teaching situations is through the type of knowledge that is uniquely contributed from each subject area. That contribution is a powerful contribution of knowledge from that specific subject area. The contribution of powerful knowledge from a combination of three different areas makes it possible to also understand the nature of the concept of epistemic quality in collaborations. Here, epistemic quality is understood as the quality in educational content that one subject area itself is not capable of offering to pupils in thematic teaching such as ESD. Increased epistemic quality in ESD teaching occurs when pupils are offered powerful knowledge consisting of the three different characteristics simultaneously. Based on these findings, we argue that the differences in the characteristics of powerful knowledge in combination hold a greater potential to provide a holistic ESD of high epistemic quality in collaborative cross-curricular work than when ESD is only taught in one or two subject areas independently. For ESD teaching, this means that in the process of developing pupils' *action competence* for sustainability (Jensen 2002) this type of collaboration is likely to make it easier for pupils to learn powerful knowledge and to use that knowledge, that is, thus becoming 'knowledge of the powerful'. Action competence in this study context is one way of working towards the capacity to empower pupils that Young (2015) discusses in relation to the need to focus on powerful knowledge in education.

Acknowledgements

This research was supported by ROSE (Research on Subject-specific Education), Karlstad University.

References

Bernstein, B. (1999), 'Vertical and Horizontal Discourse: An Essay', *British Journal of Sociology of Education*, 20 (2): 157–73.

Bladh, G., Stolare, M. and Kristiansson, M. (2018), 'Curriculum Principles, Didactic Practice and Social Issues: Thinking Through Teachers' Knowledge Practices in Collaborative Work', *London Review of Education*, 16 (3): 398–413.

Borg, C., Gericke, N., Höglund, H. and Bergman, E. (2012), 'The Barriers Encountered by Teachers Implementing Education for Sustainable Development: Discipline Bound Differences and Teaching Traditions', *Research in Science and Technological Education*, 30 (2): 185–207.

Borg, C., Gericke, N., Höglund, H. and Bergman, E. (2014), 'Subject- and Experience-Bound Differences in Teachers' Conceptual Understanding of Sustainable Development', *Environmental Education Research*, 20 (4): 526–51.

Education, T. S. N. A. f. (2011), *Curriculum for the Compulsory School, Preschool Class and the Leisure-time Centre 2011*. Retrieved from https://www.skolverket.se/publikationsserier/styrdokument/2018/curriculum-for-the-compulsory-school-preschool-class-and-school-age-educare-revised-2018?id=3984

Gericke N., Huang L., Knippels MC., Christodoulou A., Van Dam F. and Gasparovic S. (2020), 'Environmental Citizenship in Secondary Formal Education: The Importance of Curriculum and Subject Teachers', in Hadjichambis A. et al. (eds), *Conceptualizing Environmental Citizenship for 21st Century Education*, 193–212, Environmental Discourses in Science Education, Vol 4. Cham: Springer.

Gericke, N., Hudson, B., Olin-Scheller, C. and Stolare, M. (2018), 'Powerful Knowledge, Transformations and the Need for Empirical Studies across School Subjects', *London Review of Education*, 16 (3): 428–44.

Giddings, B., Hopwood, B. and O'Brien, G. (2002), 'Environment, Economy and Society: Fitting Them Together into Sustainable Development', *Sustainable Development*, 10: 187–196.

Gough, S. (2002), 'Increasing the Value of the Environment: A Real "Options" Metaphor for Learning', *Environmental Education Research*, 8 (1): 61–72.

Hopmann, S. (2007), 'Restrained Teaching: The Common Core of Didaktik', *European Educational Research Journal*, 6 (2): 109–24.

Hudson, B. (2016), 'Didactics', in D. Wyse, L. Hayward and J. Pandya (eds), *The SAGE Handbook of Curriculum, Pedagogy and Assessment*, 107–24, London: Sage Publications.

Hudson, B. (2019) 'Epistemic Quality for Equitable Access to Quality Education in School Mathematics', *Journal of Curriculum Studies*, 51: 24.

Jensen, B. B. (2002), 'Knowledge, Action and Pro-environmental Behaviour', *Environmental Education Research*, 8 (3): 325–34.

Jensen, B. B. and Schnack, K. (1997), 'The Action Competence Approach in Environmental Education', *Environmental Education Research*, 3 (2): 163–78.

Klafki, W. (1995), 'Didactic Analysis as the Core of Preparation for Instruction' (Didaktische Analyse als Kern der Unterrichtsvorbereitung), *Journal of Curriculum Studies*, 27 (1): 13–30.

Klafki, W. (2000) 'Didaktik Analysis and the Core of Preparation of Instruction', in Westbury, I., Hopmann, S. and Riquarts, K. (eds), *Teaching as a Reflective Practice. The German Didaktik tradition*, 139–60, London: Routledge.

MacMath, S. L. (2011), *Teaching and Learning in an Integrated Curriculum Setting: A Case Study of Classroom Practice's* Doctor of Philosophy, University of Toronto.

Munby, H. and Roberts, D. (1998), 'Intellectual Independence: A Potential Link between Science Teaching and Responsible Citizenship', in D. Roberts and L. Östman (eds), *Problems of Meaning in Science Curriculum*, 101–14, New York: Teachers College Press.

Oulton, C., Day, V., Dillon, J. and Grace, M. (2004), 'Controversial Issues – Teachers' Attitudes and Practices in the Context of Citizenship Education', *Oxford Review of Education*, 30 (4): 489–507.

Sjøberg, S. (2009), *Naturvetenskap som allmänbildning: en kritisk ämnesdidaktik*, Lund: Studentlitteratur.

Stables, A. and Scott, W. (2002), 'The Quest for Holism in Education for Sustainable Development', *Environmental Education Research*, 8 (1): 53–60.

Summers, M., Corney, G. and Childs, A. (2004), 'Student Teachers' Conceptions of Sustainable Development: The Starting-Points of Geographers and Scientists', *Educational Research*, 46 (2): 163–82.

Sund, P. (2008), 'Discerning the Extras in ESD Teaching: A Democratic Issue', in J. Öhman (ed.), *Values and Democracy in Education for Sustainable Development – Contributions from Swedish Research*, 57–74, Stockholm: Liber.

Sund, P. and Gericke, N. (2020), 'Teaching Contributions from Secondary School Subject Areas to Education for Sustainable Development – A Comparative Study of Science, Social Science and Language Teachers', *Environmental Education Research*, 26 (6): 772–94.

Sund, P., Gericke, N., and Bladh, G. (2020). Educational content in cross-curricular ESE teaching and a model to discern teacher's teaching traditions. *Journal of Education for Sustainable Development*, 14(1), 78–97.

Sund, L. and Öhman, J. (2018), 'On the Need to Repoliticise Environmental and Sustainability Education: Rethinking the Postpolitical Consensus', in K. Van Poeck, J. A. Lysgaard and A. Reid (eds), *Environmental and Sustainability Education: International Trends, Priorities and Challenges*, 639–659, London and New York: Routledge.

Sund, P. and Wickman, P.-O. (2008), 'Teachers' Objects of Responsibility – Something to Care about in Education for Sustainable Development?', *Environmental Education Research*, 14 (2): 145–63.

UNESCO (2017), *UNESCO Global Action Programme on Education for Sustainable Development*, Paris: UNESCO

Wals, A. and Kieft, G. (2010), *Education for Sustainable Development: Research Overview*, Stockholm: Edita 2010.

Young, M. (2009), 'Education, Globalisation and the "Voice of Knowledge"', *Journal of Education and Work*, 22 (3): 193–204.

Young, M. (2013), 'Overcoming the Crisis in Curriculum Theory: A Knowledge-based Approach', *Journal of Curriculum Studies*, 45 (2): 101–18. doi: http://dx.doi.org/0.1080/00220272.2013.764505

Young, M. (2015), 'Powerful Knowledge as a Curriculum Principle', in M. Young, D. Lambert, C. Roberts, and M. Roberts (eds), *Knowledge and the Future School: Curriculum and Social Justice*, 2nd ed., 65–88, London: Bloomsbury Academic.

11

Trajectories of Epistemic Quality and Powerful Knowledge across School Subjects

Niklas Gericke, Brian Hudson, Christina Olin-Scheller and Martin Stolare

Introduction

In reflecting on the studies outlined in this book, we return to the KOSS research questions with respect to how the nature of powerful knowledge and epistemic quality in different school subjects can be characterized. We also consider how one may describe the transformation processes related to powerful knowledge and epistemic quality. As we do so, we develop a theoretical framework based on the concepts outlined earlier in the volume: *powerful knowledge, transformation processes* and *epistemic quality*. Our ambition with this book, and this chapter in particular, is to help create a common conceptual framework as well as a language for subject-specific research and scholarship as concerns different disciplines and school subjects. In this way, we try to find common ground for use by teachers, scholars and educational researchers interested in subject-specific research.

In this final chapter, we will not once again go over what we already know about powerful knowledge, transformation processes and epistemic quality. Instead, we encourage the reader to read the first chapter of this book (Gericke et al. this volume) to become familiar with that background. Also, much of the analysis in this chapter builds on the other nine chapters in which these concepts are operationalized in empirical studies representing the school subjects of Chemistry, Education for Sustainable Development (cross-curricular teaching), Language (L1 and L2), Mathematics, Physical Education, and Social Studies. Here we address the various studies and conduct further analysis to determine the ways in which these studies inform us about similarities and differences associated with use of the theoretical concepts between and across different school subjects. At the end of the chapter, we propose how the concepts may be described in a common theoretical framework for use across disciplines and school subjects of subject-specific research and scholarship.

At first sight, the studies presented in the various chapters appear quite different, covering a range of aspects of powerful knowledge and epistemic quality for curriculum innovation. Yet, every chapter addresses the KOSS network research questions (see below), drawing on the theoretical framework by using the concepts of *powerful knowledge, transformation processes* and *epistemic quality*. In the next section, we analyse how the studies have operationalized these theoretical concepts, as specified by the two first research questions of KOSS:

1. How can the nature of powerful knowledge and epistemic quality in different school subjects be characterized?
2. How can the transformation processes related to powerful knowledge and epistemic quality be described?

Powerful knowledge and epistemic quality in different school subjects

As discussed in Chapter 1 (Gericke et al. this volume), powerful knowledge is a concept most prominently developed as a curriculum principle by Michael Young (2009, 2015). In this endeavour, he concludes that 'in all fields of enquiry, there is better knowledge, more reliable knowledge, knowledge nearer the truth about the world we live in and to what it is to be human' (Young 2013: 107). Hence, powerful knowledge is a normative concept with the aim to distinguish what is better knowledge in the sense that it provides students with knowledge otherwise inaccessible from their everyday experience. The concept is based on two key characteristics, both expressed in the form of boundaries. First, this knowledge is specialized in how it is produced and transmitted and, second, this specialization is expressed in terms of the boundaries between disciplines and school subjects that serve to define their focus and objects of study. It is stressed that powerful knowledge is not general knowledge and that the boundaries are not fixed and unchangeable (Young 2013). Subsequently, we proposed in a previous article (Gericke et al. 2018) that the way this body of (powerful) knowledge is defined in various school subjects should be an empirical question for subject-specific education research to pursue. Some studies already carried out in this direction include several school subjects like geography (Maude 2018, 2020), physics (Yates and Millar 2016), music (McPhail 2017) and history (Bertram 2019; Chapman 2021; Nordgren 2021). This volume may be seen as a contribution to develop these ambitions further.

The reason for incorporating the *epistemic quality* concept in this work is to further elaborate on powerful knowledge so as to explicitly address the concept's normative aspect. We thereby consider that epistemic quality might be useful as a tool for exploring and describing normativity. Brian Hudson (2016, 2018, 2019) in his previous work has elaborated on this aspect to define epistemic quality in mathematics education. Furthermore, the concept of *quality* has seen extensive use as an analytical tool in much educational research that explicitly tries to measure and distinguish aspects of education due to it being 'better' in the sense of more effective or productive (Cochran-Smith 2003; Croninger, Valli and Chambliss 2012). Therefore, we believe the term *quality* links well with other areas of educational research interested in the normative aspect of teaching, and that use the concept of epistemic quality as a way of introducing the same idea of normativity in subject-specific research.

Powerful knowledge in language education

This chapter brings a comparative perspective on school subjects. We thus highlight similarities and differences in our conceptual framework's expression in the different school subjects. Accordingly, to begin the overview of the contributing chapters we consider the concept of powerful knowledge in language education because four of the nine chapters include language education. In Chapter 4, powerful knowledge is only mentioned twice as an overarching idea that manifests the potential to empower students: 'all pupils will have epistemic access … to powerful knowledge through the curriculum' (Wegner et al. this volume: 59). In the study of migration in mother-tongue textbooks in Chapter 5, Ljung Egeland and Iversen Kulbrandstad (this volume) take their point of departure from Young's claim that '[powerful] knowledge which can provide young people with new ways of thinking about the world' (Young 2009: 110). Furthermore, in their analysis of the textbooks (on page 87) they identify topics that might meet this criterion. They describe possible contributions to powerful knowledge, such as 'discovering new ways of thinking', 'potential invitation to reflect on, generalize and develop identity' and 'becoming action oriented'. The authors focus on what the teaching can do for the students and state that the students should 'explore new worlds'. The analysis revolves around what experiences textbooks provide and what role the textbook offers its readers. Here, these characteristics of the content define whether it is powerful knowledge or not.

In Chapter 6 on the study of reading literature in first language education, Grünthal et al. (this volume) claim the subject specificity of powerful knowledge. However, similarly to Ljung Egeland and Iversen Kulbrandstad, they relate powerful knowledge to the aim to take pupils beyond their existing experiences into the 'unknown'. Moreover, they claim that 'powerful knowledge comprises not just one kind of knowledge but rather a mastery of knowing how different approaches are brought together. Because critical thinking promotes multiliteracy and vice versa' (Grünthal et al. this volume: 102). Thus, in their view powerful knowledge in the area of language and literature relates considerably to skills and methods and that the powerful disciplinary knowledge of 'teachers of L1 needs to be enlarged towards interactional, group-oriented methods of teaching literature' (Grünthal et al. this volume: 106).

In neither of these studies is a conceptual subject-specific content, that is, *knowing that*, defined. Rather, methods, approaches and skills that focus on empowering students are emphasized. Interestingly, the comparative study in Chapter 10 provides similar results. Sund and Gericke (this volume: 190) find that 'language teachers did not have a disciplinary ESD - related content to offer' in sustainability education. Instead, the what-question was filled with 'media content such as news and nature TV channels, a *what* question, that was assumed to be close to the pupils' everyday lives' (Sund and Gericke this volume: 190). Further, the language teachers focused on the *why*-dimension of teaching, concerning pupils' personal development, and identity making.

To conclude, all the studies in language education focus on the *how* question. Thus, knowing how seems to be the most prominent aspect of knowledge, rather than knowing that, and the defining principles are more related to students' experiences at large. Expanding their living world is the aim, rather than taking a disciplinary perspective, and the perspective is directed outwards towards society. However, it is also important to recognize that language education is diversified in L1, L2 and L3 education, which may possibly be reflected in variations in how powerful knowledge is understood among teachers of these different school subjects.

Powerful knowledge in other school subjects

The remaining chapters that address other school subjects pay less attention to the concept of powerful knowledge. This may be somewhat unexpected since powerful knowledge often focuses on disciplinary knowledge, making it possibly easier to translate into the knowledge domains of these school subjects. In Chapter 2, Hudson (this volume) considers powerful knowledge as a long-term aim that is analytically discerned with use of the epistemic quality concept. Hudson argues that: 'this resulted from the high quality of the teacher–student(s) joint action and the high epistemic quality of the content, which in turn can be seen to have produced an evolution in mathematical thinking and epistemic access / ... / to powerful knowledge *for all*' (Hudson this volume: 32). Similarly, Loquet et al. (this volume) in Chapter 3 note the importance of students' epistemic access to powerful knowledge in physical education. Likewise, Golding (this volume: 149) concludes in Chapter 8, within the context of mathematics, that 'importantly, we searched in particular for evidence of access to *epistemological ascent*, without which learners cannot fully participate in, or appreciate, the powerful culture of the discipline'.

With respect to social studies, Nilsberth et al. (this volume) in Chapter 7 address powerful knowledge as a potential outcome of education, and that different teaching aids like digital tools hold varying ability to release this potential. Furthermore, Hardman et al. (this volume) in Chapter 9 use a similar position in chemistry education and from a material dialogic position claim the materials used in laboratory work in chemistry are entangled in the teaching and learning process, which influences the potential outcome of that emergent process. In a study of cross-curricular teaching of a multidisciplinary topic, such as sustainable development, Sund and Gericke (this volume) suggest that powerful knowledge can here be understood as educational content relating to the questions of what, how and why this content is selected, hence not only knowing that, but also knowing how, as argued by Winch (2013), and also knowing why. To keep with the subject-specialist criteria of powerful knowledge, Sund and Gericke (2020) also argue that in collaborative teaching powerful knowledge could be 'the type of knowledge that is uniquely contributed from each subject area' (Sund and Gericke this volume: 194).

Among these studies, we can see that very few have chosen to define the nature of powerful knowledge relating to a specific subject or discipline as in propositional knowledge, or as knowing that. Golding comes the closest by providing some lists of characteristics of mathematics of high quality (see Golding this volume: 140 and 149–150). However, these characteristics are closely connected to the teaching practice and the development of skills. A similar approach may be seen in the chapter by Hudson (this volume) as well as in a study about physical education (Loquet et al. this volume). In their study, Sund and Gericke (this volume) show topics of propositional knowledge that teachers themselves define as powerful knowledge in sustainability education. Yet, the teachers also add the how and why dimensions of educational content. This means we cannot see a study in any of the contributions solely focusing on propositional knowledge, but rather they focus on knowing how, as well as the power dimension, that is, what the knowledge can do for the learner, is also always present.

We see the same tendencies while relating our findings to previous studies in other school subjects. Maude (2018, 2020), for instance in geography education, argues for a learner-centred view point to the issue and suggests we should look at what the knowledge can establish for empowering the learner. In physics education, the same arguments can be found, as shown in a study by Yates and Millar (2016). Although they found argument for a specific disciplinary core curriculum, many teachers also emphasize physics as a field of inquiry, that is, more to the practice than content, and questions of values, interest and identity were also raised as important for defining powerful knowledge.

Epistemic quality in different school subjects

When turning our focus to how the concept of epistemic quality is used in the chapters, more information can be extracted. Chapters 2, 3 and 4 of this book form part of the same project that draws on Joint Action Theory in Didactics and epistemic quality in three different subjects: mathematics, physical science and language. These three studies apply a similar deductive approach, making it interesting to see what kind of results and conclusion presented for each respective subject. Are similarities, or differences, in epistemic quality observable among these three very different school subjects?

There are some distinct similarities in the progression suggested for these three subjects. The knowledge of low epistemic quality in all three cases relates to fixed predetermined knowledge, where the students are supposed to mimic, rather than transform, adapt and reflect on the knowledge at hand. Wegner et al. (this volume) argue about language education that 'the repetition of three rules which are very narrow and reductive illustrates content in relation to language and language use of low epistemic quality' (Wegner et al. this volume: 68). Similarly, Hudson (this volume) describes mathematics education of low epistemic quality that is characterized by an approach that overemphasizes rule following, superficial memorized reasoning and right or wrong answers.

At the other end, the examples given of high epistemic quality in the contexts of language and mathematics education show some similarity. In both chapters, the knowing how seems to be a prominent characteristic of high epistemic quality, such as critical thinking, problem-solving and creative reasoning. Here, we may see many similarities with the previous descriptions of powerful knowledge discussed earlier, especially in L1 and L2 education. Yet, some interesting differences are also visible among the three studies. In the chapter by Loquet et al. (this volume), the language game of imitation between the teacher and the students is found to be of high epistemic quality. At first, this might be seen to be more in line with what is described as low epistemic quality in language (Wegner et al. this volume) and mathematics (Hudson this volume). Still, this difference seems to stem from the teaching tradition. In physical education, imitation is an essential teaching method, but if the student is also able to both grasp and enact the creative symbolism of dance as an art form the interaction transforms into high epistemic quality. This kind of variation in the teaching approach is one example of differences between school subjects. Moreover, physical education and subjects such as art and music involve more of an apprentice relationship between teacher and student where the understanding of epistemic quality might differ from more classical school subjects that are often taught from a more traditional transmissive approach.

In Chapter 6, the reading practices in secondary schools of Finland are studied and high epistemic quality is identified as the 'awareness of different aspects and stances of texts and the ability to discuss these using skilfully justified arguments [that] can be described as high epistemic understanding' (Grünthal et al. this volume: 103). The epistemic quality here seems to be located within the individual, rather than as an interaction or a content. But Grünthal and colleagues view the epistemic quality of content as related to a reflective trait, an ability, knowing how, more than knowing what, as exemplified in the following words: 'all subject teachers should ... make their pupils aware of the epistemic quality – not only the content but the interpretations – of the texts they read' (Grünthal et al. this volume: 103). Moreover, epistemic skills are explicitly referred to (ibid.: 106), as well as attitudinal aspects. Grünthal et al. (this volume: 112) advocate that they 'see pupils' engagement and motivation for reading as one of the most important aspects of high epistemic quality'. Here, epistemic quality can take the shape of knowledge, skills, processes and even dispositions. In the amalgam of successful teaching, all of these aspects are of course important, although the concept's analytical aspect as a research tool may be weakened if it can take all these different meanings.

In the chapter on digitalization in social studies, epistemic quality is once again, like in Loquet et al. (this volume) and Wegner et al. (this volume), defined by interactions in the classroom, as expressed in the following ' ... content to societal issues and aspects of being a citizen in a democratic society in ways that could increase the epistemic quality of their [students] dialogue' (Nilsberth et al. this volume: 128). Epistemic quality here is the outcome of teaching, with Golding (this volume) similarly arguing that epistemic quality may be viewed in action as the quality of teaching: 'we frequently observed, and teachers reported, lessons where the epistemic quality was apparently limited by teacher capacity' (Golding this volume: 148). However, in the context of mathematics education, Golding places the ability to accomplish high epistemic teaching in the skills of the teachers, and most of these skills are related to the epistemological aspects of the mathematical knowledge. Golding (this volume: 152) points out as a result 'that even "specialist" teachers often marginalized epistemological considerations in the classroom'. This provides one of the few references to the subject-specific epistemologies of the parent university discipline (in this case mathematics).

In the comparative chapter on sustainability education, Sund and Gericke (this volume) propose that, in contexts of cross-curricula teaching, epistemic quality becomes visible in complex questions in which knowledge for decision-making must come from different disciplines/subjects. This leads them to argue that the use of a multidisciplinary teaching content, that is, including expert knowledge from several subject domains, the quality of the problem-solving ability, denoted here as action competence, becomes strengthened, which may be a sign of high epistemic quality.

The importance of transformation processes

As shown above, the empirical studies challenge the idea of disciplinary powerful knowledge, a *knowing that*, which can easily be defined and put in practice. Instead, the way powerful knowledge is described and used in the chapters strengthens our argument (as developed in Gericke et al. 2018) that powerful knowledge in school subjects can only be understood and defined in the light of transformations, that is, as part in the process of recontextualizing, to use Bernstein's terminology (Bernstein 2000), whereby disciplinary and/or other forms of knowledge are transformed for an educational purpose. This is the focus of the second research question that is discussed in the section below.

Transformation, as we previously defined it, is an integrative process through which specialized knowledge, developed in subject disciplines, is reshaped and re-presented in educational environments – through various processes outside and within the education system (Gericke et al. this volume). We argue that in subject-specific education, that is, when the focus is neither on the knowledge itself nor on *producing* new knowledge, but on *reproducing* existing knowledge, that is, to engage the knowledge in the endeavour of teaching and learning, the transformation process becomes inevitable. This is because knowledge taught in school cannot be seen as a mere reduction of an academic discipline; rather, while teaching, the knowledge must be adapted to the relationship between the teacher, learner and content. This aspect is the core of the theory of Didaktik (Hopmann 2007).

The transformation process is influenced by students' understanding and their previous experience of the content, which is connected to the students' life world and relevant to the teacher–student relationship, but also to the teacher's notion of the students' relationship to the content (Klafki 1995). While considering these relationships, three important analytical questions emerge: (1) what content should be taught?; (2) why should we select the content taught?; and (3) how should we teach that selected content? These are the three basic questions to address while defining and enacting a curriculum and are expanded on in greater detail in the paragraphs below.

Biesta (2009, 2015) denotes the three main aims of education as qualification, socialization and subjectification. The aim of qualification is to empower students to be able to qualify for a life at and beyond school, the aim of socialization is to empower students to be able to understand and act within social practices at and beyond school, whereas the aim of subjectification is to empower students to be able to understand and create meaning in relation to school practices. The point here is that the particular aim being addressed by a school subject will influence the answer to *why*, and this means there are different answers to the *what* question, that is, what to teach. Consequently, school subjects must undertake a transformation process aligning to these aims, and the powerful knowledge and epistemic quality of school subjects must address the why question, that is, the aim of education, before being defined.

Likewise, the *how* question will influence the *what* question. A teacher has to include the content in a teaching activity or the content will not be taught. Different teaching practices, habits or traditions have evolved over time and been described as selective teaching traditions (Sund 2016) because the way teaching is practised will inevitably influence which content will be taught. For example, if literature teachers think it essential to connect to the students' life world, and this might be an overarching aim of their education, modern contemporary literature – or at least texts with themes connected to their lives – will probably be used in teaching rather than classical literature and literature that promote a distance while reading. If so, the teachers could develop a selective teaching tradition via which they select content that matches their existing aim and practices, rather than content that does not.

Transformation processes in relation to powerful knowledge and epistemic quality

This allows us to conclude that the questions of what, why and how to teach are intertwined, and the latter two will most often influence the what question. Therefore, we think it is important to view the normative concepts of powerful knowledge and epistemic quality in the light of transformation. The normative aspects of powerful knowledge and epistemic quality are a direct consequence of the transformation, that is, that the knowledge taught needs to fulfil the predefined goals of education, which are typically not the same as for the academic discipline. Thus, in this section we turn to the second KOSS research question by outlining how transformation processes relate to powerful knowledge and epistemic quality.

We now go back to the empirical contributions made by this volume and see how and in what way the transformation influenced their understanding of powerful knowledge and epistemic quality. With regard to school mathematics, in Chapter 2 Hudson (this volume) clearly distinguishes that epistemic quality can be seen first after the transformation has taken place, when saying: 'This process of mutation is seen as a transformation process ... The mutated version of mathematics is characterized by an approach that presents the subject as infallible, authoritarian, dogmatic, absolutist, irrefutable ... ' (Hudson this volume: 20). Hudson thus sees that the transformation process is in itself responsible for the outcome of mathematics content of low or high epistemic quality, and the source of the resulting epistemic quality in his study is found in both the teaching and the content. In Chapter 3, Loquet et al. (this volume) do not explicitly refer to the transformation process as a concept, although the whole study is about the transformation in action when a student is learning dance through an imitation process, which can be described as a very direct form of transformation.

Language learning in primary school is the focus of Chapter 4 where Wegner et al. (this volume) connect the transformation process to the theory of Bildungsgangdidaktik. Wegner et al. see transformation on different levels of teacher–student interaction that should expand into the institutional level. Wegner et al. (this volume: 57) point out that 'the first level of classroom interaction must be transformed into a *second*, communicative *level* in order that students and teachers come to see instruction as a shared experience and joint action'. This may be understood as the third level of teacher–student interaction needed in order to describe the processes of Bildung. 'The purpose is to use knowledge as a transformative tool for unfolding the individuality and sociability of the learner. In the long run, students thus will develop their own world views and self-concepts in a transformative process' (Wegner et al.: 57). These levels mirror the development of high epistemic quality in language education, and they conclude: 'High epistemic quality furthermore would imply that students are given the right, time and space to develop epistemic capacities, to stabilize or transform language and language use' (Wegner et al. this volume: 59). What can be drawn from these quotes is that the epistemic quality is seen in the teaching practices as they occur in the transformation processes. Hence, in this perspective it is more the epistemic quality of the teaching, the *how* that determines the epistemic outcomes. Teacher-led instruction involving an over-emphasis and memorization and rule following is of low epistemic quality, while the transformation of 'joint reflection and negotiation of language and language use in linguistically diverse contexts' (Wegner et al. this volume: 59) is of high epistemic quality.

In Chapter 5, Ljung Egeland and Iversen Kulbrandstad take their starting point from the very idea of transformation in language education and undertake a comparison based on the academic discipline: 'To identify areas of focus for the textbook study, we analysed the content of university courses in Swedish and Norwegian as a second language' (Ljung Egeland and Iversen Kulbrandstad this volume: 83). This analysis leads the authors to identify activities in the training textbooks for middle school children that 'explore whether focussing on these activities will add new perspectives to the understanding of possible transformations of powerful knowledge through teaching materials' (Ljung Egeland and Iversen Kulbrandstad this volume: 86). As discussed above, they identify powerful knowledge as knowledge that provides new ways of thinking about the world, and they analyse the textbooks to see if the books provide opportunities for students to take roles that achieve this in the area of migration. Powerful knowledge in their study becomes visible in the transformation process and in the practices these textbooks enable. Hence, it is in the potential knowledge construction of the teaching process that powerful knowledge can be identified following the transformation process, according to Ljung Egeland and Iversen Kulbrandstad (this volume), as expressed as follows: 'The role perspective on learning activities has helped us better understand how transformations of powerful knowledge can be achieved through teaching materials' (Ljung Egeland and Iversen Kulbrandstad this volume: 93).

In Chapter 6, L1-education is also in focus, this time in Finland regarding reading practices (Grünthal et al. this volume). Transformations are briefly mentioned in this chapter with regard to students: 'such teaching has a transformational and emancipatory impact on the pupils' (Grünthal et al. this volume: 110). Here, it is the epistemic quality of the teaching that leads to the students' transformation, rather than the opposite perspective that various transformations lead to different epistemic quality in teaching, as exemplified in the chapter by Nilsberth et al. (this volume). The reason for this diversification of views is that the term transformation has also been used by several scholars with respect to various learning theories as a concept describing the aim of education, to transform the learner, more or less similar as the subjectification aim of education described by Biesta (2009, 2015). From this perspective, transformative learning theory is a psychological theory about how individuals learn by changing their frames of reference to critically reflect on their assumptions and beliefs and consciously construct new ways of defining their worlds (Mezirow 2000). This is similar to the way Grünthal et al. (this volume) use it in their chapter while relating transformation to epistemic quality.

In their study of literacy engagement in social studies, Nilsberth et al. (this volume) investigate how the transformation might take another direction due to digitalization of the teaching process. A highly digitalized classroom in secondary school is studied. The aim of the study in Chapter 7 is to 'deepen knowledge of *what* and *how* content is represented in a digitalized classroom and discuss how transformation processes can enable knowledge of high epistemic quality' (Nilsberth et al. this volume: 118). In the chapter, the authors investigate how, why, and with whom people communicate and interact about the theme 'law and order' through different kinds of texts and how this might be mediated by digitally transformed teaching practices. Thus, it is the interaction patterns formed in the teaching that are studied. The authors claim that 'the digital devices also offer the teacher the possibility to transform the academic subject content in order for it to be accessible to the students as well as a chance to stick to the pre-planned teaching trajectory without being interrupted' (Nilsberth et al. this volume: 133). The claim being made is that transformation can take different trajectories, leading to different epistemic quality, or ascent (Winch 2013). Nilsbert and colleagues (this volume) argue digital learning resources hold the potential to improve the students' awareness of, and control over, the academic language, which may be defined as powerful knowledge. However, in this study the teachers do not release this potential because they take another trajectory where the transformation resembles a traditional teaching sequence. The authors see the first trajectory as a sign of high-quality teaching, and the second, enacted in the study, as representing low-quality teaching. Therefore, here epistemic quality seems to translate more into the teaching process.

In Chapter 10 involving a study of teachers' possible contribution to cross-curricular teaching, the transformation process of the same topic, sustainable development, was shown to take different paths in the three school subject areas of language, social science and sciences (Sund and Gericke this volume). A similar way of understanding transformation is used here as in several of the chapters of this book, for example, in Nilsberth et al. (this volume), Golding (this volume) and Grünthal et al. (this volume). Furthermore, the outcome of the transformation process in each of these subject domains may be seen as representing powerful knowledge within the boundaries of that specific subject area, while the aggregated educational content of these three subject areas together was described as knowledge of higher quality, that is, representing knowledge of high epistemic quality. The reason for this is that the knowledge stemming from different disciplines is more likely to empower a student with a greater ability to deal with complex sustainability problems, thereby providing an action competence. Here, the authors validate the normative aspect of epistemic quality based on the skills it can provide the students, as also reported in other chapters.

Transformation as intended or emergent

In most studies discussed in the previous section, transformation can be understood as a conscious process that the teacher stages in the classroom. Accordingly, transformation thereby becomes an intended outcome of the teaching, more of a skill on the part of the teacher. In relation to mathematics education, in Chapter 8 Golding (this volume) discusses the transformation between academic discipline and the school subject. She writes that: 'stage-specific "transformation" of the appropriate epistemic substance was integral to the genesis of the studied curricula' (Golding this volume: 144). Golding also relates here to different, yet intended, transformations that can lead to transformed content of different epistemic quality, that is, 'appropriate epistemic substance'.

One of Golding's major conclusions in her chapter is that teacher education should ensure teachers' 'transformation of those qualities for effective classroom use so that they "know the mathematics" in epistemically and pedagogically powerful ways appropriate to their learners and contexts' (Golding this volume: 153). Golding thus suggests that transformation can be viewed as a skill of an excellent teacher, that is, a teacher able to adapt the content to the context and students in order to facilitate learning. Transformation becomes a skill, and a purposeful act, where the outcome is to teach content and practices of high epistemic quality, including epistemological aspects of mathematics. Still, as Golding claims 'curriculum transformation processes can be constrained by curriculum communication, and by teacher capacity – their knowledge, skills and beliefs' (Golding this volume: 138). An important improvement in education is therefore to teach becoming teachers about these transformation processes and also content and skills that mirror high epistemic quality.

A similar way of understanding the relationship between transformation, epistemic quality and powerful knowledge is also found in Chapter 9. 'Our contention is that the notions of transformation and epistemic quality hold the potential to frame the ways in which disciplinary knowledge and epistemology manifest in the classroom' (Hardman et al. this volume: 158). However, in their study the authors take a material-dialogic perspective on transformation and 'argue against any stratification of disciplinary knowledge and school knowledge in how transformations might be characterised: they are not ontologically distinct' (Hardman et al. this volume: 159). From this perspective, transformation becomes an emergent process rather than a purposeful one guided by the teacher, as outlined in most chapters in this volume. In the transformation process, 'emergence involves the coming together of different influences in a dynamic and unpredictable way such that new meanings emerge' (Hardman et al. this volume: 159). This means that in the view of Hardman and colleagues the transformation process is not about representing the academic knowledge in a pedagogical way, but rather that in the classroom teaching is an emergent process in which 'the complexity of transformations by framing teacher, pupil and content as entangled within the material circumstances of classrooms' occurs (Hardman et al. this volume: 159).

Furthermore, the authors argue that considering transformations involves recognizing the agency of material aspects of the classroom such as in this case the science laboratory and the use of chromatography. In the study, it is shown that transformations display that the disciplinary knowledge and pedagogic knowledge of the teacher are intra-acting continuously within a dynamic context involving students' ideas and material resources. Finally, they conclude that 'our case study suggests that powerful, disciplinary knowledge is manifest in the models and dialogue which emerge in the classroom, and which support student understanding' (Hardman et al. this volume: 171). This is quite a different take on the conceptual framework than in most of the other chapters in that the concepts can be viewed more as analytical concepts discerning a teaching sequence, including less normative aspects for the possibilities of defining the more powerful knowledge or knowledge of higher epistemic quality. These aspects are more 'to be found' in a study as an emergent process that is difficult to predict or plan for.

To conclude, in all empirical studies presented in this volume powerful knowledge and epistemic quality is first discerned after the transformation process, rather than before, seeing the issue of power become more important in the interpretation of powerful knowledge. The transformation process can be discerned as intended or emergent, although the former dominates in the studies. Based on how the nine studies in this volume addressed our two research questions, we now try to develop a common framework for how powerful knowledge, epistemic quality and transformations can be used in subject-specific education research across different disciplines and school subjects.

Towards a framework for researching trajectories of powerful knowledge, transformations and epistemic quality across school subjects

In this section, we outline some proposals for ways to use the conceptual framework of powerful knowledge, epistemic quality and transformations as a tool for curriculum innovation and research. First looking at powerful knowledge, we may see that in most contributions in this volume the concept is defined based on what it can do for the students. Hence, it is the concept of power that comes to the fore, rather than knowledge, in the concept of powerful knowledge. Most scholars contributing to this book seem to hold the view that powerful knowledge becomes visible first after the transformation in a classroom, and more specifically in relation to what this knowledge can bring about for the students in their own life world (see for example Chapters 4, 5, 6 and 7). In other words, it relates to the ways in which, by possessing powerful knowledge, the students can transform their experience and interaction with the social world, which they would not have been able to do without possessing that particular knowledge.

In this way, several contributions focus on the power aspect of powerful knowledge rather than the knowledge aspect. This approach to defining powerful knowledge has come quite a long way from Young's (2009, 2015) original definitions that primarily focused on the knowledge aspect, proposing that powerful knowledge concerns knowledge structures, boundaries between disciplines, school subjects, and everyday knowledge. Instead, it is more strongly defined, based on its 'end-user' rather than the discipline or school subjects. Powerful knowledge is thereby becoming more closely related to the idea of transformative education (Mezirow 2000), which in one of this research area's most seminal journals is described with the aim to 'foster deep engagement with and reflection on our taken-for-granted ways of viewing the world, resulting in fundamental shifts in how we see and understand ourselves and our relationship with the world' (https://journals.sagepub.com/home/jtd). Accordingly, powerful knowledge in several studies is not strongly connected to a specific body of knowledge within an academic discipline, and this is especially observable in the studies on language education.

In the more recent work by Young, in collaboration with Johan Muller, they give greater recognition to the importance of power in powerful knowledge compared to their previous work (Muller and Young 2019). They themselves claim the earlier emphasis on knowledge was not intentional, but an artefact of the ambition to 'bring knowledge back' in the discussion on curriculum-making. Interestingly, Muller and Young (2019) identify two ways in which 'power' has been understood and used in the literature on powerful knowledge, and a third way that would be possible to argue for. The first sense Muller and Young (2019) found is denoted as 'power and academic disciplines' where they claim that power may be seen in the light of the generalizable power of specialized disciplinary knowledge, in comparison to context-dependent concepts. The second sense is 'power and the school curriculum' and relates to how powerful knowledge is argued for by sequencing and pacing the curriculum in a way that represents a systemic and holistic aspects of the discipline, that is, of a powerful curriculum. Third, Young and Muller (2019) identified 'power as a generative aspect: the capacity to generate new ideas' as a possible way to understand 'power' in powerful knowledge. Here, Young and Muller look at powerful knowledge after its transformation, in the created capacity of the student. Which new connections, insights and new generated ideas are enabled for the students are of interest in this respect.

Muller and Young (2019) did not find any literature relating to this last sense of power in powerful knowledge. Interestingly, in this volume most empirical studies adhere to this definition and use power in this sense in order to define powerful knowledge. What we see is that in most empirical work on powerful knowledge the aspect of power, in the sense of capacity-building and its transformative aspects come to the fore, and this is even more accentuated in the studies on language, social science and physical education, although also referred to in the studies on mathematics and science education.

White (2018, 2019) commented on the problem of defining 'core concepts' in disciplines and school subjects outside of science and mathematics. He claims that History does not include a system of interrelated concepts, while many concepts in Geography 'can be elucidated at a superficial level in non-technical terms, and more fully by drawing on concepts from natural science' (White 2018: 327). Moreover, as regards Language education, White claims that 'studying literature at school, students rarely if ever get to grips with aestheticians' concepts: the novelists, dramatists and poets they read use everyday, non-technical ones' (White 2018: 328). Based on these differences between various school subjects, White criticizes the idea of finding common ground for defining powerful knowledge based on conceptual interrelated structures. The findings of this volume provide empirical support for his arguments. Yet, we would argue that a solution to these definitional problems outlined in the studies of this volume is to give more attention to the power dimension in defining powerful knowledge, at least in school subjects where systems of interrelated concepts might not exist. As discussed in Chapter 1, this is also evident in other empirical studies, such as Maude (2018, 2020) and Yates and Millar (2016).

We now turn our attention to the transformation process. Due to their focus on the empowering of students, most studies herein empirically investigate the transformed knowledge emerging after the transformation process as an outcome of what students learned, rather than looking at powerful knowledge as a curriculum principle. Only the contributions about mathematics education, Chapters 2 and 8, and sustainability education in Chapter 10, touch on the selection of content to some degree.

While investigating the transformed knowledge, *knowledge how* is most often addressed and illustrated through competencies and abilities such as reasoning, problem-solving or role play. This is evident in all of the studies, but even more so for language education and physical education. *Knowing that*, the transformation of concepts and their interrelationship, is also addressed in the studies on mathematics, science and social science studies. This resembles what Winch (2013) describes as the development of subject expertise and epistemic ascent. What we may discern are descriptions of different transformation trajectories in the various studies. This might be related to 'a continuum that reflects a trajectory of the epistemic ascent in the development of subject expertise' (Hudson this volume: 17) from the restricted 'knowledge by acquaintance' of the novice, the primary mode of knowledge being experienced through the senses, towards the sophisticated higher-order 'knowledge that' and 'knowledge how' of an expert in the subject as illustrated explicitly through the example in Chapter 2. Moreover, the two studies in Chapters 7 and 9 describe how the educational or material setting contributes to the outcome of this transformation process. Nilsberth et al. (this volume) show the potential of digital learning environments to provide possibly varying epistemic access to these different knowledge domains, and Hardman et al. (this volume) describe how the laboratory setting can influence the learning taking place.

What we may conclude is that these transformation processes are fundamentally similar across different school subjects, even though the constituents or elements of that process relating to the overall aim of education and how powerful knowledge is defined might vary, meaning the transformation process takes different trajectories. We might be able to more specifically outline these different trajectories if we develop analytical tools able to discern these different trajectories in greater detail. It would be important to better differentiate different aspects of the 'power' and 'knowledge' in powerful knowledge as well as how they relate to epistemic quality. Furthermore, in line with the critique by White (2018, 2019), a common framework would allow comparative studies across different disciplines and school subjects, an aspect we elaborate on in the next section.

Trajectories of epistemic quality in different epistemic games

The third construct in our framework is epistemic quality and, as discussed above, this concept is seen here as a way to deal with the normative aspect of powerful knowledge. As Young (2009, 2015) claims, there is 'better' and more valid knowledge. Yet, as presented in many contributions in this volume, epistemic quality is observable in the learning process in the classroom in the teacher–student interaction, see Chapters 2, 3, 4, 7, 8 and 9. Not so much in the nature of the knowledge. Hence, it seems that in our studies epistemic quality is not chiefly to be found in the knowledge structure, but in the practice of how this knowledge structure might be taught in the classroom. At first glance, this might seem unexpected, but the epistemology of knowledge often becomes important in the practice of reproducing the knowledge, not only in the production of new knowledge. This dualism is shown in a common definition of epistemic: 'of or relating to knowledge or the conditions for acquiring it' (http://www.Dictionary.

com). Thus, epistemic issues come into play while disciplinary knowledge is being taught in the classroom.

In connecting our main concepts of powerful knowledge, epistemic quality and transformations together in a common framework, we wish to add the concept of *epistemic game* (Sensevy et al. 2005, 2008, 2011). Epistemic game is a concept used in science and mathematics education research and further developed in the work of Gérard Sensevy and colleagues on the Joint Action Theory in Didactics. An epistemic game may be described as a generic epistemic game within the academic discipline, here denoted as *source epistemic games*, that is, disciplinary knowledge that is first created in the practices of the academic discipline (Santini et al. 2018). This source epistemic game is then recreated in the school subjects as an epistemic game in the classroom. We would describe the investigations of epistemic quality in the studies in this volume as studies in characterizing specific epistemic games that unfold both practices and their meaningful content in order to promote powerful knowledge. Therefore, it makes sense that most studies investigate the practices or activities, along with associated interactions between students and teachers, in the search for epistemic games that provide a transformation of powerful knowledge into knowledge of the powerful.

A conclusion based on the research studies in this volume is that there is a stress on the practices and activities in the classroom to transform powerful knowledge. This volume thereby embraces the 'practice turn' in educational research, as exemplified by many scholars (e.g. Bruner 1983; Bourdieu 1990; Wittgenstein 1997). This practice turn consists of instituting the notion of a game as a valuable model to describe human enterprise, such as teaching and learning. We can therefore model the findings of this volume accordingly where pedagogical practices are modelled as learning games, and epistemic practices are characterized as enacted epistemic games emerging through the unfolding of learning games in the classroom (Santini et al. 2018). Accordingly, we define the learning of powerful knowledge as a learning game in which the enacted epistemic game creates a learning situation that is successful. By this, we mean a game that connects the students' everyday knowledge, knowledge of acquaintance, with the disciplinary knowledge, subject-specific *know that* and *know how*, in a way that facilitates students' learning and the acquisition of that knowledge, for potential use in their future life worlds.

This resonates with Muller and Young's (2019) third sense of power in powerful knowledge, that is, power as a generative aspect or a capacity-builder. In our framework, epistemic quality becomes the specific way, a trajectory, to transform powerful knowledge in successful epistemic games embedded within the learning game of a specific school subject, in contrast with other transformations not leading to this outcome, and thus representing transformation trajectories of low epistemic quality. In teaching of high epistemic quality, the disciplinary knowledge meets the knowledge by acquaintance, creating an understanding by the student that interconnects the different knowledge types of the disciplinary powerful knowledge with the student's previous experiences and knowledge of their own life world. A better understanding consisting of higher-order knowledge thereby evolves with the learner and creates meaning for their future experiences of the world, leading to a capacity to act in the future, that is, knowledge of the powerful. Such learning games of high epistemic quality demand a connecting interaction between the teacher, the student and the powerful knowledge of the discipline and life-world knowledge, all being important constituents or elements in developing knowledge of the powerful. One exemplar of a trajectory of high epistemic quality is illustrated in Figure 11.1 based on that by Hudson (this volume) in Chapter 2.

If we now turn to the cases of less successful teaching, of low epistemic quality, we may argue that the capacity-building of powerful knowledge into knowledge of the powerful has failed. The reason of this failure might stem from many different factors. First, the selection from the planned/intended curriculum might fail at targeting powerful knowledge. Here, the selection of potentially powerful knowledge as part of the planned curriculum is important. One might, for example, only select a list of concepts without any structure, as often done in a Future-1 curriculum (Young and Muller 2010), see the discussion in Chapter 1 of this volume. This is also discussed by Hudson (this volume) in Chapter 2 and shown by Wegner et al. (this volume) in Chapter 4 – see Figure 11.2. Alternatively, the knowledge might be drawn from the life world only, as in a Future-2 curriculum (Young and Muller 2010), see the discussion in Chapter 1 of this volume. This is also discussed by Sund and Gericke (this volume) in Chapter 10.

Teachers might lack the necessary level of content knowledge, pedagogical content knowledge (Shulman 1986) or subject-specific educational content knowledge (Stolare et al. 2022), to select or transform the content according to the epistemic game that is necessary. The teacher must thus be able to draw from the powerful knowledge, as part of the source domain of the epistemic game, which is often represented by *know that* and *know how*, and from that create an epistemic game in the classroom in which this knowledge is connected to the students' life world. This is exemplified by Golding (this volume) in Chapter

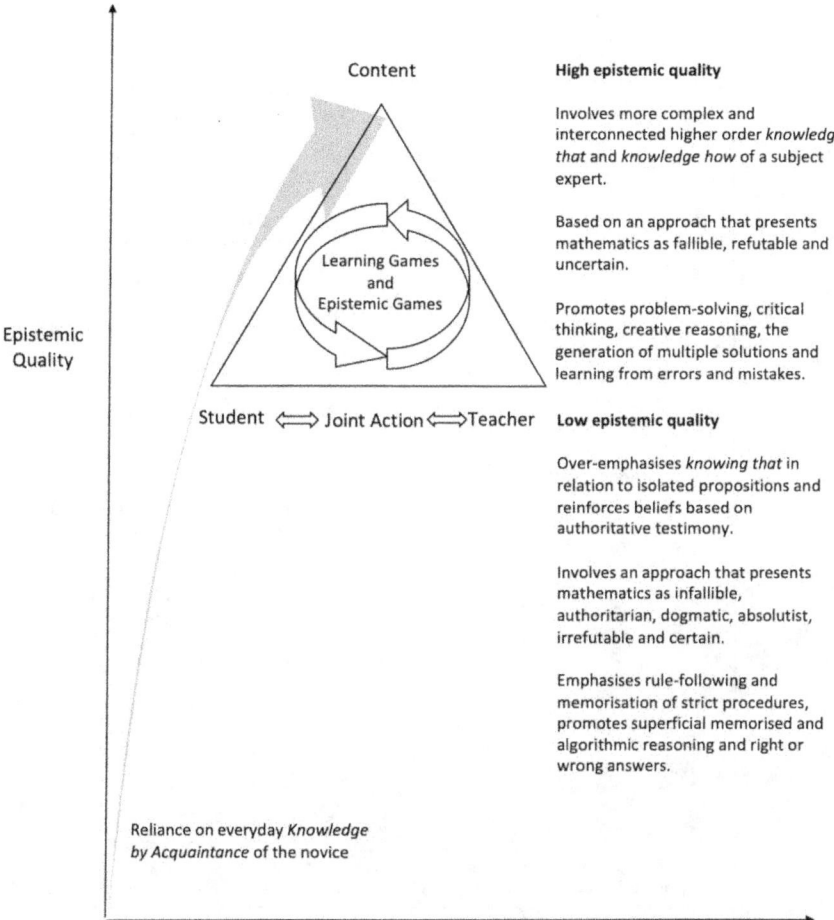

Figure 11.1 Trajectory in the development of subject-specific powerful knowledge in mathematics (Hudson this volume).

8 for mathematics education, and Nilsberth and colleagues (this volume) in Chapter 7 for social studies. However, the epistemic game is embedded within the larger context of the learning game, and the aspects of this game might induce learning failures, as discussed in relation to teaching materials by Ljung Egeland and Iversen Kulbrandstad (this volume) in Chapter 5 and by Hardman et al. in Chapter 9.

Still, the epistemic quality of the transformative trajectory might also be influenced by the quality of the teacher–students interaction in the epistemic and learning games underway. This is addressed in Chapter 3 by Loquet et al.

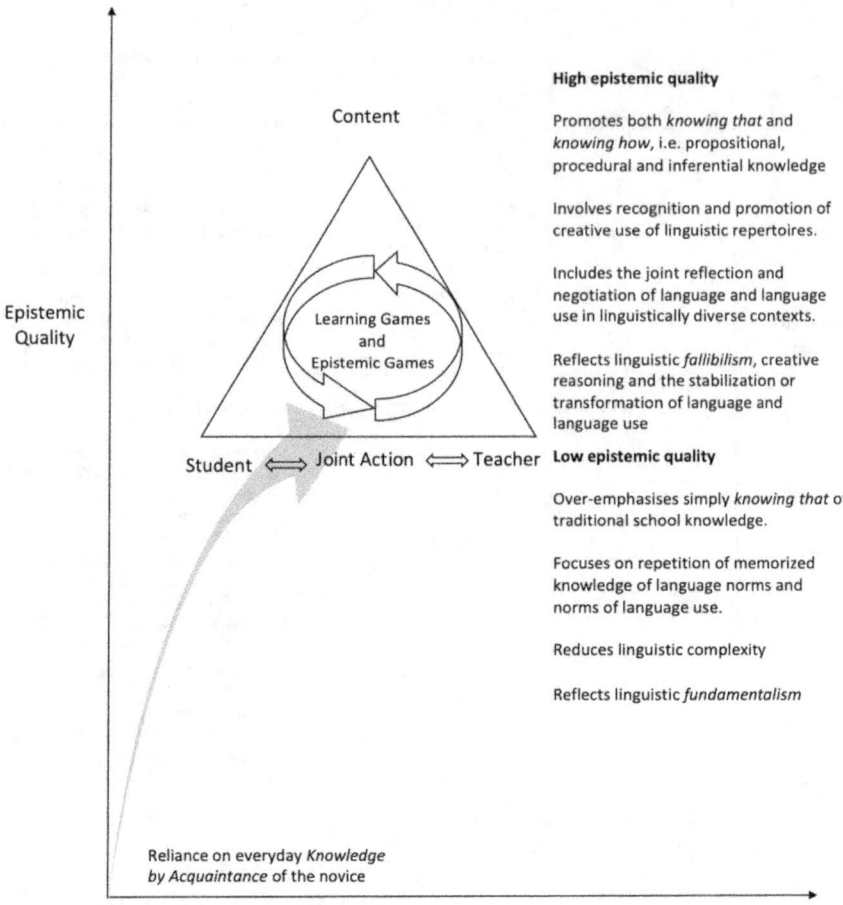

Figure 11.2 Trajectory of development in relation to language and language use (Wegner et al. this volume).

(this volume) for physical education, and by Grünthal et al. (this volume) in Chapter 6 for reading.

With the examples given in this volume, we wish to illustrate this conceptual framework's usability and how powerful knowledge, epistemic quality and transformations can be connected to the concepts of epistemic games and learning games. The framework may be applied to different aspects of teaching and learning, making it potentially useful across disciplines and school subjects.

This framework is able to handle the normative aspect of subject specific teaching. In addition, because we developed the framework in a multidisciplinary context we have tried to incorporate the differences in powerful knowledge and epistemic quality that are inherent to different disciplines and school subjects, as noted by White (2018, 2019). We hypothesize that different aspects of this framework will be weighted differently, and be given more or less attention in different school subjects. Therefore, we believe that it is especially useful in comparative studies. By providing space for both the discipline, the life world of the student, as well as the differentiation between the epistemic game, the learning game and the interaction in the classroom, one can analytically discern the transformation process of powerful knowledge in greater detail according to a trajectory of high epistemic quality leading to knowledge of the powerful.

References

Bernstein, B. (2000), *Pedagogy, Symbolic Control and Identity: Theory, Research, Critique*, rev. ed., Lanham, MD: Rowman and Littlefield.

Bertram, C. (2019), 'What is Powerful Knowledge in School History? Learning from the South African and Rwandan School Curriculum Documents', *The Curriculum Journal*, 30 (2): 125–43.

Biesta, G. (2009), 'Good Education in an Age of Measurement: On the Need to Reconnect with the Question of Purpose in Education', *Educational Assessment, Evaluation and Accountability*, 21 (1): 33–46.

Biesta, G. (2015), 'What is Education for? On Good Education, Teacher Judgement, and Educational Professionalism', *European Journal of Education*, 50 (1): 75–87.

Bourdieu, P. (1990), *In Other Words: Essays towards a Reflexive Sociology*, Cambridge: Polity Press.

Bruner, J. (1983), *Child Talk*, New York: Norton.

Chapman, A., ed. (2021), *Knowing History in Schools: Powerful Knowledge and the Powers of Knowledge*, London: UCL Press.

Cochran-Smith, M. (2003), 'Teaching Quality Matters', *Journal of Teacher Education*, 54 (2): 95–8.

Croninger, R.G., Valli, L. and Chambliss, M. (2012), 'Researching Quality in Teaching: Enduring and Emerging Challenges', *Teachers College Record*, 114 (4): 1–15.

Gericke, N., Hudson, B., Olin-Scheller, C. and Stolare, M. (2018), 'Powerful Knowledge, Transformations and the Need for Empirical Studies across School Subjects', *London Review of Education: Special Issue on Knowledge and Subject Specialist Teaching*, 16 (3): 428–44. UCL IOE Press. doi.org/10.18546/LRE.16.3.06.

Hopmann, S. (2007), 'Restrained Teaching: The Common Core of Didaktik', *European Educational Research Journal*, 6 (2): 109–24.

Hudson, B. (2016), 'The Epistemology and Methodology of Curriculum: Didactics', in D. Wyse, L. Hayward and J. Pandya (eds), *SAGE Handbook of Curriculum, Pedagogy and Assessment*, 107–24, Sage Publications.

Hudson, B. (2018), 'Powerful Knowledge and Epistemic Quality in School Mathematics', *London Review of Education: Special Issue on Knowledge and Subject Specialist Teaching*, 16 (3): 384–97. UCL IOE Press. https://doi.org/10.18546/LRE.16.3.03

Hudson, B. (2019) 'Epistemic Quality for Equitable Access to Quality Education in School Mathematics', *Journal of Curriculum Studies*, 51 (4): 437–56. https://doi.org/10.1080/00220272.2019.1618917

Klafki, W. (1995), 'Didactic Analysis as the Core of Preparation for Instruction' (Didaktische Analyse als Kern der Unterrichtsvorbereitung), *Journal of Curriculum Studies*, 27 (1): 13–30.

Maude, A. (2018), 'Geography and Powerful Knowledge: A Contribution to the Debate', *International Research in Geographical and Environmental Education*, 27 (2): 179–90.

Maude, A. (2020), 'The Role of Geography's Concepts and Powerful Knowledge in a Future 3 Curriculum', *International Research in Geographical and Environmental Education*, 29 (3): 232–43.

McPhail, G. J. (2017), 'Powerful Knowledge: Insights from Music's Case', *The Curriculum Journal*, 28 (4): 524–38.

Mezirow, J., ed. (2000), *Learning as Transformation: Critical Perspectives on a Theory in Progress*, San Francisco: Jossey-Bass.

Muller, J. and Young, M. (2019), 'Knowledge, Power and Powerful Knowledge', *The Curriculum Journal*, 30 (2): 196–214.

Nordgren, K. (2021), 'Powerful Knowledge for What? History Education and 45-degree Discourse', in A. Chapman (ed.), *Knowing History in Schools: Powerful Knowledge and the Powers of Knowledge*, 177–201, London: UCL Press.

Santini, J. T., Bloor, T., and Sensevy, G. (2018), 'Modeling Conceptualization and Investigating Teaching Effectiveness', *Science and Education*, 27 (9–10): 921–61. https://doi.org/10.1007/s11191-018-0016-6

Sensevy, G. (2011), 'Overcoming Fragmentation: Towards a Joint Action Theory in Didactics', in Hudson, B. and Meyer, M. A. (eds), *Beyond Fragmentation: Didactics, Learning, and Teaching*, 60–76, Opladen and Farmington Hills: Verlag Barbara Budrich.

Sensevy, G., Tiberghien, A., Santini, J., Laubé, S. and Griggs, P. (2008), 'An Epistemological Approach to Modeling: Cases Studies and Implications for Science Teaching', *Science Education*, 92 (3): 424–46.

Sensevy, G., Schubauer-Leoni, M.-L., Mercier, A., Ligozat, F. and Perrot, G. (2005), 'An Attempt To Model the Teacher's Action in the Mathematics Class', *Educational Studies in Mathematics*, 59 (1–3): 153–81.

Shulman, L. S. (1986), 'Those Who Understand: Knowledge Growth in Teaching', *Educational Researcher*, 15 (2): 4–14.

Stolare, M., Hudson, B. Gericke, N. and Olin-Scheller, C. (2022), 'Teachers' Powerful Professional Knowledge as Subject-Specific Educational Content Knowledge', in B. Hudson, N. Gericke, C. Olin-Scheller and M. Stolare (eds), *International Perspectives* on *Knowledge and Quality: Implications for Innovation in Teacher Education Policy and Practice*, 225–41, London: Bloomsbury Publishing plc.

Sund, P. (2016), 'Discerning Selective Traditions in Science Education: A Qualitative Study of Teachers' Responses to What is Important in Science Teaching', *Cultural Studies of Science Education*, 11 (2): 387–409.

White, J. (2018), 'The Weakness of Powerful Knowledge', *London Review of Education*, 16 (2): 325–35. doi:10.18546/LRE.16.2.11

White, J. (2019), 'The End of Powerful Knowledge?', *London Review of Education*, 17 (3): 429–38. DOI https://doi.org/10.18546/LRE.17.3.15

Winch, C. (2013), 'Curriculum Design and Epistemic Ascent', *Journal of Philosophy of Education*, 47 (1): 128–46.

Wittgenstein, L. (1997), *Philosophical Investigations*, Oxford: Blackwell.

Yates, L. and Millar, V. (2016), 'Powerful Knowledge' Curriculum Theories and the Case of Physics', *The Curriculum Journal*, 27 (3): 298–312.

Young, M. (2009), 'Education, Globalisation and the "Voice of Knowledge"', *Journal of Education and Work*, 22 (3): 193–204. doi:10.1080/13639080902957848

Young, M. (2013), 'Overcoming the Crisis in Curriculum Theory: A Knowledge-based Approach', *Journal of Curriculum Studies*, 45 (2): 101–18. http://www.tandfonline.com/doi/full/10.1080/00220272.2013.764505

Young, M. (2015), 'Powerful Knowledge as a Curriculum Principle', in M. Young, D. Lambert, C. Roberts, and M. Roberts (eds), *Knowledge and the Future School: Curriculum and Social Justice*, 2nd ed., 65–88, London: Bloomsbury Academic.

Young, M. and Muller, J. (2010), 'Three Educational Scenarios for the Future: Lessons from the Sociology of Knowledge', *European Journal of Education* 45: 11–27.

Index

academic disciplines. *See specific disciplines*
academic knowledge 81, 210
academic language 119, 121, 123, 131–3, 208
activities, textbook (roles of students)
    active citizen (writing blogs) 86–8, 90–3
    empathetic individual 86–8
    personal expert 86–7
    subject-specific apprentice 86–8, 93
        with empathetic individual (illegal refugee) 90, 92–3
        learning alphabets 88–9, 92
        with personal expert (multilingualism) 89–90, 92–3
actual epistemic game 19–20, 38, 58–9. *See also* epistemic games; source epistemic game
aesthetics 6
    aesthetic reading 102–3
anti-discrimination education 80, 91
Arabic writing system 88. *See also* writing systems
art education in France 42, 42 n.1. *See also* Physical Education (PE) in France

Bakhtin, M. M. 160, 171
Barad, K. 159–60, 171
    agential realism 159–60
    phenomena/phenomenon 160, 168
    rejection of representationalism 161
    relational ontology 160
Bernstein, B. 7, 141, 148, 157, 204
Biesta, G. J. J. 4, 158–9, 205, 208
Bildung processes 56–7, 61, 73, 207
Bildungsgangforschung and -didaktik (BDG) 7, 11, 55–8, 61, 206
    normative/scientific dimension 56
    reconstruction of learning 56
    sprachliche Bildung 59, 73
    teacher–student interaction 56–7
Boaler, J., *The Elephant in the Classroom* 20

Charmaz, K. 41
chemistry education 183, 186, 197, 201
Chevallard, Y. 20, 110
Cilliers, P. 158–9
citizenship 6, 42–4, 46, 127, 131, 192
classroom-based action research 18, 43
classroom interaction 19, 24–32, 58, 74, 118, 206–7. *See also* teacher–student interaction
    levels of 57–8, 61
classroom organization/environment 62, 73, 214
collaborative game 39
communication 21, 68, 91, 140, 145, 151, 192
    classroom 73, 146
    curriculum 138, 210
    digital 42
    epistemic/epistemological 137, 147
    intergenerational 57, 59, 72
    language 57, 59
compulsory schooling 79, 144, 151, 180–1
conceptual knowledge 101, 178, 188
content knowledge (CK) 3, 24, 84, 103, 179, 185, 216
cross-curricular context xv, 10, 12, 37, 177–8, 180–1, 185–6, 193–4, 201, 204, 209. *See also* interdisciplinary context; multidisciplinary context
cross-disciplinary approach 4, 10, 118, 153
cross-subject education 100
cultural diversity 37, 79, 82
Cummins, J. 94, 119
Curriculum for Excellence Development partnership group 18
curriculum innovation 1, 3, 17, 30, 33, 153, 198, 211
    in language/language use 55, 72–4
    and teacher education 12, 93–4
curriculum principle 1, 3, 82, 178–9, 181, 192, 198, 213
curriculum system policy 137–9, 153

curriculum theory, crisis in xvi, 1, 3
curriculum transformation processes 138, 210

deferent reading 102. *See also* efferent reading
democracy 88, 189, 193
   democratic quality of instruction 55, 61, 71, 73–4
Developing Mathematical Thinking in the Primary Classroom (DMTPC) project 17–18, 20, 24, 32–3
didactics system 7–9, 19, 56, 60–1, 82
   didactic contract 38–9
   didactic game 38–9
   didactic transposition theory 20, 157
   French 8, 19–20, 38, 58 (*see also* Physical Education (PE) in France)
   German 11, 55–6
   principles of teaching and learning 62–3, 65
      clear structures 65
      day schedule (*Tagesstruktur*) 63–4
      individualized learning 65
      joint learning 65
      keeping overviews 65
      learning fields 63
      setting 63
      visualizing learning 63
   subsystems 19, 38
   teaching and learning 107
   transactions 39
Didaktik theory 161, 178–81, 192, 205
digital resources/digitalization in instruction 117, 208. *See also* social science, digital teaching and learning
   Challenges in the connected classroom 120
   communication/interaction 119–20
   Connected Classroom Nordic (*CCN*) 120
   digitalized classrooms 118–19, 208
   enacted curriculum 119, 134
   epistemic quality 203–4
   Google search 130–2
   instruction 119, 123–8
   literacy 119–20
   method and materials 120–1
      NVIVO software 120
      OneNote 121, 127
      Prezi software 121–4, 127, 133
   multimodal texts 121, 127, 131–3
   phases of
      introduction 121–3
      seat work in pairs/small groups 128–32
      teacher lecture 123–8
   results 121–32
   tiny cards (digital memory game) 128–30, 133
   transformation processes in 119–20, 134
   video recordings 120
   Wikipedia 130–2
   YouTube clips 121, 124, 126
disciplinary knowledge xviii, 2, 4, 7, 106–7, 118, 138, 157–8, 200, 215–16
   transformation (*see* transformations of disciplinary knowledge in classrooms)
disciplines, subject. *See specific disciplines*
diversity 10–11, 37, 79, 91, 93, 101, 103
   cultural 37, 79, 82
   linguistic 59, 72, 74, 79–83, 85, 91, 94
   societal 79, 81, 91–2
   super-diversity 80

Early, M. 94, 119
educational knowledge 117, 180, 185
education for sustainable development (ESD) 177, 197. *See also* sustainable development (SD)
   and action competence 181–3, 185, 194, 209
   cross-curricular settings 177–8, 180–1, 185–6, 193, 197
   collaboration 183–6
   collaborations between teachers 191–4
   co-operation 183–4
   overlapping collaboration 183–4
   didactical dimensions of 185–6, 188–91
   educational aspects of 187–8
   educational content 180, 183–4, 186–7, 202
      analysis of (what/how/why) 184–5
      in language 189–90
      powerful knowledge *vs.* epistemic quality 189–91
      in science 188, 190
      in social science 188–90

empirical study 185–6
epistemic quality 179, 185–6, 194
powerful knowledge 178–9, 180–1, 185, 192, 194
subject areas 183–4
    contributions (common/unique) 190–2
    data analysis 187–8
    results (didactical dimensions) 188–91
    selection of teachers 186–7
transformation 177, 179–81, 193
education system 1–2, 6–7, 204. *See also specific countries*
societal diversity and 79–80, 91, 180
efferent reading 102–3. *See also* deferent reading
emergent method 41, 209–11
empirical studies xvii, 2, 6, 12–13, 18, 177, 192, 197, 204, 211–13
Enders, M. 73
    Individuell lernen – gemeinsam arbeiten. Ein kompetenzorientiertes Unterrichtsmodell aus der Grundschulpraxis 62
England. *See* mathematics (school) curriculum in England
English curriculum structure 137–8
epistemic access 10, 17, 19, 32, 39, 59, 142, 148, 199, 201, 214
    impact of curriculum texts on 146–7
epistemic ascent 10, 17, 22, 24, 61, 137, 144, 149–50, 153, 213
epistemic capacity 22
    of choreographic activities 40–1
epistemic games 8, 19, 38–9, 52, 58, 214–19. *See also* actual epistemic game; language games; learning games; source epistemic game
epistemic kinship 51
epistemic quality (EQ) 1–3, 8–12, 17, 94, 118, 134, 162, 165, 197–8, 211
    characterization of 137, 140, 142, 152
    of content 24, 41, 49–50, 61, 71, 74, 203
    in epistemic games 214–19
    in ESD 179, 185–6, 194
    high/low 9, 21, 32, 50, 59–60, 72, 101–2, 110, 139–40, 149–50, 152, 184–5
    in language education 202

    of language learning (*see* language teaching/learning (EQ) in Germany)
    of literature education in Finland 112
    in mathematics (*see* mathematics curriculum in England, epistemic quality (high) in)
    physical education (*see* Physical Education (PE) in France)
    primary school mathematics (*see* mathematics education in Scotland)
    in school subjects 199, 202–4
    of teacher–student interaction 31–2, 61, 71, 74
epistemology 4, 138, 159, 161, 210, 214. *See also specific knowledge*
epistemological ascent 137, 144, 148–52, 201
epistemological knowledge 147, 151–2
epistemological quality in classroom 149–51
knowledge by acquaintance (knowing who/what) 100, 110, 214
mathematical 140–1, 143, 145–7, 151–2
procedural knowledge (knowing how) 22, 100–1, 110
propositional knowledge (knowing that) 100–1, 110, 201–2
of science 171
European Conference on Educational Research (ECER) Conference 62
everyday knowledge 4, 6, 22, 41, 46, 49–50, 82, 87, 89, 178, 212, 215
experienced/achieved curriculum 137
expertise, subject 10, 17, 22–4, 32, 61, 213

Finnish Cultural Foundation 103 n.5, 112
Finnish National Agency for Education 104
first language and literature (L1), Finland 11, 99, 200. *See also* literature education in Finland
    age group of students 100 n.3
    book choices 107
    critical thinking 101–2, 108, 200
    deferent reading 102
    efferent reading 102–3
    epistemic quality 203
    fact-based textbooks 109
    fiction/nonfiction (factual prose) 100, 100 n.3, 103, 103 n.5, 108–9, 112

Index

Finnish National Curriculum 100 n.2, 101–3, 107
inferential knowing how 101
knowing how/knowing that/knowing what 108–9, 111, 200
motivation for reading 11, 99, 103–4, 103 n.5, 106, 110–12, 203
PIRLS survey 106
powerful reading 103–7
primary school teachers 100 n.4, 103 n.5, 104, 105 n.7, 107, 109–11
procedural knowing how 101
qualifications of teachers 100 n.3, 107
Reading Clan project 103, 103 n.5, 105–6, 111–12
reading literacy
  and powerful knowledge 100–3
  skills 111–12
school subjects 99
secondary school teachers 99, 100 n.4, 103 n.5, 104, 105 n.7, 106–7, 106 n.9, 109–11
teacher education 109–10
transaction theory 102
transformation processes 208
France
  art education in 42, 42 n.1
  French didactics 8, 20, 38, 58 (*see also* German didactics)
  physical education in (*see* Physical Education (PE) in France)
Future 1 curriculum 4, 216
Future 2 curriculum 4–5, 216
Future 3 curriculum xvii, 5

geography education 2, 5, 183, 186, 199, 202, 213
German didactics 11, 55–6. See also France, French didactics
Goodson, I. F. 3–4
grounded theory approach 41, 61

high-quality education 10, 17, 72, 142, 209
history education 2, 6, 183, 186, 213
Hudson, A. 8–9

integrative process. *See* transformation processes
interdisciplinary context 102, 180, 183. *See also* cross-curricular context; multidisciplinary context
intergenerational communication 57, 59, 72

Joint Action in Didactics in Europe (JADE) project 37, 55, 61
Joint Action Theory in Didactics (JATD) 8, 11, 19, 24, 58, 202, 215
  abstract–concrete relationship 42
  contract 38–9
  games 38–9
  milieu 38–9

knowledge 58, 80–1, 119, 128, 133, 148–9, 178, 198, 214. *See also* epistemology
  academic 81, 210
  building 1, 91–2
  conceptual 101, 178, 188
  content 3, 24, 84, 103, 179, 185, 216
  disciplinary (*see* disciplinary knowledge)
  educational 117, 180, 185
  epistemological 147, 151–2
  everyday (*see* everyday knowledge)
  memorized knowledge of language 59, 73
  non-specialized 100
  pedagogical 73, 145, 147, 161, 170–1, 210, 216
  personal 87, 89
  powerful (*see* powerful knowledge)
  predetermined 202
  prior 30–2, 81, 87, 92, 122, 161, 166, 168
  professional 3, 93, 171
  school 6, 68, 159, 178, 187, 193, 210
  scientific 189–90
  specialized 118, 178, 204
  structure 148, 212, 214
  subject 41, 61, 92–3, 117, 149, 177
  transfer/transformation of (*see* transformation processes; transformations of disciplinary knowledge in classrooms)
KOSS program (*Knowledge and Quality across School Subjects and Teacher Education*) 2, 12, 17, 178, 197–8, 206

language awareness 74, 91, 94, 100
  and multilingualism 80–1
language education 11, 212–13
  EQ in 202, 207

powerful knowledge in 199–200, 203
transformation in 207
language games 19, 24, 38, 203. *See also* epistemic games; learning games
language teaching/learning (EQ) in Germany 41, 58–61, 206
   Bildungsgangforschung and -didaktik 11, 55–8, 206
      acceptance of 'otherness' 55
      community of practice 57
      individual development pathway 56
      individual sense construction 56–7, 72–3
      institutional educational pathway 56
      institutional requirements 56
      intergenerational communication 57
      levels of teacher-student interaction 57–8, 61
      'seeing as' 57
      subjective educational pathway 56
   creative reasoning 59–60, 72
   data analysis (quiz sequence) 67–72
   data collection 65–7
   democratic discourse 59–60
   didactic principles 62–3, 65 (*see* didactics system, principles of teaching and learning)
   first/second 11
   high/low EQ in language 59–60, 72
   individuality of learner 57–8, 207
   individualized learning 62, 68, 72–3
   knowing that/knowing how 60, 72
   knowledge that/knowledge how 61
   language/language use 11, 59, 74, 207
      curriculum innovation 55, 72–4
      trajectory of development 60–1, 218
   linguistic change 59, 72
   linguistic diversity (*see* linguistic diversity)
   linguistic fallibilism 59
   linguistic fundamentalism 60, 68, 73
   memorized knowledge of 59, 73
   mother tongue 59, 62
   research design 61–2
   self-organized learning 62, 73
   sociability of learner 57, 207
   study 62–5
   teaching material in classroom 63
learning games 8, 19–20, 38–9, 58–9, 215–19. *See also* epistemic games; language games
linguistic diversity 59, 72, 74, 79–83, 85, 91, 94
literacy engagement model 11, 119–20, 122, 128, 132–4, 208
literacy skills 102, 109
   enhancing reading 111–12
literature education in Finland 99–100, 103 n.5, 104, 107
   collaborative method of reading 104, 106, 109–10
   epistemic quality in 112
   group-oriented method 106, 111–12, 200
   interactional method 104, 109, 111–12
   and L1 103, 200
   language and 101
   national curriculum for 107
   powerful knowledge in 112
   teaching methods
      book circles/literature circles/reading clubs 105–6, 105 n.8, 106 n.9, 111
      book diplomas 104–5
      book snakes/trees 105, 105 n.7
      book tippings 104
      drama methods 105
Lithner, J. 21
Local Education Authorities (LEA) 18

Marsh, C. J. 3–4, 119
mathematics (school) curriculum in England 137–8
   empirical study 138–9
   enacted curriculum 137–8, 146–7
      epistemic and epistemological ascent 148–9
      EQ in classroom 149–51
   epistemic quality (high) in 139–42, 204
      in curriculum texts 142–5
      in enacted curriculum 148–52
      impact of curriculum texts (epistemic access) 146–7
   expansive learning 142, 147
   higher education courses 140
   intended curriculum 137, 139, 142, 144–8, 151, 153

intensive courses 141
interpretation 148, 151
know-that/know-how 144, 152–3
materials and assessments 137–9, 144–7, 149, 151–4
mathematical fluency 138, 143–6
mathematical reasoning 21, 143, 145–6
national curriculum 137, 139, 142–3, 151
parent discipline 138, 140–1
problem-solving 138, 143–6, 203–4, 213
programmes of study 143–5, 151
purpose statement of curriculum 142–3
specifications (11–16 and A-Level) 143, 145, 147
subject/non-subject specialists 147–8, 151–2
teacher educative resources 145–6, 148, 153
mathematics education in Scotland 9–10, 12, 17, 206, 213
algorithmic reasoning 21, 51, 59
creative reasoning 9, 21, 31–3, 49, 59, 203
critical thinking 9, 21, 33, 203
DMTPC project 17–18, 20, 24, 32–3
epistemic quality 19–24, 202
of content 30–1
of teacher–student(s) joint action 31–2
imitative reasoning in 21, 49, 51
knowledge by acquaintance 10, 22, 24, 30
know-that/know-how 10, 22–4, 30–2
mathematical fallibilism 9, 20–1, 33, 59
mathematical fundamentalism 9, 20–2, 32, 179
mathematical thinking 8, 25–9, 31–2, 201
memorization 9, 20, 22, 32
memorized reasoning 21, 51, 59
'The Rainforest' project 17, 24–5, 30
study (classroom interaction) 24–5
data analysis 30–2
data collection 25–9
subject-specific powerful knowledge in 23
topic-based approach 8, 17, 24, 33

Maude, A. xvii, 5, 202
McPhail, G. J. 6
meaning-making processes 101–3, 132–3, 158–60
Meyer, M. A. 57–8, 74
migration, language and (Sweden, Norway textbooks) 79
diversity (*see* diversity)
equality/equal rights for education 80
multilingualism and language awareness 80–1
national curriculum 80
second language learners 79
super-diverse societies 80, 93
teaching aids 79–80
textbook study 80–2, 199–200, 207
activities (*see* activities, textbook (roles of students))
area of focus 83
content analysis 84
content knowledge 84–6
material and method of 83–4
transformations of knowledge 81–2, 86
Millar, V. 5–6, 202
monolingual tradition 79, 81, 85–6, 93–4
mother tongue 59, 62, 85, 99, 186, 199
Muller, J. xvii, 4–5, 8, 212, 215
multidisciplinary context 107, 180, 182, 201, 204, 218–19. *See also* cross-curricular context; interdisciplinary context
multilingualism 11, 83, 85–6, 94
and language awareness 80–1
and linguistic diversity 81
textbook activities 89–91
multiliteracy 100–3, 200
multimodal texts 101, 121, 127, 131
music education 6, 199, 203

National Council of Teachers of Mathematics (NCTM) 21
national curriculum 80, 88, 99, 107, 137, 139, 142–3, 151
Ndary Lo 43–4
new digital media 117
non-specialized knowledge 100. *See also* specialized knowledge
Norway. *See* migration, language and (Sweden, Norway textbooks)

Oates, T. xvii
omstilling 7, 119, 157
Osberg, D. 158–9

pedagogical content knowledge (PCK) 74, 216
pedagogical knowledge (PK) 73, 145, 147, 161, 170–1, 210, 216
pedagogy 3, 5, 7, 51, 118, 140, 148, 159, 178, 180
personal knowledge 87, 89
Physical Education (PE) in France 37, 197, 201, 213, 218
   choreographic activities 37, 40–4
      oeuvre 41–3, 42 n.1
   Dance and Citizenship study 42–3
   epistemic quality 39–49, 203
      data analysis 44–9
      research design 41–2
      study 42–4
   imitation and creation 49–52
   JATD 38–9
   symbolic gestures 45–50
physics education 2, 5–6, 141, 159, 186, 199, 202
powerful knowledge xvii, 1–12, 17, 19, 22, 39, 59, 80–3, 86, 91, 93–4, 109–10, 157, 159–60, 165, 169, 171, 197–8, 208, 211–12, 214–15, 218–19
   in epistemic games 216
   in ESD 178–80, 194
   in language education 199–200, 203
   in literature education 112
   in mathematics 217
   power and knowledge in 212–14
   and reading literacy 100–3
   in school subjects 198–202, 205
   subject-specific 102
   and transformation 81–2, 86, 93, 158, 177
predetermined knowledge 202
pre-planned teaching trajectory 133, 208
prior knowledge 30–2, 81, 87, 92, 122, 161, 166, 168
problem-based curriculum structure 138
professional knowledge 3, 93, 171
progressive focussing process 42, 62

qualification, education 107, 205
quality, educational research 199

reading literacy 99–103, 109–12
real-world representations 21, 158
reciprocal semiosis 38
reconstruction 7, 56, 157, 161, 171
re-contextualization 157, 171, 204
Research on Subject-Specific Education (ROSE) 81, 194
Rosenblatt, L. 102

scholarship 2, 197–8
school knowledge 6, 68, 159, 178, 187, 193, 210
school subjects 2–8, 12–13, 17, 79, 81–3, 86, 91–2, 94, 118–19, 149, 157, 159, 168, 171, 179–80, 197–8, 209, 211–13, 219. See also specific disciplines
   EQ in 199, 202–4
   on L1 99
   powerful knowledge in 198–202, 205
   transformation in classrooms 119
scientific knowledge 189–90
Scotland
   primary school mathematics in (see mathematics education in Scotland)
   Scottish Survey of Literacy and Numeracy 18, 32
second-language learning 11, 79, 83–4, 83–5
self/self-concepts 56–8, 207
Sensevy, G. 19, 215
Shulman, L. S. 73–4
socialization 205
social science, digital teaching and learning 11–12, 118–32, 197, 213. See also digital resources/digitalization in instruction
   educational content of ESD in 188, 190
   phases of (law and order)
      introduction 121–3
      seat work in pairs/small groups 128–32
      teacher lecture 123–8
      tiny cards game 128–30, 133
source epistemic game 19, 38, 58, 215. See also actual epistemic game; epistemic games
specialized knowledge 118, 178, 204. See also non-specialized knowledge
subjectification 205, 208

subject knowledge 41, 61, 92–3, 117, 149, 177
subject matter 9, 22, 93, 181
  artistic and cultural education (France) 42
subject-specific education 2–3, 7, 10, 13, 23, 51, 110, 118, 198, 204, 211. *See also specific subjects*
substantive mathematics 138
super-diverse societies 80, 93
sustainability education. *See* education for sustainable development (ESD)
sustainable development (SD) 10, 17, 177, 181–2, 193, 201, 209. *See also* education for sustainable development (ESD)
  and dimensions 182
Sweden/Swedish curriculum
  compulsory schooling 181 (*see also* compulsory schooling)
  digital/digitalization, teaching (*see* digital resources/digitalization in instruction; social science, digital teaching and learning)
  language and migration (*see* migration, language and (Sweden, Norway textbooks))
  secondary school teachers in 183
syntactical mathematics 138, 144

teacher education 12, 62, 79–80, 93–4, 209
  and curriculum innovation 93–4
teacher–student interaction 11–12, 17, 24, 39, 41, 49, 72–3, 118, 206, 214–15, 217. *See also* classroom interaction
  co-operation in instructional process 55, 57–8, 73
  digitalization 117, 119–20
  epistemic quality of 31–2, 61
    language learning (*see* language teaching/learning (EQ) in Germany)
    levels of interaction 57–8, 61
  imitation and creation 49–52
  symbolic gestures 45–50, 52
teaching practices/traditions 117–18, 181, 183, 193, 201, 203, 205–9
technology. *See* digital resources/digitalization in instruction
transaction theory 102

transformation processes 1–3, 7, 9–13, 20, 56, 58, 94, 118–19, 197–8, 209, 211, 213–15, 218–19
  curriculum 138
  in digitalized classrooms 119–20, 134
  disciplinary knowledge in science classroom (*see* transformations of disciplinary knowledge in classrooms)
  in ESD 179–81, 193
  importance of 204–6
  as intended/emergent 209–11
  of knowledge 57–8, 81–2, 137
    powerful knowledge 81–2, 86, 93, 158, 177
    with powerful knowledge and EQ 206–19
    and selection of knowledge 80
  subject knowledge 92
  teacher–student relationship 205
  through student roles 87
transformations of disciplinary knowledge in classrooms 157–8, 210
  artefacts model 169
  dialogic education 160
  embodied cognition 169
  empirical study (chromatography) 162–70, 172
  interactive whiteboard material 165–7, 170, 172
  intra-action/interaction 160–1, 165–6, 168, 170
  material-dialogic frame 12, 158–62, 164–6, 168–72, 210
  material-discursive process 160–1, 164
  matter 162, 168, 171–2
  mini whiteboards 165–6, 168, 172
  model-based learning 169–70
  new materialism/new materialist 159–60, 164
  phenomena/phenomenon 160, 168–72
  pupil verbal protocols 164, 166
  research design 162–3
  teacher verbal protocols 164, 166, 170
  through non-human materials 165–8
  top-down/bottom-up 161
triangle/triad process 107

UN Sustainable Development Goal 4 17, 19, 39, 59

whole class teaching 28, 67, 86, 168
Winch, C. 22, 149, 213
Wittgenstein, L. 23
　'seeing as' 57
writing systems 88. *See also* Arabic writing system

Yates, L. 5–6, 202
Young, A. 80, 91
Young, M. xvii, 3–8, 12, 87, 92, 159, 178, 194, 198, 212, 214–15
　everyday knowledge (*see* everyday knowledge)
　powerful knowledge (*see* powerful knowledge)

www.ingramcontent.com/pod-product-compliance
Lightning Source LLC
Chambersburg PA
CBHW062139300426
44115CB00012BA/1978